Volume 95 Number 3 September 2023

American Literature

Senses with/out Subjects

Edited by Erica Fretwell and Hsuan L. Hsu

Essays

Book Reviews

Erica
Fretwell
and
Hsuan L.
Hsu

Redistributions of the Sensible:
An Introduction to "Senses with/out
Subjects"

Across Octavia Butler's *Xenogenesis* trilogy, touch, chemosensation, and sensitivity to DNA itself offer a basis for building kinship relations that stretch across both species and interplanetary boundaries. In *Dawn* (1987), for instance, surviving a planetary apocalypse and centuries of racial capitalist violence and war making requires the reeducation of the senses. When she wakes up on a spaceship after nuclear war has made most of Earth uninhabitable, the protagonist Lilith Iyapo must slowly overcome her conditioned visual responses ("Look at me," insists Lilith's Oankali companion) and then learn to interact with a being whose face is filled with "sensory tentacles" (Butler [1987] 2000: 15). She is genetically recoded thanks to the preternatural sensitivity of the third gender known as ooloi (who can sense and manipulate DNA) and becomes capable of communicating through chemical cues. Through the transmission of olfactory chemical signals, "Strangers of a different species [are] accepted as family" (196). By challenging the supremacy of vision as a tool and metaphor for knowledge, by centering a Black woman's struggle for survival and reproductive futurity as a site of relationalities that exceed the sensorium of Enlightenment "Man," and by exploring the embodied sensorium (including nonconsensual chemosensation) as a pathway toward more-than-human kinships, Butler's novel offers a generative model for emergent scholarship in sensory studies, an interdisciplinary field organized around the premise that sensory perception is a social rather than strictly neurological construct.

This special issue hazards the hypothesis that literary criticism and sensory studies are mutually sustaining fields of inquiry. That the senses and the symbolic are coextensive is a truth so obvious as to be

American Literature, Volume 95, Number 3, September 2023
DOI 10.1215/00029831-10679195   © 2023 by Duke University Press

invisible; sensation is inscribed into the etymological meaning of aesthetics (*aisthetikos* in Greek) as "of or relating to sensation." To be
sure, reshaping sensory aesthetics has long been a vital concern in
the theory and practice of US literature: along with Butler's speculative experiments with sensorial estrangement, we might think of the
"howling wilderness" invoked by Cotton Mather to animate Puritan
exceptionalism, Walt Whitman proclaiming the holiness of his touch
and armpit aroma, Herman Melville on the homoerotic and interspe-
cies communion of squeezing spermaceti, Henry David Thoreau's
effort to "[train] into his writing the alertness of his senses" (Matthiessen 1941: 93), the "most terrible spectacle" of Frederick Douglass's
(1845: 6) primal scene, and Saidiya Hartman's (1997: 3) refusal to
reproduce it. Nonetheless, the field of American literary studies has
only occasionally engaged with work in sensory studies. Given the
long-standing Western dichotomy between form and matter, between
representation and experience, and between artistic mediation and
lived immediacy, this oversight among literary scholars is perhaps
unsurprising. Literary criticism's tendency to focus on matters of textual representation, in conjunction with its origins in liberal humanism, has often directed critical attention away from the diverse sensory
modes in which we interact with literature—and which literature itself
enacts. Several questions motivate this special issue: How does poetic
language extend rather than reflect sensory experience? Is literature
itself not a sensitizing mechanism, a means of cultivating attention to
more kinds of feelings within and outside us? What methods might we
use to engage with the sensory dimensions of literature—including
nonrepresentational and more-than-human sensory interactions—
without universalizing historically and culturally particular sensoria?
And, conversely, how might attuning to literature's sensory pleasures
shift our methods of reading and contextualizing texts, as well as how
we teach and write about literature?

It is no mere coincidence that Butler imagined a posthuman future
requiring the activation of new sensations in the same decade that
sensory studies took shape as a research field: when the Reaganite
neoliberal order hastened environmental crises and exacerbated racial
and class disparities, and scholars responded to the limits of linguisti-
cally focused poststructuralist analysis by examining the lively materiality of human and nonhuman worlds. Grounded in the anthropological
studies of David Howes and Constance Classen—as well as the foundational scholarship of media theorist Marshall McLuhan, psychologist
J. J. Gibson, and ecophenomenologist David Abram, among others—
sensory studies investigates the historical contingency, cultural variety,

and biopolitical deployment of sense perception. As Howes (2022) writes, sensory studies scholars seek to "liberate the senses from the artificial confines of the psychology laboratory" and explore how they function across a range of everyday contexts. By attending to the social variability of sensory experience and discourse, this interdisciplinary field has demonstrated how sensory discipline—for example, the hierarchy of the five classical senses—has been mobilized in the service of colonial, racist, and heteronormative models of embodiment and epistemology.

Yet, until recently, sensory studies has not engaged with formative research on these topics in fields such as critical ethnic studies, postcolonial studies, and Indigenous studies. Gus Stadler's (2015) provocation "On Whiteness and Sound Studies" resonates across the entire field of sensory studies: "I'm struck . . . by the relative absence of a certain strain of work . . . an approach that is difficult to characterize but that is probably best approximated by the term 'American Studies.' Over the past two decades, this field has emerged as an especially vibrant site for the sustained, nuanced exploration of forms of social difference, race in particular." As shown by recent work on topics ranging from the "sensory practices of colonialism" (Hacke and Musselwhite 2017) and "slavery, segregation, and the senses" (Smith 2006) to "the sonic color line" (Stoever 2016) and "the felt politics of racial embodiment" (Sekimoto and Brown 2020), the modern sensorium cannot be disentangled from the histories of racial and colonial capitalism. In addition to exploring the senses as tools of violence, extraction, and exclusion, critical ethnic studies scholars—for example, Amber Jamilla Musser (2018), Ren Ellis Neyra (2020), and Dylan Robinson (Stó:lō/Skwah) (Robinson 2020)—have also explored the queer, antiracist, and decolonial potentialities of sensory experience.

This important and growing body of scholarship on the power asymmetries embedded in the classical sensory hierarchy has facilitated efforts to interrogate sensory experiences excluded from Western sensory orderings—for example, proprioception, thermoception, interoception—and has shown how they vary across historical, cultural, and biopolitical divides. Contra the Aristotelian model of the senses as a means of extracting information from the outside world, these embodied senses focus more on perceiving how we neuronally and metabolically interact with our surroundings. As Desiree Förster (2021: 75) explains, "Interoception senses changes in the hormonal, chemical, and thermoregulatory states that impact the way we feel and how much physical energy we have in a situation, and therefore influences our intentions and actions. The body thereby enables sensory experience not only external to itself in the environment, but also sensory experience of internal biochemical processes." Nicole Starosielski (2022: 8, 7) has modeled an approach to "critical temperature studies" that can attune us to the vital role of thermoception in sustaining media infrastructures and in the production of "gender, race, class, ethnicity, and other forms of social difference." While thermal sensation goes some way toward explaining forms of infrastructural and embodied violence, the atmosphere itself (not only temperature and humidity but also light and sound) has become an object of calibration and a means of managing the circulation of bodies through specific environments. The scientific and artistic manipulation of "what counts as a habitable environment and for whom that environment appears livable," media theorist Yuriko Furuhata (2022: 4) has demonstrated, operates by turning sensory stimuli into a mode of social control. At the heart of this new generation of sensory studies, then, sensation—in all its ineffability and raucousness— is the hinge upon which the more-than-human world and the all-too-human world pivot.

As the contributors to this special issue demonstrate, when literary critics attend to the aesthetic and political contexts of sensory perception, not only do new heuristics emerge for studying sensory embodiment in a variety of aesthetic and cultural contexts but also new texts and textualities, new literary genealogies, and new ways of reading become available. This special issue showcases the literary and textual practices that simulate as well as stimulate sensory experiences to recalibrate relations between aesthetics and violence, being and knowing, and space and time. Authors consider gustatory encounters, atmospheric volatility, tactile communication, and psychotropic substances that pressure the bounds of human subjectivity at scales both personal and planetary, historical and ecological.

Crucially, the sensory experiences described in this special issue advance posthumanist perspectives while also resisting them. A Deleuzian philosophy around which the new materialisms, object oriented ontology, and agential realism constellate, posthumanism gathered force at the turn of the twenty-first century by taking the liveliness of matter (rather than the instability of signification) as an entry point into social analysis. In so doing, it rejected a key epistemological condition facilitating the Western fantasy of human mastery: anthropocentrism. As propounded by thinkers like Jane Bennett, Brian Massumi, and Karen Barad, to theorize the conditions of human and nonhuman being through materiality is to affirm a specific set of beliefs: that the material world is composed of dynamic assemblages, not static subjects; that agency is distributive, not unidirectional; that biological processes are transformative, not deterministic; that bodies are potential becomings, not bounded entities; and that affect is a pre-conscious intensity, not a meaningful emotion. These beliefs constitute what might be called the "posthumanist thesis": that the material world, intra-active in its formation and nonhierarchical in its organiza-tion, contains within it the means for dismantling anthropocentric and Eurocentric epistemologies. Athwart transcendental and humanist traditions of thought, the posthumanist subject is not a self-sovereign agent but an enfleshed, fluctuating site of external influences and out-wardly unfolding affects.

But decoupling the world of matter from the anthropocentric telos of history does not come without risk. In fact, many Indigenous scholars have pointed out that there is very little new about new materialisms. Reproducing a kind of disciplinary colonialism in the very act of claim-ing to dismantle Eurocentric binaries of matter/spirit, posthumanist criticism typically has called upon its own genealogy of thought— with the troublesome effect of erasing the First Nations and Indige-nous knowledge traditions that long preceded Western thought. Rosi Braidotti (2000: 159), for instance, has described new materialisms as "Descartes' nightmare, Spinoza's hope, Nietzsche's complaint, Freud's obsession, Lacan's favorite fantasy." Thus, even as posthumanism in general and feminist new materialisms in particular have examined the entanglement of bodies in relations of power, privileging relations of matter and decentering the human has involved white scholars' appropriation of Asian, Indigenous, and African ontologies and episte-mologies. Indeed, one of the most thoroughgoing criticisms of the new materialisms is that it has abandoned the human stakes of alive-ness in a historical present haunted by the colonial fungibility of peo-ple and things, of converting certain people into objects while imbu-ing some objects with personhood.

As suggested by its title, "Senses with/out Subjects," rather than cede the ground of humanism, this special issue explores the neces-sary incompleteness of the human and the refusal of all living things to being perceptually and politically apprehended in their entirety. The articles included in this issue offer important contributions to the "post-posthumanist" scholarship that critically engages with new materialisms—from Mel Chen's (2012) examination of the racialized materiality of animacy and Dolleen Tisawii'ashii Manning's (Kettle and Stoney Point First Nation) work on Indigenous worlding practices (Manning 2017) to Neel Ahuja's (2016) study of the entanglement of species and environments within the biopolitics of empire. In so doing, these essays participate in a critical genealogy that blends postcolonial and race studies perspectives with posthumanism in its rejection of anthropocentrism. In their challenges to the liberal conception of Man as a rational subject and an ideal citizen, Black thinkers such as Frantz Fanon and Sylvia Wynter have argued that the human is neither a universal category nor a transcendent truth but a historical construct wielded by empires to delimit who is (white people, men) and is not (women, disabled people, people of color) worthy of human rights, social membership, and democratic citizenship. Crucially, the ordering of the senses played an essential role in this project: as Wynter (2003: 260) explains, the overrepresentation of "Man" as the bearer of freedom and rationality requires a sharp distinction between this white, patriarchal, bourgeois figure of the human and those Others who "are made to embody the postulate of 'significant ill' of enslavement to the lower, sensory aspects of 'human nature.'" All the while, sensation itself indexes state violence against those relegated to the "lower" sensory order of humanity. Take, for instance, the connection identified by prison abolitionist Mariame Kaba (2015) between summer heat and hypersurveillance: warm weather invites young Black people to inhabit contested public spaces where "residents collude with law enforcement to police and enforce boundaries." This dynamic tradition of minoritarian critique establishes the ontological fragmentation, epistemic ruptures, and temporal discontinuity generated by sensory materiality as integral to practices of human survival, especially when recovery or overcoming (a narrative arc that invariably leads back to Man) is neither desirable nor readily available.

The contributions to this special issue constitute a decisive redistribution of the sensible. In his influential formulation of the "distribution of the sensible," philosopher Jacques Rancière (2004: 13) linked sense perception to politics by arguing that aesthetics "is a delimitation of spaces and times, of the visible and the invisible, of speech and noise, that simultaneously determines the place and the stakes of politics as a form of experience." The aesthetic, in other words, is inherently political because it reorganizes the sensible; it redraws the bounds of what is sayable, visible, and audible and which groups can be seen, can speak, can be heard. While aesthetics has the capacity to upend regimes of truth and representation, as Rancière claims, it also has the potential to generate what Kandice Chuh (2019: xi) calls "illiberal humanisms": the apprehension of uncommon sensibilities that run athwart liberal common sense by materializing relationality (rather than individuality) as the grounds of human ontology. In varying ways, each author in this special issue takes up Chuh's (2019: 22) call to disentangle humanism from its liberal iteration in order to recover "a human subjectivity formed in fuller, embodied relation to the world." By examining the illiberal sensibilities formalized in minoritarian literatures, from twentieth-century Ho-Chunk autobiography and disability writing to contemporary Vietnamese American poetry and Black feminist speculative fiction, these articles bring the insights of critical new materialisms to bear on the literary study of sensation, offering a redistribution of the sensible that illuminates the transitivity of subject and objecthood, that rethinks representational histories, and that instantiates new ways of proliferating accounts of the human (in all its variations and iterations) in a more-than-human world. What emerges is both a new "sense" of sensation as formalizing some of the broadest debates underpinning racial modernity and new literary histories that plot an enfleshed aesthetics shaped by nature, culture, and power.

In "Moved by Another Life: Altered Sentience and Historical Poiesis in the Peyote Craze," Sylvie Boulette reads the General Allotment Act as a chronobiological project intended to impose settler-capitalist framings of individuated, cumulative time and to "extract Native lives from the sacred durations of the earth and the animacy of living environments." Against this context, Boulette details the unruly "sonic, kinesthetic, and transsensory pathways" opened up by the Peyote Road, which enabled access to a sense of time and embodiment irreducible to "the regularity and immediacy of regimes of work and rest." Through nuanced readings of episodic structures and sensory descriptions of peyotism in Sam Blowsnake's (Ho-Chunk) *Autobiography of a Winnebago Indian* (1920), Boulette develops a fascinating account of "an Indigenous medium of mobile association and persistence through ecstatic discontinuations of the already-accumulated future."

In "Extra Consciousness, Extra Fingers: Automatic Writing and Disabled Authorship," Clare Mullaney reads Gertrude Stein's and Lucille Clifton's practices of automatic writing as sites of productive intersection between disability and embodied sensory experience. Mullaney argues that Stein and Clifton harness the creative potential of embodied "extra" senses—sensorial experiences that exceed patriarchal, white supremacist, and ableist taxonomies of sensation. Theorizing automatic writing not as an absence of subjectivity but as an extra consciousness, "Stein reclaims . . . the sensing body as a neglected source of knowledge production." Clifton, by contrast, positions herself as a medium for her ancestors' voices, channeled in part through her additional finger that was removed at birth. Reading these authors' work as feminist revisions of the gendered and ableist hierarchies that grounded nineteenth-century Spiritualism, Mullaney shows how they practiced writing not as a mode of liberal individual authorship but as a way of channeling embodied sensation and feeling, as well as "what is told by others through their bodies."

Sunhay You's "Sweetness of Race: On Synesthesia, Addiction, and Self-Possessed Personhood in Monique Truong's *Bitter in the Mouth*" frames synesthesia as both a literary and a neurological experience that has the potential to interrupt and reorganize racial sensoria. Focusing on Monique Truong's representation of a transnational Vietnamese adoptee's lexical-gustatory synesthesia in *Bitter in the Mouth* (2010), You considers how both white supremacy and its violent appetite for racial intimacies are sustained by a cultural addiction to sweetness. Synesthesia unsettles the racial sensorium's reliance on visual and gustatory regimentations of intersectional identity, instead highlighting "the body's materiality and its sheer capacity to feel in excess of those preestablished networks of meaning." The plasticity and errancy of Linda's sensory experience activate possibilities for interiority, cross-racial affiliation, and queer intimacy that refuse the defensive psychic structures of whiteness and its addictive racial intimacies.

In "Touching Ash in Vietnamese Diasporic Aesthetics," David Pham explores the sensorial qualities of fire and ash as vital "matter metaphors" in recent works by the poet and novelist Ocean Vuong and the artist Tuan Andrew Nguyen. Turning aside from the centrality of water in Vietnamese refugee imaginaries, Pham traces how haptic encounters with fire and ash open onto a "pyric ontoepistemology of the refugee" that blends personal knowledge, histories of imperial violence, and material being. While Vuong and Nguyen attend to fire's shattering, traumatizing, and even apocalyptic capacities, they also dwell on the paradoxical experience of touching ash—an insensible, opaque material whose beauty punctuates the world so that something else might yet follow. Pham's work models a generative dialogue between sensory studies and Edouard Glissant's theorization of opacity, inviting us to sit with that which escapes or refuses existing terms of perceptibility not as a problem but as a source of confounding beauty.

Shouhei Tanaka's "Black Feminist Geohaptics and the Broken Earth" brings sensory studies into generative dialogue with new materialist and Black feminist approaches to theorizing the Anthropocene. Through striking readings of Alexis Pauline Gumbs's *M Archive* (2018) and N. K. Jemisin's *Broken Earth* trilogy, the article makes a compelling case for "the centrality of sensory praxis to ecological thought." For Tanaka, these works bring forth new sensorial and ecological futures through geohaptics—a reciprocal, ecological touch that refuses the instrumentalist distribution of the sensible that has sustained racial capitalism's violent and extractive conceptions of environment, geology, and the human. Thus, Gumbs renders the ongoing ecologies of the Middle Passage through intimate and reciprocal relations of breath and touch, and Jemisin instantiates an insurgent, anticolonial sensorium attuned—through sensuous "temperatures, pressures, [and] reverberations"—to the sensorial agency of geological materials. More broadly, Tanaka's article exemplifies the political and aesthetic stakes of an approach to speculative literature that centers techniques of sensorial world making.

Collectively, these contributions demonstrate what we might call a post-posthumanist sensory studies that has the potential to reorient literary studies toward our varied, contingent, and sometimes transformative modes of sensorial interaction. Indeed, they register broader efforts within the expanding field of sensory studies to bring the disability, gender, and racial politics of the "bodymind" (Price 2014) to bear on the seemingly apolitical "earthbodies" (Mazis 2002) that populate nonhuman environments. By attuning to the senses as malleable capacities of relationality and world making, the authors articulate the generative modes of ecological relation, historical inquiry, speculative praxis, temporal possibility, and ontoepistemology articulated by a diverse literary archive. In a moment of planetary crisis shaped by racial capitalism's ongoing projects of sensory bureaucratization, commodification, surveillance, hierarchy, denigration, and simulation, these contributions exemplify generative approaches to engaging with literature as a powerful site for experimenting with more equitable, ecologically responsible, and illiberal redistributions of the senses.

Erica Fretwell is associate professor of English at the University at Albany, SUNY. She is the author of *Sensory Experiments: Psychophysics, Race, and the Aesthetics of Feeling* (2020). Her current research is on sentimentality and anaesthetics, and on haptic literacies.

Hsuan L. Hsu is professor of English at the University of California, Davis. He is the author of *The Smell of Risk: Atmospheric Disparities and the Olfactory Arts* (2020), *Sitting in Darkness: Mark Twain, Asia, and Comparative Racialization* (2015), and *Geography and the Production of Space in Nineteenth-Century Literature* (2010). He is currently writing a book on air conditioning for Bloomsbury.

References

Ahuja, Neel. 2016. *Bioinsecurities: Disease Intervention, Empire, and the Government of Species.* Durham, NC: Duke Univ. Press.

Braidotti, Rosi. 2000. "Teratologies." In *Deleuze and Feminist Theory,* edited by Ian Buchanan and Claire Colebrook, 156–72. Edinburgh: Univ. of Edinburgh Press.

Butler, Octavia. (1987) 2000. *Dawn.* In *Lilith's Brood,* 1–248. New York: Warner Books.

Chen, Mel. 2012. *Animacies: Biopolitics, Racial Mattering, and Queer Affect.* Durham, NC: Duke Univ. Press.

Chuh, Kandice. 2019. *The Difference Aesthetics Makes: On the Humanities "After Man."* Durham, NC: Duke Univ. Press.

Douglass, Frederick. 1845. *Narrative of the Life of Frederick Douglass.* Boston: Anti-Slavery Office.

Förster, Desiree. 2021. *Aesthetic Experience of Metabolic Processes.* Lüneberg: Meson Press.

Furuhata, Yuriko. 2022. *Climatic Media: Transpacific Experiments in Atmospheric Control.* Durham, NC: Duke Univ. Press.

Hacke, Daniela, and Paul Musselwhite. 2017. *Empire of the Senses: Sensory Practices of Colonialism in Early America.* Leiden: Brill.

Hartman, Saidiya. 1997. *Scenes of Subjection: Terror, Slavery, and Self-Making in Nineteenth-Century America.* New York: Oxford Univ Press.

Howes, David. 2022. *The Sensory Studies Manifesto.* Toronto: Univ. of Toronto Press.

Kaba, Mariame. 2015. "Summer Heat." *New Inquiry,* June 8. https://thenew inquiry.com/summer-heat/.

Manning, Dolleen Tisawii'ashii. 2017. "Mnidoo-Worlding: Merleau-Ponty and Anishinaabe Philosophical Translations." PhD diss., University of Western Ontario.

Matthiessen, F. O. 1941. *American Renaissance: Art and Expression in the Age of Emerson and Whitman.* London: Oxford Univ. Press.

Mazis, Glen. 2002. *Earthbodies: Rediscovering Our Planetary Senses.* Albany: SUNY Press.

Musser, Amber Jamilla. 2018. *Sensual Excess: Queer Femininity and Brown Jouissance.* New York: NYU Press.

Neyra, Ren Ellis. 2020. *The Cry of the Senses: Listening to Latinx and Caribbean Poetics.* Durham, NC: Duke Univ. Press.

Price, Margaret. 2014. "The Bodymind Problem and the Possibilities of Pain." *Hypatia* 30, no. 1: 268–84.

Rancière, Jacques. 2004. *The Politics of Aesthetics: The Distribution of the Sensible*. Translated by Gabriel Rockhill. London: Continuum.

Robinson, Dylan. 2020. *Hungry Listening: Resonant Theory for Indigenous Sound Studies*. Minneapolis: Univ. of Minnesota Press.

Sekimoto, Sachi, and Christopher Brown. 2020. *Race and the Senses: The Felt Politics of Racial Embodiment*. New York: Routledge.

Smith, Mark. 2006. *How Race Is Made: Slavery, Segregation, and the Senses*. Chapel Hill: Univ. of North Carolina Press.

Stadler, Gus. 2015. "On Whiteness and Sounds Studies." *Sounding Out!*, July 6. https://soundstudiesblog.com/2015/07/06/on-whiteness-and-sound-studies.

Starosielski, Nicole. 2022. *Media Hot and Cold*. Durham, NC: Duke Univ. Press.

Stoever, Jennifer Lynn. 2016. *The Sonic Color Line: Race and the Cultural Politics of Listening*. New York: NYU Press.

Wynter, Sylvia. 2003. "Unsettling the Coloniality of Being/Power/Truth /Freedom: Towards the Human, after Man, Its Overrepresentation—An Argument." *CR: The New Centennial Review* 3, no. 3: 257–337.

Sylvie Boulette

Moved by Another Life:
Altered Sentience and Historical Poiesis
in the Peyote Craze

Abstract This article follows the transsensory pathways opened by peyote, a mood-altering entheogen, as it diffused among Native peoples living under and along the edges of colonial occupation around the turn of the twentieth century. It traces that movement through the pulsions of temporal and sensorial animacy created in the episodic narration of *The Autobiography of a Winnebago Indian* (1920), the life story of a Ho-Chunk man named Sam Blowsnake. Apprehended by settler governance as a "craze," anti-assimilationist currents of the Peyote movement met with intensifying attempts to constrain the biochemical flux of "intoxication" through Native bodies. Modern campaigns against "peyote worship" mounted by government agents, progressive reformers, and sensationalist press in the early twentieth century exploited scripts of revulsion and prurient fascination to target the border-crossing "mind poison" for prohibition. Just beneath the scenes of psychotoxicity and sexual disorder projected by the antinarcotic imaginary of the craze, this article posits, there ran an ongoing struggle over the restrictive capacitation of property and personhood within the settler-capitalist regime of allotment. Against the norms enforced by that policy, in peyote meetings the alteration of sentience could unbind the day-to-day reproduction of property-bearing personhood. Lines of collective transport opening from the passage of ecstasy thus composed a historical moment in refusal of allotment drives for schizochronic individuation.

Keywords ecstasy, drug war, settler capitalism, chronobiopolitics, transsensory

Near the end of *The Autobiography of a Winnebago Indian* (1920), the life story of a Ho-Chunk man named Sam Blowsnake, the narrator has a strange experience. After taking peyote, a visionary medicine, he dies. In death he is "moved by another life": his body goes on "to move about and make signs," animated by the mescalinic sacrament or the living word of Earthmaker. Whatever inspires the body to speak also displaces the experience from its ostensible subject. "(My) body spoke of many things and it spoke of what was true," it says (447). At once seizing and vacating the authorial

American Literature, Volume 95, Number 3, September 2023
DOI 10.1215/00029831-10679209 © 2023 by Duke University Press

voice, the body's ecstatic resonance derails the grammar of dis/possessive subjectivation inserted (in parentheses) by Paul Radin, the ethnologist behind the *Autobiography*. Narrative time comes undone here: the peyote experience neither resolves an "inside view" of a mind typifying the "primitive community" (383), the telos of Radin's salvage project, nor even fully feeds its episodic "influence" into Blowsnake's redemptive script of conversion (446). As a device of sensuous estrangement, peyote releases aberrant streams of speech, feeling, and movement from the anthropomorphism that normally shapes first-person narration, ceding the voice of Radin's "native informant" (383) to an unseen source, the acousmatic *it*: "It was not I and I could not see it. . . . I would be confessing myself a fool if I were to think that I had said all this, it (my body) told me" (447).[1] Only once he resumes his "normal human condition"—once the sinuous time-space of ecstasy reverts to a temporary disturbance, once the confessing *I* recovers its perspectival grasp on the *it* Radin glosses as *(my body)* —only then does Blowsnake realize that some of his friends had feared he'd "gone crazy." "Others had liked it," though. They believed the "'shaking' state" may carry divine insight (447). Alternately dreaded as a pathology of lost self-possession and exalted as a conduit for the vitalizing power of Earthmaker, the tremor is a seismograph recording the forces of spatiotemporal rupture working to assimilate its subject to settler-capitalist modernity. Yet in so doing the narrative yields an extraneous mobility it can neither hold in nor shake off. Not just reflected but suffused and reanimated by the metamorphic sentience of Peyote, the ecstatic sensorium opens an exit from colonial schemas of chronoception.[2] Altered senses here make contact with currents of historical time that resound across dissentient practices of subaltern consciousness and announce modes of living beyond the privative realism allocated by settler regimes of chronic fracture.

As it oscillates between a sort of craziness and something one might like, the passage of ecstasy amplifies the historical moment of its solicitation—a peyote craze, as settler publics saw it.[3] Newspapers first noted the rise of the craze on the Winnebago Reservation in Nebraska around 1906, about a year before Blowsnake took peyote and seven years before he drafted the manuscript that became the *Autobiography*. John Rave, another Ho-Chunk Peyotist, introduced ritual use of the medicine to Wisconsin (where Blowsnake lived) around the turn of the century, carrying forward lines of spiritual and bodily transport—the Peyote Road—that had reached the Nebraska Winnebago Reservation as early as 1889 (La Barre 1989: 121; Stewart 1987:

148–62). Moving by rail or post from peyote gardens on the Mexico-Texas border, through Indian Territory and across the Northern Plains, the Peyote Road was turning the infrastructure of territorial settlement inside out. Agents of settler-capitalist rule had come to rely on the postal and transit systems to coordinate the long-range incorporation of Native lands and peoples under federal jurisdiction. Yet this same infrastructure also afforded the followers of Peyote a way to disseminate the counterterritorializing energies of what Gerald Vizenor (Anishinaabe) (1998: 15) calls "native transmotion," a sovereignty elicited not from "dominance over nature" but in visionary transfers of "creation with other creatures" (183).[4] Locating the autonomous trajectories of the Peyote Road as a threat to the assimilation of the national interior, the US settler bureaucracy, led by the Bureau of Indian Affairs (BIA), in turn arrayed new protocols of interception and intervention in the biochemical spread of the "Aztec narcotic" (Safford 1915) through Native populations. As histories of *peyōtl* in colonial Mexico attest, since the sixteenth century Spanish missionaries had condemned the *raíz diabólica* (diabolic root) as an intoxicant vehicle of idolatry, witchcraft, revolt, wildness, sexual license, and hallucinatory derangement (Dawson 2018; Jay 2019; Nesvig 2018; Snow 2016). Modern campaigns against "peyote worship" (Pierson 1915) conducted by government bureaucrats, progressive reformers, and sensationalist press exploited similarly paranoid scripts of revulsion and prurient fascination as they lobbied to eradicate the border-crossing "mind poison" (*Washington Times* 1918) in the early twentieth century. Just beneath the projections of psychotoxicity and degenerate sexuality invoked by the antinarcotic imaginary of the craze, this article posits, there ran an ongoing struggle over the racializing projects of restrictive capacitation that promised to disappear the native transmotion of Peyote into the unidirectional history and day-to-day reproduction of settler rule.

My argument in what follows speaks to how the practices of sensuous transport diffused along the Peyote Road could defy emplotment in the habitual regularities of property-bearing personhood administered and fantasized by the chronic architecture of allotment (1887–1934). Allotment was a program of land expropriation whereby the US federal government broke tribal reservations into a grid of privately owned parcels, granting individual plots to former "wards," who thus assumed American citizenship, and selling off the ensuing "surplus" to white settlers (McDonnell 1991: 14, 121). As the first part of this article argues, allotment interpellated its subjects in an ethnological idiom of schizochronism (Fabian 1983: 38), splitting Indigenous life from intersubjective time not by relegating it to a state of immutable exception but by scattering it across variable loci of social-evolutionary lag. Land privatization led a tectonic shift in the instrumental rationality and aesthetic form of what Dana Luciano (2007: 9) calls *chronobio-politics*, the "sexual arrangement of the time of life." Allotment, by contrast to the removal-era regime of anachronism she examines, was schizochronic: its policy was not to expel Native lifeworlds from national copresence but to fade them into indistinction with the normative habitus of settler-capitalist futurity. If still driven by a necropolitical logic of elimination, its ruptural process would no longer embed indigeneity in the ontological inertia of brute matter. At issue here is a torsion in the biopolitics of racial malleability. Kyla Schuller and Jules Gill-Peterson (2020) maintain that biocapitalist governance hinges on stratifications of plasticity that invest white bodies with a morphogenetic potential despoiled from racialized populations, which are cast as too rigid, erratic, or monolithic to create and retain complex form. Maldistribution of the malleable thus ossifies indigeneity as "a remnant of past growth" (2)—an archaic mass bound for extinction because incapable of the "dynamic instability" (3) that adapts individual bodies to living conditions. Near the end of the nineteenth century, however, the rise of residential schooling and other arenas of assimilationist capture would recast the anachronistic survival of Native life as a site of biopolitical manipulation or, as Schuller (2016: 243–44) puts it, "somatic transformation from savagery to civilization." Malleability surfaced in this moment not as the eminent domain of whiteness but as its mimetic reflex, extracted from the dead weight of racial ancestry by remedial exposure to disciplinary environments. Arraying protocols for the reform of sensorial, energetic, sexual, and rhythmic comportment, assimilation meant the abduction of Native subjects into a lifetime of propriative individuation—a strategy to accelerate the shattering of "tribal mass" into alienable shards of land and labor.[5] Not the racial aggregation of indigeneity, then, but the controlled demolition and plunder of its deracinated vitality defined the schizochronic matrix of allotment.

Linking that chronobiopolitical order to state renditions of competency and susceptibility, the second part of this article turns to the archive of Ho-Chunk peyotism to trace emergent drug-war protocols of restrictive capacitation. My lines of questioning unfold around the motifs of psychic and social-reproductive breakdown that succeeded models of spectral and prehistoric remainder as the governing configuration of Native viability under allotment. Norms appraising fitness for the life of propertied citizenship primed the apprehension of peyote as a cause of individual and familial collapse and hence a disabling threat to the absorption of Native subjects by settler society. Antinarcotic imaginaries seeded this aura of precarious incorporation with circuits of surveillance and reportage assembled around 1906, when white authorities first caught wind of the Peyote movement among Ho-Chunk people in Nebraska. Serial expansion of those circuits resulted in congressional hearings in 1918 on a bill to outlaw peyote (H.R. 2614). Kindling scandalized alarm via ethnopornographic images of toxic delirium and perverse frenzy, missionary groups called on apparatuses of state care and criminalization to extirpate the "peyote cult" (US Congress 1918: 20) before its malign influence could spread any further.[6] An ascetic rationality underpins the effort to expose that influence as a potentiation of communal hedonism fueled by individually damaging losses of sensorial fidelity, sexual continence, energetic hygiene, and rhythmic unison with the diurnal cycle of work discipline. Lapsed self-possession thus took form on the stage of state-racist investigation both as reversion to the archaic—an atavism—and as anarchic trespass, orgy, or subterfuge in need of legislative correction.[7] In its hyperbole the charge of anarchism fabricates a scenario that nonetheless suggests how the diffusion of Peyote across sensoria could subvert the compulsion to subordinate the many-bodied ecstatic potentiality of live presence to an individuating calculus of redemptive futurity. Attuning to the autonomous movements this altered sentience may generate, the final part of this article circles back to *The Autobiography of a Winnebago Indian*. Narrative digression from confessional to episodic form here dilates ecstatic temporality around the voice of another life—a life whose exteriority to the present at once foils the ascription of autological subjecthood and eludes the audit of its extrahuman body for echoes of primitive stasis or developmental relapse.[8] Against the work of schizochronic individuation, encounters with Peyote call forth sonic, kinesthetic, and transsensory pathways that let the autoaffective pulsation between interior receptivity and somatic resonance multiply without returning to a self-reflexive center of consciousness.[9] Movements along such pathways not only stray outside the biological closure of the organism and the mechanism of abstract time, I argue, but also choreograph a historical moment that could in turn draw past anticolonial resistance toward incipient horizons of Indigenous world creation.

Allotment and the Schizochronism of Competency

In May 1916, a "competency commission" sent by the US Department of the Interior arrived at the Yankton Sioux Reservation in South

Dakota to stage the inaugural performance of a "Ritual on Admission of Indians to Full American Citizenship." Its mission was to grant Indian "wards" the status of "free American citizens" by leading new allottees through a sex-bifurcated script of renunciation. Men shoot their "last arrow" and take hold of "the plow," thus affirming that "only by work do we gain a right to the earth or to the enjoyment of life." Laden with the duty of making a home for the "future of our Nation," women accept a "work bag and purse" to avow that "she and her children will not starve" only if she "saves her money." Men trade their *"Indian name"* for a *"white name"*; the representative addresses women by the latter alone (US Department of the Interior [1916] 1929).[10] At work throughout the ritual is, to adapt Audra Simpson (Kahnawà:ke Mohawk)'s (2014: 24) critique, an injunction to enjoy the "gift" of minoritarian citizenship and contort Native self-governance to satisfy the affective criteria of a settler-capitalist "theater of apprehension." Native voice may embrace simultaneity with the "shared, unified 'now'" of the nation only on the condition that it relinquish any remaining tie to what Mark Rifkin (2017: 2, 110) calls "temporal sovereignty." More than that, the ritual dictates a rule of ascetic restraint wherein the allottee can only survive if he or she is liberated from the "ethnic past," as Rey Chow (2002: 49) might put it—pledging not just to endure but to internalize work discipline as the sole ground of pleasure and habitation. Luciano's (2007: 74) chronobiopolitical analysis might observe that, for women, the ritual grounds the "linear-accumulative" time of asceticism—figured by the mortal duress of saving money—in a "cyclical-repetitive" time that subordinates futurity to the biological reproduction and loving maintenance of home life. If her study concerns a regime of anachronism that apprehended the Native voice as both an echo of the archaic past and an exception to linear history as such, however, here we find a related but distinct regime of *schizochronism*, a mode of biopower administered via the proliferation of temporal breakages.[11] Allotment compelled not the removal of Native vitalities to a federally bounded space outside national time, I argue, but their progressive adequation to rationalized futurity via the revocation of any tendencies ascribed to the social-evolutionary past.

Mystifying the coercion of propriative citizenship as a consensual act of transformation, the ritual envisions allotment as a kind of laissez-faire tutelage in the white agrarian ethos of improvement.[12] Assimilation draws energy here from the severance of tribal bonds and exposure to "the habits of civilized life" (US Department of the Interior [1916] 1929), a phrase the ritual lifts verbatim from the General Allotment Act (Dawes Act; ch. 119, §6, 24 Stat. 388, 390 [1887]).

Mere proximity to white neighbors was supposed to instill a self-reliant work ethic in allottees. For instance, the reformer Merrill Edwards Gates (1886: 141–42) declared that allotment would let "life-giving currents of civilized life" cut through the "sticky layers" of vice that insulated reservations from the good exemplarity of neighboring settlements. Not only did Gates extol the moral education of landownership but he also called for policies that would cut off rations and annuity payments, pry apart extended kin groups to make heteronuclear families (Phillips 2009), criminalize Native religions (Wenger 2014), and summon people to punitive equality in the US court system—all to liquidate Indians' "savage communism" (Gates 1897: 9). According to Eric N. Olund (2002: 142), reformers like Gates advanced a "redemptive vision of the law" that hinged on the association of Indian Country with "lawlessness" in need of a "law that would individuate its inhabitants." Jessica R. Cattelino (2018: 280–81) holds that allotment's "money-property-government complex" answered that need in part because it furnished economic and legal subjects who had no choice but to "extend the temporality of their desires" into a precarious future. No matter whether they yearned for national belonging or just dreaded starving, allottees would have to conform their appetites to the abstract self-continuity needed to improve their lot in and after life. Landownership held the promise of producing that desiring subject from the regularities of the labor it compelled, the horizons of expenditure and accumulation it unfolded, and the normalizing contact with white civil society it obligated. Over time, reformers thought, such associations would blend Native bodies into a civilized habitus that could hope to live into the settler-national future and would deserve to live on in the Christian eternity.

Many schizochronic mechanisms converged in settler society's attempts to disintegrate bodily comportments attuned to the time of Indigenous lifeworlds. Among the most powerful coalesced in the racializing fracture of kinship, the heteropatriarchal division of labor time, and the anthropocentric extinction of environmental vitality. Native land rights came to depend on assimilationist norms of racial fitness between 1906, when the Burke Act authorized the issuing of "fee patents" to allottees deemed capable of managing property without federal oversight, and 1917, when Cato Sells, the commissioner of Indian affairs, granted competency to "all Indians with less than one-half Indian blood" (Ellinghaus 2017: 57). Allotment realized the commensuration of land with the discrete rectilinear divisions of the survey map in part by generating "sanguinary documentation" of an "individual subject located within a linear and collateral family," as Nicole Tonkovich (2012: 185) has argued vis-à-vis the Nebraska Winnebago cases processed by special agent Alice Fletcher from 1887 to 1889. Not only did Fletcher straighten Ho-Chunk kinship along lines amenable to a patriarchal logic of inheritance, but she also played an intimate, often deceitful role in the "recruitment" of Ho-Chunk children for removal to settler boarding schools like the Hampton Institute and the Carlisle School (Jacobs 2009: 199). K. Tsianina Lomawaima (Mvskoke/Creek Nation) (1994: 86) examines in her study of Chilocco Indian School how such institutions subjected Indian girls to "training in dispossession under the guise of domesticity, developing a habitus shaped by the messages of subservience and one's proper place."[13] At stake in the cultivation of Native women's capacity to bear and find their bearings in "bodily submissions" to the rule of property, Beth Piatote (Nez Perce) (2013: 112) contends, was a "performative taxonomy of citizenship" that threw private domains open to public inspection by a liberal state invested in normalizing any perceived aberrance in Native "family forms." More abstractly, we might say that the state fixed its gaze on a racial ontology of blood and the coerced performance of private time's sacralizing regularity to stem the fallout of a concomitant effort to extract Native lives from the sacred durations of the earth and the animacy of living environments.[14] Allotment schizochronism thus came into effect along multiple fault lines, wherever the conduct of "civilized life" dislocated the sense of time from traditional rhythms of inhabitance. In this way its normative agenda was to bind habit-forming bodies to a colonial order in which Native survival could never achieve sovereign presence but, rather, hinged on the exhibition of lineal and libidinal attachments to earned or inherited claims on heteroreproductive futurity.

Unfit for Daily Life: Regulating the Peyote Craze

Just as agents of settler-capitalist rule collocated racializing metrics and assimilationist norms in the abandonment of allottees to property-bearing citizenship, so too did they administer new legal controls to enforce the biochemical consistency of schizochronic comportment.[15] The year the Department of the Interior put on the first citizenship ritual in South Dakota, 1916, was also the year Harry Gandy, the representative of that state, brought H.R. 10669 to Congress. If passed, the bill would have enabled the government to fine or imprison anyone convicted of transporting, selling, or using peyote. Likening its effects to alcohol and the menace of opium, antipeyote reformers tied to the Society of American Indians and the Lake Mohonk Conference lobbied for the Gandy bill with a rhetoric of narcotic peril that cast the "drug" as a cause of acute intoxication, chronic physical injury, mental deterioration, and impending social breakdown. Acting as a representative of the Society of American Indians during the 1918 congressional hearings on a later version of the bill, H.R. 2614, Yankton Dakota writer and activist Gertrude Bonnin (Zitkála-Šá) verified a lurid scenario imagining that "[peyote] use leads to the wildest intoxication and all kinds of orgies in which men, women, and even children take part, to the degradation of their minds" (*Washington Times* 1918). Much of her testimony (US Congress 1918) revolves around the extrapolation of "'data against peyote'" from this ur-scene of primitive sexual degeneracy. It substantiates, for Bonnin, an obscene reality of racial debasement usually veiled from settler authorities by self-conscious "restraint" (124), or what her interlocutor calls "subterfuge" (128). Known to government agents as *mescal buttons* up until the 1910s, the Anglophone excavation of the loanword *peyote*, from the Nahuatl *peyōtl* (Nesvig 2018), enmeshed official scrutiny of Peyotism in an ethnopornographic fascination with its aura of archaic origins in pre-Columbian Mexico. Antinarcotic rhetoric, fueled by concurrent expansions in federal drug law (i.e., the Pure Food and Drug Act of 1906, Smoking Opium Exclusion Act of 1909, and Harrison Narcotics Tax Act of 1914), lent that aura an edge of seductive transmissibility.[16] Yet these tropes of vicious influence and diffusion succeeded not only in inflaming moral panic but also in further spreading the autonomous tempos of peyote ecstasies—their anarchaic potential to reroute the lucid progression of settler-capitalist modernity through the occult proliferations of the peyote habit.[17] In the following analysis, therefore, I approach the craze not just as an ideological distortion but also as a genre for the making of subaltern history, set in motion through practices of sensuous transport that could at once deflect and disorder the assimilation to allotted time.

Around the turn of the century reports of a "mescal craze" began spilling out of Indian Territory. To describe the spread of Peyotism as a craze was to constrain its world-making potentials by, at best, reducing them to an "artificial paradise" (Ellis 1898) or, at worst, equating them with the mental instability of aspiring citizen-subjects. Newspapers cited the reports of white experimenters like S. Weir Mitchell and Havelock Ellis in an effort to pathologize the altered comportments and ecstatic structures of feeling Peyote meetings were known to generate. One of the first stories to profile the craze, headlined "Color Visions in Mescal Bean," claims that peyote "gives the Indians strong hallucinations that influence their daily conduct, frequently toward violence, and on this account white settlers living in their vicinity are alarmed for their own safety" (*Chicago Daily Tribune* 1899). Just living in the vicinity of white settlements was, according to the ideology of allotment, supposed to reform the "lawless" reservations by environing them with examples of the good life of propriative citizenship. Accesses of ecstasy registered as alarm for white sensoria because they opened lines of transport that cut across the privatizing allocation of somatic proximities and territorial boundaries. Not only that, but these transports could disturb the "daily conduct" that made settler rule feel like a routine occupation. To yield to the craze, on this view, was to go crazy—not just for the moment but permanently debilitating the possessive binding of desire in habits of rational self-continuity across space and time.

January 1906 saw the craze resurface after years of relative latency. Now the revulsive alarm of newspaper publics and state agencies closed in on the upsurge of "Mescal Society" at the Winnebago Reservation in Thurston County, Nebraska. As far west as Los Angeles, catastrophic scenarios of drug-crazed violence rescripted the mescal rite as a "gateway to lunacy" that might lead to "armed rebellion" if not shut down by federal authorities (*Los Angeles Times* 1906). Not many stories were quite so paranoid. Most framed the craze as a source of "demoralizing" superstitions and incapacitating excitements, not a hotbed of anticolonial insurrection. A story originally published in the *Sioux City Tribune* and circulating under the title "Insidious Mescal Fatal to Indians" claimed in June 1906, for example, that the "outraged bodies" of mescal eaters usually took days to recover from the aftereffects of the "horrible orgy" (*Forest City Press* 1906). Insofar as they detached vital energies from a habitus that measured every expenditure in the present against what it allotted for the future, these "wild orgies" seemed to endanger the day-to-day reproduction of settler-capitalist forms of life. Linking "religious ecstasy" to "the horrors of insanity," "racial extinction," "inevitable physical decline," and "more crime, more licentiousness, and more devil-may-care wildness," the story ends by blaming "mescal buds" for "destroying the Indians who own 100,000 acres of the finest and most fertile lands on which the sun has ever shone."[18] To some extent this final note of pathos simply rehearses the genocidal fantasy that Winnebago self-destruction would clear new land for white settlement. But in calling for state intervention the story also preoccupies itself with the impairment and recuperation of competence for individual landownership. News coverage of the peyote craze sought, in other words, to delimit and reincorporate a plane of collective sensuousness that allowed Indigenous people to escape or abandon the schizochronic work of allotment.

Affidavits on Ho-Chunk Peyotism submitted to the BIA in late 1911 appeared to verify the public intuition that the craze was interfering in the allotment process. In 1918 Bonnin entered a copy of the file into the record during Senate hearings on a provision to suppress liquor traffic (US Congress 1919). Medical commentary given by the mission doctor Rev. Walter Clark Roe, physiological tests conducted by the government chemist E. B. Putt, and tribal data tabulated by Albert H. Kneale, superintendent of the Winnebago and Omaha Agency, are interspersed in the BIA file with depositions from John Semans, Harry Rave, and other Ho-Chunk people. All try to assess the extent to which the passions of "mescal worship" sexually debase, mentally debilitate, or otherwise delay progress toward a civilized life. Not surprisingly, Roe stresses how the "all-night character of their worship unfits the peyote eaters for active service the following day." Something besides the "industrial efficiency" of the body is at issue, however. Because peyote "excites the imagination and relaxes the will," Roe deduces, it must be an aphrodisiac, leading to "sexual immorality" and "scenes of unbridled libertinism" (33). Semans corroborates these speculations. Nocturnal meetings, on his account, conceal intimacies that stray outside the reprosexual enclosure of the married couple. More than simply accommodating extramarital sex, though, the meetings generate a promiscuous surplus of feeling that "makes [the young men] very crazy after the girls" and "affects the girls the same way," Semans attests (35). According to Rave, too, eating peyote lets people "think more or want more about what they are thinking" and thus risks giving those who think "bad things" license to "lose all their ashamed," like the two women he says "tore off their clothes right in the meeting" and "pulled out their hair" (37). Loss of shame divests the subject of self-possession, here, not by making her thoughtless but by amplifying desire for the sensuous thinking the body does on its own. As the settler bureaucracy saw it, these acute intensifications of shamelessness enabled an excitement so draining that it threatened to wear out the peyote eaters' nervous systems both in everyday life and in the progressive evolutionary time of racial assimilation.

Nevertheless, if the pathologization of Peyote rituals depended on the charge of improper conduct, that charge set off mechanisms of state care whose more general aim was to rehabilitate, or at least recontain, subjects who had lost the capacity for economic independence. To that end Rave closes his statement by naming a number of people whom he alleges the craze had driven insane. One woman known only as "Taylor Houghton's wife" was even committed to the Norfolk Asylum in Nebraska after she "got crazy" (37) from eating mescal. As data tabulated in the BIA file on Ho-Chunk Peyotism suggests, the settler bureaucracy would have apprehended this reaction less as a lapse of disciplinary order than as a class of irregularity in the total record of each tribe member's "degree of competency." After first separating out the "nonablebodied," the classificatory matrix found here assigns its subject population one of three grades: "A-1 signifies that the Indian is self-supporting by his own efforts"; "A-2 signifies that the Indian is partially self-supporting"; "A-3 signifies that the Indian is making no effort at self-support" (44–46). Only men populate this list; women are implicitly subsumed under male heads of household. Not unlike the ritual discussed in the first section, the tabulation of competency assimilates women to a position of subservience. At other points in the report, though, the sexual overexposure of women's bodies marks a breakdown in their ability to sustain the affective restraint and material reproduction of heteronuclear forms of home life. In this dialectic of invisibility and hypervisibility, women's bodies screen the gendered divisions of labor time and comportment that were to prop up the appearance of self-sufficiency in those the state deemed competent. Wherever the craze disheveled settler norms of feminine propriety, then, it also signaled a failure of conjugal and maternal care severe enough to require the intervention of the care of the state.

No scenario recurred more obsessively in the campaign against peyote than that which depicted Indigenous women debased by the animalistic shamelessness of drug-crazed abandon. Journalists, missionaries, and reformers lobbying for a federal suppression of peyote derived the choreography of that scenario from the BIA file discussed above, feeding excerpts from Semans's and Rave's affidavits through the propaganda machine they built in preparation for the 1918 congressional hearings. Anonymous passages from the file had come into public circulation at the Lake Mohonk Conference four years earlier (Daiker 1914), framing the peyote habit as a cause of death and intoxicant debility but also laying an amorphous charge of "immoral" (68) conduct on the "Peyote Society" (67). Latent deviance takes shape, in a version of Rave's deposition that surfaced a year later, as the peripheral abjection of women who "'lie around the corners of the room like a lot of dogs,'" "'like they lose all their ashamedness'" (Pierson 1915: 203–4). Another, more widely circulated piece, "Peyote Worship: An Indian Cult and a Powerful Drug" (Seymour 1916), would reprise this misogynist display of racial depravation.[19] Now the gaze mortifies the forfeit of propriety not as idle disgrace but as rabid bestialization: again they "'lose all their ashamedness,'" but here the loss inflames "animal passions" that see the women fall to "tearing their clothes and pulling out their hair" (Seymour 1916: 182). And again, in a newspaper exposé that relocates the scenario from Nebraska to Utah, "possessed of animal instincts," Ute women "lose all sense of modesty." Kneale, the agent associated with the original BIA file, even shows up here to stage a report from a Ft. Duchesne man who says he beat his wife because, "'crazed'" by peyote, she "'tore the clothing from her body and danced about almost naked in the presence of all the others'" (Matson 1916). In its pornotropic structure this scenario draws a libidinal surplus from the insinuation of unbound enjoyment kept just out of frame, only to purge that excess through the stigmatic breakdown from woman to flesh. Marked by a racializing logic of atavism, the "animal instincts" that possess her body also expropriate it from subservience to white norms of domestic and conjugal intimacy. Across each iteration the scenario projected a sense of chronic crisis by magnifying the retroactive humiliation of Indigenous women who let their flesh unravel from the individuating circuits of shame that held together the private life of settler heteropatriarchy.[20] Mobilizing an abusive correction of female deviance, the aim of the image was to both evince and preempt a more general divestiture of Indigenous sensoria from the sociosexual fabric of private property relations compelled by allotment.

Moralizing reflexes ingrained by assimilationist discourse impel the fixation of this scenario on the comorbidity between the dancing women's "total abandonment of virtue" and the "'waste [of] time, strength, and money'" in "nocturnal debaucheries" (Indian Rights Association 1916: 38–40; US Congress 1918: 20–21). Assimilationism, as Tisa Wenger (2014: 138) has shown in her work on attempts to suppress Pueblo dances in the 1920s, displaced biological theories of permanent racial inferiority in favor of a cultural racism that sought to end the "degrading" continuation of tribal practices, which Indigenous leaders therefore had to defend, in Euro-American terms, as religious. Layered into this reform discourse, despite its posture of virtuous concern, is a strain of prurience that derives from inaugural acts of scopic colonization. An imperial pornotropics, as Anne McClintock (1995: 22) construes it, sets up the placement of Indigenous women's bodies as "boundary markers" (24) on the "liminal scene" (26) of orgiastic dance insofar as that scene oscillates around their absolute sexual vulnerability and border-dissolving voracity. Joining the assimilationist script to this obscene undercurrent is a vortex of attraction and revulsion spiraling toward the fantasmatic ruin of sexed bodies' energetic, sensorial, and temporal self-containment in the intensification of ecstasy. Antipeyote campaigns thus recirculated the scenario of crazed naked dancing as if it were intuitive evidence for the urgency and generality of the vague causal nexus posited among idol worship, promiscuous sex, injurious expenditure, and reversion to a state of incompetency. Lapses of propriety slide, in the lurid redundancy of that scenario, toward an impending collapse of the Native subject's present and future viability for the daily life of propriative citizenship. As a means to overcode craze wherever it arrived, the scenario at once reinforced the imaginary coherence of peyotism and incited the anticipation of an incalculable radius of effect that demanded correspondent expansions in the assimilationist project of restrictive capacitation.

Yet if this antinarcotic imaginary scripted the craze as a regression from the civilizing work of allotment, the apprehension of crisis was more than a reaction to a perceived reversal on the timeline of cultural-economic development. To frame the spread of peyotism as a craze was to anticipate both its contagious volatility as an event *in* and its tendency to derange the rational periodization *of* historical time. As an instance of what Jennifer L. Fleissner (2004: 129) calls "fad culture," a craze designates an inflation of the "self-determining individual" (124) by the all-consuming caprice of mass culture at a given moment in history. Like the "ghost-dance craze" (US Congress 1918: 147) of the late 1880s, however, the proliferation of Peyote rites looked dangerous to settler domination not because they resembled the loss of agency in frenzied consumption but because they contravened the governing consensus that colonial subjugation would soon reach its supposedly inevitable end point: the disappearance of Native peoples. In its diffusion across the Northern Plains from the 1890s forward, Peyote's lines of transport carried enduring affinities with the same wave of "pan-Indian cultural resistance" to US assimilationism that, Scott Richard Lyons (Ojibwe/Dakota) (2010: 63) argues, coalesced in the Ghost Dance.[21] Lyons (1999: 152) elsewhere interprets Peyotism as the creation of a "new pan-Indian body" through "unmediated religious experience made in metis space," a cultural space intermixing "tribal, extratribal, and non-Indian elements." In clearing the way for a form of embodiment unaccountable to the time-based agendas of racial assimilation, Lyons suggests, Peyote offered to heal the "Western mind/body split" and solidify a renewed sense of collective wholeness. As a zone of historical intermixture, too, Peyote meetings could open paths around that split—a schizochronic split, dividing the timeless from the time bound—by at once invoking roots in precolonial tradition, carrying forward the resistant energy of movements from the recent past, and welcoming the autonomy of an incipient future unrestricted by settler-capitalist rule.

Another Life: Historical Poiesis in the Episode of Ecstasy

Most readings of *The Autobiography of a Winnebago Indian* sketch this moment only in passing. So far neither the reverberation of scenes from the Winnebago "craze" in the national antinarcotic imaginary nor, conversely, the historical poetics of peyote ecstasies has received extensive study.[22] Instead critics focus on the vexed configuration of autobiographical, ethnographic, and Indigenous genres in which Blowsnake's text emplots the discursive action of its confessional subject. My reading of the *Autobiography* argues for the perspectival and temporal convolution of that subject by the transsensory movement of "another life"—the life of bodies in ecstasy, overtaken and moved to speak by Earthmaker, God, or Peyote itself, among other spirits. Amidst these bodies unfold episodes of collective transport that lose the plot of an individuated life story as much as they escape the stasis of the ethnopornographic present. But if these ecstasies may seem to hold out a scene of spiritual exception from linear temporality, in practice they were never sealed off from mundane loci of association and rhythms of gathering. Altered senses of time and embodiment in the Peyote meeting no doubt concentrated the intensities of a sacred ritual setting (meetings lasting all night, in a circle, around a fire), but they also spilled over into the more amorphous horizons of the next day, the next night, the next weekend. Narratively speaking, the *Autobiography* reenacts this contiguous pacing through a succession of episodes that both take the senses beyond and run them alongside allotted time frames. Letting one day lapse into the next, peyote ecstasies stretch the amplitude of the present. In this way they could lift sensuous capacities out of the day-to-day regulation of settler-capitalist life and pull apart the tissue of temporal breakages that would otherwise divide bodily sentience up for allotment regimes of work and rest.

Not many analyses of the *Autobiography* examine its episodic structures in much detail. As a consequence, this work conflates the life animating the life story with the voice of a confessional subject corresponding to a person named Sam Blowsnake. The question, then, becomes how the confessional voice mediates the power asymmetries Blowsnake confronted as a "native informant" (Radin 1983: xx) for Paul Radin, the anthropologist who assembled, annotated, and arranged for the publication of the *Autobiography* in 1920. All of this editorial work, to complicate things further, was based on the translations that Radin's interpreter, Oliver Lamere (Ho-Chunk), made from a manuscript in Hočąk syllabary, which Radin had induced Blowsnake to compose in 1913. It was not until 1926 that a retranslated and enlarged version of the text entered circulation under the title *Crashing Thunder: The Autobiography of a Winnebago Indian*. These multiple loci of composition merge, for Radin, to form an "ethnological and psychological document" of a "multiple personality" that belongs to Blowsnake alone but also stands to typify the "primitive people" he represents (xxxiii–iv).[23] Against this documentary impulse, Michelle Burnham (1998: 470) stresses how Ho-Chunk trickster mythology works in *Crashing Thunder* to deconstruct the criteria for social scientific "accuracy" that are supposed to authenticate the veridiction of the confessional *I*. If trickster discourse may tease out and undo the colonial relations of the autobiographical subject to ethnographic authority, however, Burnham does not yet situate the "irresolvable paradox" of confessed deception in the contradiction it reflects. As Grant Arndt (2012: 42) contends, Peyotism and the chronic dispossession it countered—a site of "Indigenous experimentation and struggle" against forced removals, massive land theft, and settler encroachment via allotment—make up the necessary sociohistorical ground for the "mise-en-abyme" (28) effect of the *Autobiography*. Arndt reads this formal device (the recursive nesting of narrated events) as the "auto-transcription" (40) of a confessional discourse Blowsnake had already rehearsed in his conversion to Peyotism, hence as a "socially distributed" mode of "representational agency" (41). Yet while this reading may allow us to follow the emergence of a confessional voice from the self-fashioning work of conversion, it does not specify how that voice maintains and loses its ability to plot episodes of ecstasy within a life story. Nor does Arndt's notion of historical context, though attuned to Ho-Chunk dispossession, account for how the moment of the craze initiated oppositional ways of living through the fragmentation of history in chronic crisis. Attending more closely to episodes of ecstasy, particularly where they skew or thin out the autobiographical plot, expands our sense of the multiple agencies that animated everyday life under allotment.

If conversion seeks to fashion another self through the semiotic repertoires of prayer, reflective suffering, and confession of sin, ecstasy sweeps the body up in the motion of a life that no longer aligns with any integral self. Moved by this life, the confessional subject edges toward a sort of decentered reflexivity, in which assembled bodies may rethink live relations from somewhere outside the possessive investment in their own discrete presence. Loss or displacement of the usual contours of somatic experience can sometimes lead to a fusion with others so seamless that each constituent body comes to feel not just indistinct but immaterial. "'My corporeal affairs are over'" is indeed how Blowsnake (1920: 442) says he felt after the apparent climax of his conversion to Peyotism. Just before dawn, he and the circle of other Peyotists had come to have "all together one spirit": "I instantly became the spirit and I was their spirit or soul." Once their spirits have circled into one, Blowsnake finds that he can know whatever the others think without having to speak with them. Not only that, but when he thinks "of a certain place, far away," he finds that "immediately [he is] there." Thought turns into a medium of instantaneous transfers. As they go out of their senses together, the ecstatics are not just disembodied but at the same time moved to reembody the spiritual powers of the other life that passes through them. But the telekinetic structures of thinking and feeling that extend from this episode bear only superficial likeness to the states of intoxication with which ecstasy was so often confounded. Neither the sacralizing excitement that Emile Durkheim (1995: 216–21) called "collective effervescence" nor the abandonment of individuation to some Dionysian substratum (Bloch 1996: 59) adequately describes the Peyotists' experience. Dissolution of the self in a transcendent or inchoate continuum of being is not the source of ecstasy here. It emerges, rather, from the transports of sensoria assembled on the verge of losing self-possession while retaining and even augmenting the capacity to think collectively through that condition.

Narrating ecstasy is tricky, though—first because episodes of somesthetic intensification tend to stray from autobiographical plotlines but also because that movement opens onto a field of alternate perspectives that carry narratorial agency outside the sphere of human sentience as such. More than deconstructing or socially redistributing the confessional subject, the episode of ecstasy allows unseen voices to speak through and confound the device of first-person narration. One such episode in the next-to-last chapter of the 1920 *Autobiography*, which Radin titles "I Have a Strange Experience," plays out like this:

I died, and my body was moved by another life. It began to move about; to move about and make signs. It was not I and I could not see it. At last it stood up. . . . (My) body spoke of many things and it spoke of what was true. Indeed it spoke of many things. It spoke of all the things that were being done (by the pagan Indians) and which were evil. A long time it spoke. At last it stopped. Not I, but my body standing there, had done the talking. Earthmaker (God) had done his own talking. I would be confessing myself a fool if I were to think that I had said all this, it (my body) told me.

After a while I returned to my normal human condition. Some of those there had been frightened, thinking that I had gone crazy. Others had liked it. It was discussed a good deal. They called it the "shaking" state. (Blowsnake 1920: 447)

Another life moves the body to speak. What the speaking body says enunciates an *it* that slips out of perspectival alignment with the narrating *I*: "It was not I and I could not see it." Ownership of the body turns into a parenthetical operation. "(My) body" comes to articulate the condition in which possession and dispossession cross over one another: the ecstasy that lets another life overtake the body also takes the body out of itself.[24] Living again through the movements of this other life does not simply dissociate the narrator from his physical and sensuous center, however. As it passes through him, the *it* wraps the *I* up in the convolutions of its speaking body. Nowhere is that coil wound tighter than in the sentence that brings the episode to an end. At this point the speaking body overtly toys with impersonating or even deposing the confessional voice, at first seeming to resuscitate the *I* only to twist back into an indirect discourse spoken by "it (my body)." Rewritten in direct discourse, the sentence reads: "'You would be confessing yourself a fool if you were to think that you had said all this,' it (my body) told me." In the original sentence, then, the *I* does not come from the body speaking in the first person but instead represents the speech act with which the body addresses the narrator as *you*. Of course, the trick here is that the use of indirect discourse conceals itself until the end of the sentence, when the *it* suddenly retracts the would-be confessional voice. But even then it remains ambiguous: "it (my body)" indicates less a single discursive agent than the convergence of "my body standing there" and "Earthmaker (God)" speaking at the same time, if not necessarily with the same voice. Moving amidst these multiple agents, each taking its own perspective on the scene, the episode of ecstasy sets the confessional subject off-center only to loop it back through a peripheral sense of the speaking body's strange animacy.

Nonetheless, it would be misleading to conclude from the preceding instances that the condition of ecstasy confined itself to climactic scenes of eccentric or incorporeal sensation. It was not just by eliciting torsions in ordinary self-presence but also by inducting its devotees in a newly elastic structure of sociohistorical experience that Peyote formed lifeworlds that at once crossed the fractures and went off the grid of the settler-capitalist everyday. As it unfolds over time, the episode of ecstasy conforms not to a teleological arc but instead to an open-ended process that curves along variably spanned crests, ebbs, plateaus, and gradations of intensity. Nowhere are the world-making dimensions of this sinuous duration better exemplified than in the account Blowsnake gives of his first time eating peyote. When he comes to visit relatives in Nebraska, his younger sister, Hinákega (Distant Flashes Standing), convinces him to join the "peyote people" (436) in their ceremony. Most of the night he experiences relatively little effect. Something feels different but he can see "nothing wrong about [him]self." Later, after midnight, people are crying and he begins to "see strange things" with his eyes closed, but the most salient alteration is a lack of sleepiness, which lasts until "the light (of morning) [comes] upon [him]" and throughout the next day. Another meeting is planned for that night, and the Peyote people entice Blowsnake to come learn how "'their spirits wander over all the earth and the heavens also.'" Though skeptical, he follows:

> So we went there again. I doubted all this. . . . However I went along anyhow. When we got there I had already eaten some peyote, for I had taken three during the day. Now near the peyote meeting an (Indian) feast was being given and I went there instead. When I reached the place, I saw a long lodge. The noise was terrific. They were beating an enormous drum. The sound almost raised me in the air, so (pleasurably) loud did it sound to me. Not so (pleasurable) had things appeared at those affairs (peyote meetings) that I had lately been attending. (437)

Central to this passage is the contrast between the solemn air of the Peyote meeting and the sonic buoyancy of the nearby feast. Much of this atmospheric divergence stems from the iconoclastic break that adherents of Ho-Chunk Peyotism made with traditional feasts and religious societies like the Medicine Dance. But in practice these social and spiritual worlds could overlap with one another in a common amplification of a present not yet flattened into the laborious routinization of the settler-capitalist everyday. Lifted on a current of sound and the afterglow of the previous night, Blowsnake's sensorium resonates with a pleasure that carries him into the next evening, this time taken up in dancing and flirting. By the end of the sequence, he and the others have spent four nights eating peyote together. Sometimes they take it as a kind of social lubricant, and sometimes they use it to elicit ceremonial suffering. Yet their sustained recurrence to the ritual time of the Peyote meeting interlaces with mundane expansions of the amplitude of the present. Settled horizons of work and rest come undone in the indefinite dilation of their ecstasies, digressing into the atelic logic of an experience that no longer keeps time with the segmented reproduction of life from one day to the next.

■ ■ ■

Lapsing into the episodic passage of ecstasy, out of the senses with which one ordinarily receives and acts on the world, is at the same time a way to let another present elapse alongside the normative rhythms of everyday life.[25] New ways of living through allotted time gather into and spread out from the interval of an alteration that brings another world to pass in the process of passing out of the world as it seemingly already is. Moments in that passage split, decenter, or multiply the autoaffective voice in which the experiencing subject would otherwise claim their experience, instead composing figurations of collective sentience that a lifeworld made up of schizochronic breakages would rather disappear. Nonetheless, nowhere do we see the semiosis of that collective fall into mere "presignifying polyvocality"—a poststructuralist motif that, as Jodi Byrd (Chickasaw) (2011: 18–19) contends, plays on the spectral trace of Indianness to manifest a *terra nullius* of metamorphic affects detached from "lived colonial conditions of Indigeneity." Allotted time was not a structure Blowsnake could dissolve, but he and his companions could nonetheless refuse to internalize its aspirational contract of experiential and somatic constriction. Led down paths of sensorial alteration by Peyote, their practice not only afforded a means to build counterinstitutions under the aegis of religious freedom (i.e., the Native American Church) but also formed an Indigenous medium of mobile association and persistence through ecstatic discontinuations of the already-accumulated future. More than simply acting out a compensatory fantasy of some more perfect world or culminating in a communal occasion to repair the sad reality of this one, the Peyote Road would instead extend the amplitude of participants' sensoria and in turn generate new currents of historical poiesis—a sense of history in the making, not yet overdetermined by the horizon of chronic dispossession.

Sylvie Boulette is a writer and scholar living in the settler-occupied homelands of the Three Fires Council, a confederacy of the Ojibwe, Odawa, and Bodéwadmi Nations. She teaches at the University of Chicago. Her work has also appeared in *American Quarterly.*

Notes

Many thanks to Edgar Garcia, Frances Ferguson, Marissa Fenley, Lauren Jackson, Jacob Harris, Brandon Truett, Mercedes Trigos, Julia Xiao Yun Cheng, and the Religions in America Workshop for their thoughtful responses to earlier versions of the manuscript.

1   Martha Feldman and Judith T. Zeitlin (2019: 6) suggest that "all voices are acousmatic, their source never visible or otherwise fully accessible to their bearers or hearers."

2   On chronoception (the sensing of time) in a context of ritual alteration, see Dorland 2017: 17–19. Anticolonial critique of realist genres of chronoception may lead us, with Bliss Cua Lim (2009: 107–8), to parse the agentic force of "preternatural anomalies" (demons, angels, or, here, Peyote) not as mere figurative residue of an alternate sensorium but, more radically, as the animate trace of "*immiscible times*—multiple times that never quite dissolve into the code of modern time consciousness" (12).

3   A note on style: in this article I capitalize *Peyote* when referring to the spirit of the entheogen itself or the spiritual movement it generates. I use the lowercase *peyote*, by contrast, to connote the vernacular reference (often made by settler authorities) to a drug, substance, or plant.

4   After buying supplies from the Laredo peyote gardens, roadmen would load them onto the Texas-Mexican Railroad and then transship them on the International and Great Northern line to Indian Territory. On rail transport, see Stewart 1987: 139–40, 61. Also see Hoxie 1992: 987.

5   Notoriously, Theodore Roosevelt (1901: 39) declared that allotment would "recognize the Indian as an individual," in this case defined as the by-product of the "mighty pulverizing engine to break up the tribal mass."

6   Apprehension of those held in "biopolitical states of care" entails, for Audra Simpson (2014: 24, 10), both immediate and deferred modes of control: the arresting grasp of the authorities that detain subjects in transit and the anticipatory reach of regulatory agencies as they predict the movement of populations. On the asymmetries of recognition, see also Coulthard 2014. On ethnographic penetration and archival distortion, see Sigal, Tortorici, and Whitehead 2019: 17.

7   On the turn-of-the-century science and culture of atavism, an evolutionary model of the resurgence of outmoded traits or instincts, see Seitler 2008.

8   As Elizabeth Povinelli (2006: 4) defines it, the *autological subject* refers to "discourses, practices, and fantasies about self-making, self-sovereignty, and the value of individual freedom associated with the Enlightenment project of contractual constitutional democracy and capitalism." On the

history of animism as an anthropological concept of "other-than-human-persons," see Harvey 2005: 17–20. On developmentalism, the administration of empty time, and the disenchantment of historical agency, see Chakrabarty 2000.

9 Autoaffection, for Patricia Clough (2000: 17), refers to how subjects cohere in the self-continuous speech and reflexive audition of an "inner voice" and hence depends on "the disavowal of the unconscious as the mark of the noncoincidence of subjectivity with consciousness." On the chemical entanglement and decolonial futurity of "alterlife" in post-industrial deathworlds, see Murphy 2018. My use of *transsensory* evokes, first, the communicability of the craze—its reverberant, contagious, or empathogenic transfer of sensory effects and affinities across bodies otherwise apprehended in severalty, as individuated subjects. Analogous mobilities and porosities of the sensible preoccupy the accounts of sensorial racecraft in recent studies by the editors of this special issue. See the argument that "sympathetic vibration turns black kinship into a transpersonal mode of consciousness" in Fretwell 2020: 115. See also Hsu 2020 for an analysis of "trans-corporeal intoxication" (22) and "molecular intimacies of empire" (118) vis-à-vis Asian racialization. Second, as an access of ecstatic temporality, in contrast, the transsensory may not only multiply sensuous relations but also stage an amodal departure from consensus reality: not a transfer across sensoria but a transport beyond the sensible. Media and sound studies scholars (Chion 2019: 134; Goodman 2012: 47–48; Ikoniadou 2014: 67, 84) have articulated the term in this latter vein.

10 Copies of the original document are held by the State Historical Society of North Dakota and in the Records of the Office of the Secretary of the Interior. See US Department of the Interior (1916) 1929 for a transcription. On competency commissions See McDonnell 1980; and Barsh 1993.

11 More or less synonymous with *allochronism* (temporal othering), for Fabian (1983: 42) schizochronism generates an "aporetic split" between two tenses in anthropological discourse: the time-sensitive present of the field and the timeless present of the archive. To parse others in the "ethnographic present" is to abstract from what they are doing now to who they are as a people, for all time. At the very moment it claims Native informants as a "necessary condition for communication," the anthropological text thus cuts their voices out of "shared, intersubjective Time."

12 On racial tutelage, see Gonzalez 2004. On laissez-faire subjection, see Biolsi 1995: 31.

13 Managerial "leadership" in the home posed an alternative to "subservience" but could also reproduce norms of settler femininity at large, as Renya Ramirez (Ho-Chunk) (2018: 95) suggests of Hampton graduate and Carlisle teacher Elizabeth Bender Cloud (Ojibwe), who espoused "colonial notions that Indigenous lands lay idle and needed to be developed."

14 Naomi Greyser (2017: 130) suggests that "allotment was embedded in a systematic, expansive reorganization of relations among animate and purportedly inanimate matter."

15 Marcel Mauss (1973: 76) includes "chemical aim" in the taxonomy of adjustments the body habitually makes as it goes through everyday life. This serves as my working definition of *habitus*.

16 On vice commissions and narcotics legislation, see Acker 2002: 24.

17 *Anarchaic* is meant to suggest the anarchic movement of the archaized Indigenous past outside the constriction of settler timelines. As Elizabeth Freeman (2019: 12) notes, the prefix *ana-* evokes "an unpredictable sense of direction"—"upward, backward, again, against"—in how sense-methods attend to "social reroutings that take place through embodied temporal recalibrations."

18 An article titled "Drug That Kills" (*Gateway* 1906: 39) that same year similarly claimed that "the wild orgies . . . are rapidly depopulating the tribe" and echoes the concern for Winnebago landholdings: "The Winnebagoes occupy 15,000 acres of as fine land as the sun ever shone on, just across the river from Sioux City."

19 Depravation is a concept Alexander Weheliye (2014: 97) uses to describe how the biopolitical materialization of "modern sexuality" routes through "the pornotropic modalities of colonial bare life" (98).

20 On shame as an affect that heightens the contours of the individual subject around breaks in a "circuit of mirroring expressions," see Sedgwick 2003: 36.

21 See also Taylor 2014 on the cultural logic of "outbreak" in regard to the Ghost Dance.

22 A historical poetics, as Mikhail Bakhtin (1981: 244, 250) understands it, does not approach the chronotopic structures of narrative discourse and those of everyday life as ontologically impermeable to one another but, rather, as interrelated through dialogic transfers.

23 Another source of confusion arising from the republication of the autobiography is the addition of a false eponym to the title. *Crashing Thunder* was the name of Sam Blowsnake's older brother, Jasper, whose Hočąk name, Warudjáxega, Radin translates as "terrible thunder crash" in Blowsnake 1913: 303.

24 Nahua (Aztec) shamanic practices used peyote and other intoxicating substances to bring about similar forms of dis/possession. When a supernatural being enters the body, the *tonalli* (part of the soul) journeys out of the body toward the dwellings of the gods. See Austin 1988: 354–60, 394.

25 Henri Lefebvre (2004: 16) associates eurhythmia with normed everydayness, where "rhythms unite with one another in the state of health."

References

Acker, Caroline Jean. 2002. *Creating the American Junkie: Addiction Research in the Classic Era of Narcotics Control*. Baltimore: Johns Hopkins Univ. Press.

Arndt, Grant. 2012. "Indigenous Autobiography en Abyme: Indigenous Reflections on Representational Agency in the Case of *Crashing Thunder.*" *Ethnohistory* 59, no. 1: 27–49.

Austin, Alfredo López. 1988. *The Human Body and Ideology: Concepts of the Ancient Nahuas.* Vol. 1. Translated by Thelma Ortiz de Montellano and Bernard Ortiz de Montellano. Salt Lake City: Univ. of Utah Press.

Bakhtin, Mikhail. 1981. *The Dialogic Imagination: Four Essays.* Translated by Caryl Emerson and Michael Holquist. Austin: Univ. of Texas Press.

Barsh, Russel Lawrence. 1993. "An American Heart of Darkness: The 1913 Expedition for American Indian Citizenship." *Great Plains Quarterly* 13, no. 2: 91–115.

Biolsi, Thomas. 1995. "The Birth of the Reservation: Making the Modern Individual among the Lakota." *American Ethnologist* 22, no. 1: 28–53.

Bloch, Ernst. 1996. *The Principle of Hope.* Vol. 1. Translated by Neville Plaice, Stephen Plaice, and Paul Knight. Cambridge, MA: MIT Press.

Blowsnake, Jasper. 1913. "Personal Reminiscences of a Winnebago Indian." Edited by Paul Radin. *Journal of American Folklore* 26: 293–318.

Blowsnake, Sam. 1920. *The Autobiography of a Winnebago Indian.* Translated by Oliver Lamere. Edited by Paul Radin. In *University of California Publications in Archaeology and Ethnology* 16, no. 7: 381–473.

Burnham, Michelle. 1998. "'I Lied All the Time': Trickster Discourse and Ethnographic Authority in *Crashing Thunder.*" *American Indian Quarterly* 22, no. 4: 469–84.

Byrd, Jodi. 2011. *The Transit of Empire: Indigenous Critiques of Colonialism.* Minneapolis: Univ. of Minnesota Press.

Cattelino, Jessica R. 2018. "From Locke to Slots: Money and the Politics of Indigeneity." *Comparative Studies in Society and History* 60, no. 2.

Chakrabarty, Dipesh. 2000. *Provincializing Europe: Postcolonial Thought and Historical Difference.* Princeton, NJ: Princeton Univ. Press.

Chicago Daily Tribune. 1899. "Color Visions in Mescal Bean." October 15.

Chion, Michel. 2019. *Audio-Vision: Sound on Screen.* New York: Columbia Univ. Press.

Chow, Rey. 2002. *The Protestant Ethnic and the Spirit of Capitalism.* New York: Columbia Univ. Press.

Clough, Patricia. 2000. *Autoaffection: Unconscious Thought in the Age of Teletechnology.* Minneapolis: Univ. of Minnesota Press.

Coulthard, Glen Sean. 2014. *Red Skin, White Masks: Rejecting the Colonial Politics of Recognition.* Minneapolis: Univ. of Minnesota Press.

Daiker, F. H. 1914. "Liquor and Peyote a Menace to the Indian." In *Report of the Thirty-Second Annual Lake Mohonk Conference.* Mohonk Lake: Lake Mohonk Conference on the Indian and Other Dependent Peoples.

Dawson, Alexander S. 2018. *The Peyote Effect: From the Inquisition to the War on Drugs.* Berkeley: Univ. of California Press.

Dorland, Steven. 2017. "Sensoriality and Wendat Steams: The Analysis of Fifteenth-to-Seventeenth Century Steam Lodge Rituals in Southern Ontario." *American Indian Quarterly* 41, no. 1: 1–30.

Durkheim, Emile. 1995. *The Elementary Forms of Religious Life.* Translated by Karen E. Fields. New York: Free Press.

Ellinghaus, Katherine. 2017. *Blood Will Tell: Native Americans and Assimilation Policy.* Lincoln: Univ. of Nebraska Press.

Ellis, Havelock Henry. 1898. "Mescal: A New Artificial Paradise." *Contemporary Review* 74: 130–41.

Fabian, Johannes. 1983. *Time and the Other: How Anthropology Makes Its Object.* New York: Columbia Univ. Press.

Feldman, Martha, and Judith T. Zeitlin. 2019. Introduction to *The Voice as Something More: Essays Toward Materiality*, edited by Martha Feldman and Judith T. Zeitlin. Chicago: Univ. of Chicago Press.

Fleissner, Jennifer L. 2004. *Women, Compulsion, Modernity: The Moment of American Naturalism.* Chicago: Univ. of Chicago Press.

Forest City Press. 1906. "Insidious Mescal Fatal to Indians." June 20.

Freeman, Elizabeth. 2019. *Beside You in Time: Sense Methods and Queer Sociabilities in the American Nineteenth Century.* Durham, NC: Duke Univ. Press.

Fretwell, Erica. 2020. *Sensory Experiments: Psychophysics, Race, and the Aesthetics of Feeling.* Durham, NC: Duke Univ. Press.

Gates, Merrill Edwards. 1885. "Land and Law as Agents in Educating Indians. An Address Delivered before the American Social Science Association at Saratoga, N.Y., Sept. 11th, 1885." *LSE Selected Pamphlets.*

Gates, Merrill Edwards. 1897. "Address of President Merrill E. Gates." In *Proceedings of the Fourteenth Annual Lake Mohonk Conference of Friends of the Indian.* New York: Lake Mohonk Conference.

Gateway. 1906. "Drug That Kills." *The Gateway: A Magazine of the Great Lake States and Canada* 7, no. 1: 39–40.

Gonzalez, John M. 2004. "The Warp of Whiteness: Domesticity and Empire in Helen Hunt Jackson's *Ramona*." *American Literary History* 16, no. 3: 437–65.

Goodman, Steve. 2012. *Sonic Warfare: Sound, Affect, and the Ecology of Fear.* Cambridge: MIT Press.

Greyser, Naomi. 2017. *On Sympathetic Grounds: Race, Gender, and Affective Geographies in Nineteenth-Century America.* Oxford: Oxford Univ. Press.

Harvey, Graham. 2005. *Animism: Respecting the Living World.* New York: Columbia Univ. Press.

Hoxie, Frederick E. 1992. "Exploring a Cultural Borderland: Native American Journeys of Self Discovery in the Early Twentieth Century." *Journal of American History* 79, no. 3: 969–95.

Hsu, Hsuan L. 2020. *The Smell of Risk: Environmental Disparities and Olfactory Aesthetics.* New York: New York Univ. Press.

Ikoniadou, Eleni. 2014. *The Rhythmic Event: Art, Media, and the Sonic.* Cambridge, MA: MIT Press.

Indian Rights Association. 1916. *The Thirty-Fourth Annual Report of the Executive Committee of the Indian Rights Association.* Philadelphia: Office of the Indian Rights Association.

Jacobs, Margaret. 2009. *White Mother to a Dark Race: Settler Colonialism, Maternalism, and the Removal of Indigenous Children in the American West and Australia, 1880–1940*. Lincoln: Univ. of Nebraska Press.

Jay, Mike. 2019. *Mescaline: A Global History of the First Psychedelic*. New Haven, CT: Yale Univ. Press.

La Barre, Weston. 1989. *The Peyote Cult*. 5th ed. Norman: Univ. of Oklahoma Press.

Lefebvre, Henri. 2004. *Rhythmanalysis: Space, Time, and Everyday Life*. Translated by Stuart Elden and Gerald Moore. New York: Continuum.

Lim, Bliss Cua. 2009. *Translating Time: Cinema, the Fantastic, and Temporal Critique*. Durham, NC: Duke Univ. Press.

Lomawaima, K. Tsianina. 1994. *They Called It Prairie Light: The Story of the Chilocco Indian School*. Lincoln: Univ. of Nebraska Press.

Los Angeles Times. 1906. "Indians Mad on Mescal Bean." January 11.

Luciano, Dana. 2007. *Arranging Grief: Sacred Time and the Body in Nineteenth-Century America*. New York: New York Univ. Press.

Lyons, Scott Richard. 1999. "The Incorporation of the Indian Body: Peyotism and the Pan-Indian Public." In *Rhetoric, the Polis, and the Global Village: Selected Papers from the 1998 Thirtieth Anniversary Rhetoric Society of America Conference*, edited by C. Jan Swearingen and David S. Kaufer, 147–54. New York: Routledge.

Lyons, Scott Richard. 2010. *X-Marks: Native Signatures of Assent*. Minneapolis: Univ. of Minnesota Press.

Matson, F. G. 1916. "Great God Peyote Draws Indians of Utah to His Lair of Dreams; Civilization Crumples under Clinging Claws of New Destroyer." *Salt Lake Telegram*, June 25.

Mauss, Marcel. 1973. "Techniques of the Body." *Economy and Society* 2, no. 1: 70–88.

McClintock, Anne. 1995. *Imperial Leather: Race, Gender, and Sexuality in the Colonial Contest*. New York: Routledge.

McDonnell, Janet. 1980. "Competency Commissions and Indian Land Policy, 1913–20." *South Dakota History* 11: 21–34.

McDonnell, Janet. 1991. *The Dispossession of the American Indian*. Bloomington: Univ. of Indiana Press.

Murphy, Michelle. 2018. "Against Population, toward Alterlife: In *Making Kin, Not Populations*, edited by Adele Clarke and Donna Haraway, 101–24. Chicago: Prickly Paradigm Press.

Nesvig, Martin. 2018. "Sandcastles of the Mind: Hallucinogens and Cultural Memory." In *Substance and Seduction: Ingested Commodities in Early Mesoamerica*, edited by Stacey Schwartzkopf and Kathryn E. Sampeck, 27–54. Austin: Univ. of Texas Press.

Olund, Eric N. 2002. "From Savage Space to Governable Space: The Extension of United States Judicial Sovereignty over Indian Country in the Nineteenth Century." *Cultural Geographies* 9, no. 2: 129–57.

Phillips, Richard. 2009. "Settler Colonialism and the Nuclear Family." *Canadian Geographer* 53, no. 2: 239–53.

Piatote, Beth. 2013. *Domestic Subjects: Gender, Citizenship, and Law in Native American Literature.* New Haven, CT: Yale Univ. Press.

Pierson, Delavan. 1915. "American Indian Peyote Worship." *Missionary Review of the World (Funk & Wagnalls)* 38: 201–6.

Povinelli, Elizabeth. 2006. *The Empire of Love: Toward a Theory of Intimacy, Genealogy, and Carnality.* Durham, NC: Duke Univ. Press.

Radin, Paul. 1983. *Crashing Thunder: The Autobiography of a Winnebago Indian.* Lincoln: Univ. of Nebraska Press.

Ramirez, Renya. 2018. *Standing Up to Colonial Power: The Lives of Henry Roe and Elizabeth Bender Cloud.* Lincoln: Univ. of Nebraska Press.

Rifkin, Mark. 2017. *Beyond Settler Time: Temporal Sovereignty and Indigenous Self-Determination.* Durham, NC: Duke Univ. Press.

Roosevelt, Theodore. 1901. *Message of the President of the United States Communicated to the Two Houses of Congress at the Beginning of the First Session of the Fifty-Seventh Congress.* Washington, DC: Government Printing Office.

Safford, William Edward. 1915. "An Aztec Narcotic (*Lophophora williamsii*)." *Journal of Heredity* 6: 291–311.

Schuller, Kyla. 2016. "The Fossil and the Photograph: Red Cloud, Prehistoric Media, and Dispossession in Perpetuity." *Configurations* 24, no. 2: 229–61.

Schuller, Kyla, and Jules Gill-Peterson. 2020. "Introduction: Race, State, and the Malleable Body." *Social Text* 38, no. 2: 1–17.

Sedgwick, Eve Kosofsky. 2003. *Touching Feeling: Affect, Pedagogy, Performativity.* Durham, NC: Duke Univ. Press.

Seitler, Dana. 2008. *Atavistic Tendencies: The Culture of Science in American Modernity.* Minneapolis: Univ. of Minnesota Press.

Seymour, Gertrude. 1916. "Peyote Worship—An Indian Cult and a Powerful Drug." *The Survey*, May 13.

Sigal, Peter, Zeb Tortorici, and Neil Whitehead. 2019. *Ethnopornography: Sexuality, Colonialism, and Archival Knowledge.* Durham, NC: Duke Univ. Press.

Simpson, Audra. 2014. *Mohawk Interruptus: Political Life across the Borders of Settler States.* Durham, NC: Duke Univ. Press.

Snow, David H. 2016. "Whole Pots Full of Idolatrous Herbs." *Kiva: Journal of Southwestern Anthropology and History* 82, no. 2: 127.

Stewart, Omer. 1987. *Peyote Religion: A History.* Norman: Univ. of Oklahoma Press.

Taylor, Matthew. 2014. "'Contagious Emotions' and the Ghost Dance Religion: Mooney's Science, Black Elk's Fever." *ELH* 81, no. 3: 1055–82.

Tonkovich, Nicole. 2012. *The Allotment Plot: Alice C. Fletcher, Jane E. Gay, and Nez Perce Survivance.* Lincoln: Univ. of Nebraska Press.

US Congress. 1918. "Peyote: Hearings on H.R. 2614 before the H. Comm. on Indian Affairs." 67th Cong., 2d sess., 125.

US Congress. 1919. "Hearings on H.R. 8696 [Indian Appropriation Bill] before the S. Comm. on Indian Affairs." 65th Cong., 2d sess., 32–47.

US Department of the Interior. (1916) 1929. "Ritual on Admission of Indians to Full American Citizenship." In *Survey of Conditions of the Indians in the United States: Hearings before a Subcommittee of the Committee on Indian Affairs* . . . , vol. 7, pt. 15, *Oklahoma*, 7013–14. Washington, DC: Government Printing Office.

Vizenor, Gerald. 1998. *Fugitive Poses: Native American Scenes of Absence and Presence.* Lincoln: Univ. of Nebraska Press.

Washington Times. 1918. "Indian Woman in Capital to Fight Growing Use of Peyote Drug by Indians—Mrs. Gertrude Bonnin, Carlisle Graduate, Relative of Sitting Bull, Describes Effects of Mind-Poison." February 17.

Wenger, Tisa. 2014. *We Have a Religion: The 1920s Pueblo Indian Dance Controversy and American Religious Freedom.* Chapel Hill: Univ. of North Carolina Press.

Clare Mullaney   Extra Consciousness, Extra Fingers: Automatic Writing and Disabled Authorship

Abstract Nineteenth-century Spiritualism championed women with chronic illnesses as the ideal conduits for mediumship due to their assumed sensitivity. Positioning the movement's many historical iterations of automatic writing as central to disability history, this article turns to Gertrude Stein and Lucille Clifton, who center extrasensory perceptions in the compositional scene. Foregrounding mind and body, they upend the privileging of the rational male subject who dominates accounts of authorship in literary studies. By modeling collaborative forms of writing that exceed consciousness, Stein and Clifton make way for embracing disabled authorship in our past and present.
Keywords Spiritualism, extrasensory perception, race, gender, bodymind

On a rainy evening in Buffalo in 1975, Lucille Clifton sat with her two oldest daughters at their kitchen table, a surface used for eating and poem making. Deterred from venturing outdoors, they decided to play a game and discovered a Ouija board when rummaging through the cabinet. After opening the box, Clifton and her daughter Sidney placed their fingers on the planchette, which began jumping. "Stop Ma. . . . Don't do this," Sidney pleas. Clifton responds, "I'm not doing anything" (deNiord 2010: 10). Having imagined that the other is responsible for the jolting, they closed their eyes to prevent human interference. Clifton's other daughter, Rica, assumed the role of transcriber and saw the board shuffle again between letters. The planchette spelled "T-H-E-L-M-A," the name of their mother and their grandmother, who passed away from epilepsy at the age of forty-four (Lupton 2006: 14).

Following this scene at the Ouija board, Clifton would receive an influx of messages after the premature deaths of her disabled loved ones, her husband and her daughter Rica (both had cancer) and her

American Literature, Volume 95, Number 3, September 2023
DOI 10.1215/00029831-10679223   © 2023 by Duke University Press

son, Channing (who died of heart failure). But as early as the late 1970s, her welcoming of what Akasha Hull (1997: 341) calls the "extrasensory realm" resulted in an entire collection of poems delivered by spirits (Lupton 2006: 72). In these instances, Clifton's hand would begin "feeling itchy," a sensation that would extend through her arm "like an electric current" (Hull 1997: 340, 341). Clifton's late twentieth-century engagement with mediumship honored the history of the Spiritualist movement, which began among enslaved populations in the antebellum South who affirmed the West African belief that "the dead can return to their living" (qtd. in Braude 1989: 29).[1] Given the disabling effects of enslavement, contact with the spirit world proved necessary for Black populations wishing to communicate with dead loved ones who were injured and then often killed by white enslavers.[2] Embracing her roots as a Dahomey woman, Clifton wrote poems drawing on the urgency of Black Spiritualism to refute not only Southern caste systems but also Western knowledge production's praising of individual rationality at the exclusion of shared extrasensory perceptions (Baer 1989: 152; Hull 1997: 331).

While within the last half century Spiritualism's ties to race and gender have been extensively documented, little critical focus has been brought to the movement's overlap with disability history. Nineteenth-century accounts of mediumship emphasize women's assumed alignment with chronic illness. The November 1866 publication of the Spiritualist magazine *Banner of Light* explains that a "feminine disposition," both "negative and passive," results in a successful channeling of the dead:

> Women in the nineteenth century are physically sick, weak and declining. They are physically inactive, sedentary, and non-manifestational. The functions depending upon force and muscle are weak, but the nerves are intensely sensitive. They dislike work, but love excitement, and culminate in weakness. Hence sickness, rest, passivity, susceptibility, impressionability, mediumship, communication, revelation! This abnormal experience educates the delicate to finer issues, while compensating them for physical limitations. . . . They improve upon the limitations of the normal, as the telescope enlarges the function of the eye, giving a local habitation and a name to things dreamed of. (*Banner of Light* 1866)

While this account of mediumship relies on the gendered stereotype that women are "weak," it reclaims the ill or disabled mind and body as necessary conduits for otherworldly communication. The presumed "passivity" of "sickness" morphs into "susceptibility"; the disabled woman's bodymind becomes a welcomed facilitator of conversation.[3] As Ann Braude (1989: 83) explains, "The very qualities that rendered women incompetent when judged against norms for masculine behavior rendered them capable of mediumship." While the *Banner of Light* later propagated the benefits of Spiritualism for women's health (mediums often challenged the logic behind medical diagnoses and treatment-based protocols), the report situates the movement's origins in illnesses' capacity to make "finer issues," or overlooked truths, newly discernable. Belief in the sensitivity of women's nerves amplified nineteenth-century investments in hysteria, but Spiritualism challenges such pathologization, which relies on what Dana Luciano describes, in conversation with Audre Lorde, as the "'exclusively European-American male tradition' . . . that dismisses emotion and sensation as legitimate sources of knowledge" (qtd. in Roudeau 2015: 3).[4] As Bettina Judd (2019: 138) explains, "Embodied technology allows for Clifton to practice forms of humanness that are beyond concepts of the human assumed in its initial, Enlightenment age formations." Spiritualism argues that women's "compromised" bodies deploy their extra senses to successfully cross between subjects.

Debates about automatic writing in the nineteenth and twentieth centuries raise questions about the role of the senses in literary and disability studies as well as histories of disabled authorship. In the pages that follow, I turn to two twentieth-century literary practitioners of automatic writing: Gertrude Stein and Lucille Clifton, who embrace mindless compositional practices that foreground the sensorium, an early modern concept that, in attempting to undermine "the classic Western split between mind and body," collapses "cognition and sensation" (Howes 2009: 1).[5] While both authors occupy different ends of the twentieth century and are rarely, if ever, discussed in tandem, they convey a shared investment in extrasensory experiences that cannot be captured within the standard five categories of sight, sound, smell, taste, and touch.[6] Stein's research investments in psychology as an undergraduate student led to experiments that aimed to excavate a subject's unconscious, what she called "xtra consciousness" (qtd. in Will 2001: 172).[7] This clinical work was followed by a personal bout with depression, which occasioned her shift away from scientific writing to literary pursuits (Katz 1971: xvii). Clifton (2012: 204) was born with "extra fingers" (six rather than five), which she believed assisted in her channeling of dead spirits. The poet's breast and rectal cancers and kidney failure also resulted in a depression that generated poems about the afterlife (deNiord 2010: 13). With extraness marking the writers' proximity to disability, their disabled bodyminds wield extrasensory perceptions to reclaim traditionally discounted forms of authorship.[8]

Historically, the senses have occupied a contentious place in disability studies. While a subset of work in the field has attended to bodily senses that have disappeared or become amplified (e.g., Deaf studies foregrounds the tactile elements of sound), scholars are reluctant to emphasize the impaired body, which they argue detracts from a necessary focus on the environmental forces that disable people (Geurts 2015; see also Freidner and Helmreich 2012). As anthropologist Kathryn Linn Geurts (2015: 162) explains, "For decades . . . disability studies actively discouraged a . . . sensory approach, favoring instead political accounts that focus on social exclusion."[9] But this turn away from the senses misses an opportunity to consider the diverse realities of disabled people's embodied experiences. Geurts advocates for scholars' engagement with sensibility, a concept that merges the concerns of the body with those of the world because it understands bodily surfaces and interiors as bearing the same political weight as their environments. Rather than resist the relegation of disabled women to their bodies, Stein and Clifton center the body and its extrasensory perceptions not as apolitical sites subject to medical manipulation but as politically motivated matter that upends rational male subjecthood. Authorship is not only the work of the mind, they argue, but of gendered, racialized, and sensing bodies that frame writerly subjectivity as exceeding consciousness.

The Death of the Thinking Author and Birth of the Sensing One

A term first used in 1855 at the height of the Spiritualist movement in the United States, *automatic writing* referred to writing produced "entirely independent of the medium's volition," with the spirits of the deceased expressing themselves through a medium's hand (Hare 1855: 181). When British Spiritualist writer and reformer Sophia Elizabeth De Morgan (1863: 53) asked "a young writing-medium" to describe "how . . . spirits write through mediums," the informant responded, "It is done by the spiritual fluid, which comes from the brain to the hand" and decides, upon explanation, to visualize the process through a drawing. In the image shown in figure 1, a scribbling medium is surrounded by a "good" spirit and a "bad" one, both simultaneously sending energy to "the muscles" (De Morgan 1863: 56). Note that the

Figure 1 A scene of automatic writing in the mid-nineteenth century. A person wearing a suit is seated at a round table with a feather pen in their right hand and a paper beneath their arm. Two spirit-like figures place their hands near the writer's head. The figure on the left is a woman with long hair in a dress who appears above the seated figure. The figure on the right is not wearing clothing and has horns on his head. Dotted lines extend from the spirits' hands to the medium's head. From Sophia Elizabeth De Morgan's *From Matter to Spirit: Ten Years' Experience in Spirit Manifestations* (1863: 54)

"bad" spirit is shaded and subject, unlike its white counterpart, to the laws of gravity. The first entraps the medium's mind, and the other, their body. The dotted lines, which stretch from spirits to medium, mark a collision between cognition and sensation; "whatever the spirit thinks," the informant concludes, "the medium writes" (De Morgan 1863: 56).

Given the historical tethering of women to bodies, the female "medium" is most often responsible for dispelling a message's textual content, her arm dutifully moving in response to received communication. Nameless female mediums haunt the pages of male authors' prose; Arthur Conan Doyle, Mark Twain, Oscar Wilde, and William Butler Yeats are famous for having their thoughts channeled automatically.[10] While their books were physically written by women, they were attributed to the male mind (and hence author) upon publication. The sketch pictured in figure 2, which appeared in the French magazine *Le Charivari* in 1865, illustrates the gendered distinction between the male message and the female medium. A woman is seated at a chair conveying the spirit of Dante while surrounded by a crowd of curious, male onlookers. Her father and another male figure fill the image's foreground, and their conversation serves as its caption. By contrast, the woman medium is depicted as passive; she is silently consigned to the room's corner, with her open mouth receiving invisible messages from above. Works in feminist disability studies and disability activism argue that women's and, more specifically, women of color's reduction to their bodies (for the sake biological reproduction or mere appearance) propagates the agency of the disembodied liberal subject who is both white and male. As Rosemarie Garland-Thomson (1993: 42) purports, our understanding of "liberal individualism as a . . . disembodied form of masculinity depends upon [the] construction of and flight from a denigrated, oppositional femininity." This excessively embodied "feminine" self curtails "the idea of an autonomous individual self," which takes shape, in the context of literary studies, as the author (42). The erasure of these women's names from books' title pages and bindings—or "Les sprites" naming of Dante rather than the daughter who channels his presence—confirms the long-standing belief that women, in having bodies but lacking minds, are deprived of the intellectual capacity to compose texts of their own creation.

Scholarship at the intersection between sensory studies and literary studies understands the body as offering valuable insight about individuals' interiors. Unlike Enlightenment-based thinkers who position the body as weight that encumbers one's selfhood, such work exposes embodied life as an expression of the invisible worlds of artists. Investigating what he describes as "the mind's 'outward turn,'" Benjamin Morgan (2017: 19) shows how individual consciousness in late nineteenth-century Britain becomes dispersed across bodies and objects. A "materialist aesthetics," Morgan explains, reveals the dual directional relationship between art and the bodies that make it (12). Similarly, Jonathan Kramnick (2018: 4) advocates that we consider minds as part of bodies and bodies as part of environments. What Stein and Clifton contribute to these conversations is their reliance on extra senses (i.e., senses both of and beyond the body) that exceed the reified taxonomy of sensation that has historically placed the white, thinking male subject in opposition to racialized, excessively embodied, and feeling women.[11]

Neither Stein nor Clifton identified as disabled, but in the words of Sami Schalk and Jina B. Kim (2020: 39), they frame "disability as a relationship to power that intersects with and is mutually constituted by race, gender . . . and sexuality." Schalk and Kim argue that "a

LES SPIRITES par DAUMIER

_ Chut ! . . ma fille entre en communication avec l'Esprit du Dante !

Figure 2 Honoré Daumier, "Les sprites" (*Le Charivari* 1865). Black-and-white drawing of a female medium who is looking upward with her mouth ajar to channel an invisible spirit through writing. The medium is positioned to the left-hand side of the image and is surrounded by male observers. Two older men stand at the forefront of the image and speak to one another. As the caption explains, the man to the left says, "Quiet! . . . My daughter is in communication with Dante! . . . " Photograph courtesy of the Metropolitan Museum of Art

feminist-of-color disability studies" encourages "thinking beyond the politics of recognition, representation, and identity" to unpack the entangled relationship between ableism and white supremacy, among others, "as they assign value or lack thereof to certain bodyminds" (37–38). Stein and Clifton transpose such lack into the extraness of exteriorized bodyminds. They understand how the world perceives disabled minds and bodies as without value but nevertheless harness such impairments' transformative possibilities via their distributive channelings.[12]

Both authors and readers alike claim that Stein's early novella "Melanctha" (1909) and Clifton's poetry collections *two-headed woman* (1980) and *Mercy* (2004) were channeled automatically, Stein drawing on her scientific background and Clifton honoring her ancestors' commitment to Spiritualism. Clifton's careful redefinition of Black bodies in the context of her own and her family's disabilities counters Stein's largely stereotypical representations of a Black community in a fictionalized Baltimore. And yet, in reclaiming bodily forms of authorship—writing with the six-fingered hand rather than the mind or with the spirit rather than the self—both Stein and Clifton collapse mind and body; their hurried strokes convey communication as a bodily behavior that supplants cerebral encounters. Stein's and Clifton's prose and poems ask that readers understand disabled women as bearing the rhetorical weight of these often nondiscursive sensations, which overthrow accounts of authorship that claim to originate in the mind.

"Xtra Consciousness"

In the final decade of the nineteenth century, twenty-two-year-old Gertrude Stein sat in a psychology laboratory at Harvard University, her hand resting on a small glass plate propped atop three wheeled casters. A metal arm extended from the plate's surface and held a pencil, which responded to movements of Stein's hand on the plate. Seated across from her, graduate student Leon Solomons slowly read a novel aloud, focusing on the blank paper resting beneath the plate supporting Stein's palm. As Stein listened to Solomons, her hand began to move slowly up, down, and around, resulting in the repeated formation of the letter *m* across the page (Solomons and Stein 1896: 495). The board's instability intensified any movement her arm made, capturing the circularity of Stein's gesture. This monotonous writing appeared mindless, with the writer's gaze detached from her hand's increasingly hurried strokes. No human subject claimed ownership over the letters, words, and often unintelligible scribbles that emerged from beneath the wandering board.

Such a scene comes from Stein and Solomons's study of "normal motor automatism," more commonly termed *automatic writing*, which was believed to reveal the status of a subject's unconscious. With the codification of the field of psychology at the century's turn, automaticity determined that the "abnormal" mind was more prone to mindless scribbling than the "normal" one.[13] If disabled women in the nineteenth century deployed Spiritualist practices to depathologize themselves (i.e., to show that their "weaknesses" enabled new modes of perception), by the twentieth century these same practices would be used to diagnose women as sick. In this vein, famous French psychologist Pierre Janet invented a writing machine, modeled after the mid-nineteenth-century Spiritualist planchette, that would measure a subject's sensations; the more they sensed, the less authority they had as a self-possessed subject and thus independent author (Thompson 2004: 4–5; see fig. 3).[14]

By contrast, Stein and Solomons's study moved away from scientific

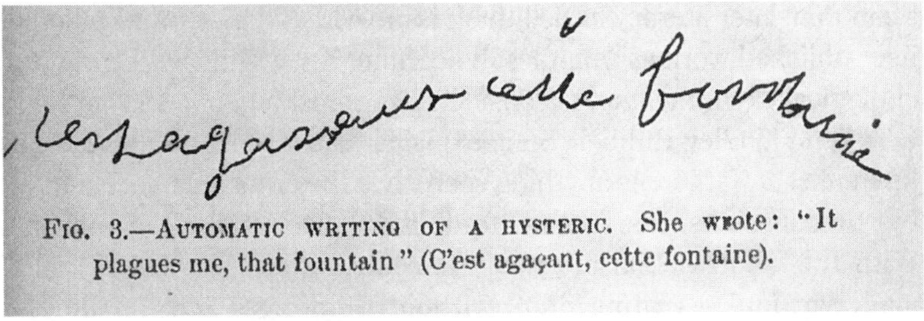

Fɪɢ. 3.—Aᴜᴛᴏᴍᴀᴛɪᴄ ᴡʀɪᴛɪɴɢ ᴏꜰ ᴀ ʜʏsᴛᴇʀɪᴄ. She wʀote: " It plagues me, that fountain " (C'est agaçant, cette fontaine).

Figure 3   Example of automatic writing with an aesthetic hand which reads, "'It plagues me, that fountain' (C'est agaçant, cette fontaine)." Black ink written in cursive on a white page. The writing is uneven; it dips and rises. The cross marks in "cette" appear detached from the lettering. From *Alterations in Personality* (Binet 1896: 191)

experiments that attempted to uncover the split personality of the "hysterical subject" who wrote without thinking. They instead turned to "normal" and "ordinary people" to see if they, too, could write automatically (Solomons and Stein 1896: 492). Unlike Spiritualist forms of writing in which the medium would channel voices of the dead, Stein and Solomons served as both the experiment's leaders and subjects, declaring themselves perfectly "normal" and ready to undertake the proper "training" to ensure clinical distance. "The only subjects we had were ourselves," Stein explains (qtd. in Ambrosio 2018: 148). Their published findings conclude that "the normal subject" bears "automatic powers" (Solomons and Stein 1896: 492). Rather than confirm the existence of a "double personality," their findings assert subjects' *"extra personality"* in which an arm's sensation supplants human consciousness (492, 495; my emphasis). Disinterested in pathology, Stein argued that human behavior exists on a spectrum of similarity; "normal" and "abnormal" minds are equally primed for automaticity.

In a 1934 issue of the *Atlantic Monthly*, psychologist B. F. Skinner published a scathing review not of Stein's scientific work but of her literary writing, which he believed was adversely influenced by her time in the laboratory. He claimed that the "secret" behind her "unintelligible" prose (full of senseless repetition and circular sentences) was that she was writing automatically. "It is clear," he professes, "that the hypothetical author who might be inferred from the writing itself possesses just those characteristics that we should expect to find if a theory of automatic writing were the right answer" (Skinner 1934: 52). He attributes this "very little intellectual content" to her authorship's source—it is, in Stein's own words, "what her arm wrote" rather than her brain (Skinner 1933: 52, 51). Despite her investment in inattention,

Stein (and later literary critics) took issue with Skinner's attribution of her published work as "mindless"; equating her writing with early psychological experiments was considered diminishing. In a 1934 letter to her friend Lindley Hubbell, Stein explains: "No it is not so automatic as he thinks. . . . If there is anything secret it is the other way. . . . I achieve by *xtra* consciousness, excess" (qtd. in Will 2001: 172; my emphasis). With this abbreviation of *extra*, Stein distinguishes between "automatic writing"—writing done without thinking—and her heightened perception of external stimuli. Automatic writing, then, is about not the absence of consciousness but its deployment in new forms. *Xtra consciousness* refers to Stein's diligent attempts to, in the words of Katherine Biers (2013: 187), "make her writing into a literal extension of the senses." A consideration of Stein's relationship to the senses is not new, but attention to "xtra consciousness" as a manifestation of the bodymind and its excesses demands new focus on Stein's underdiscussed relationship to mental disability.[15] Stein does not refute Skinner's declaration that her "literary materials are the sensory things nearest at hand—objects, sounds, tastes, smells, and so on"; rather, she takes issue with male critics' reliance on automatic writing as an invitation to dismiss her authorship and, as a result, discount her personhood (Skinner 1933: 53).[16]

Although she and Solomons once considered themselves "representative of the perfectly normal—or perfectly ordinary—being, so far as hysteria is concerned," Stein experienced depression after fleeing John Hopkins Medical School, where she was completing her study of women's nervous diseases (Solomons and Stein 1896: 494; Daniel 2009: 47, 42). Between mindless bouts of copying English novels at the British Library (an act akin to the automatic practices she performed in the laboratory years earlier), she drafted *Three Lives* (1909), an extended study of three women characters' cognition. The second novella in the trilogy, "Melanctha: Each One as She May," features a young mixed-raced woman who "wonders . . . how she could go on living when she was so blue" (Stein 2012: 340). Her name derived from "melancholy," Melanctha endures a chronic, irresolvable "despair." While the story of three college-educated women in *Q.E.D.* (an earlier version of *Three Lives*) demonstrates mental agility (its title refers to a geometrical proof, which is evidence of school-based knowledge), Melanctha, as a mentally disabled character, espouses an embodied cognition, thus suturing mind to body (Walker 1984: 54).

Drawing on her prior investments in automaticity, Stein transposes the white space of Radcliffe's laboratory into the Black neighborhood of Bridgeport. Melanctha models a form of automatic behavior as she repeatedly and often aimlessly wanders the nearby streets: "Melanctha wandered widely," and she "wandered on the edge of wisdom" (Rowe 2003: 349, 351). As she approached nearby men, "she would advance" and then "withdraw," "not know[ing]. . . . what it was that she so badly wanted" (348). Like young Stein's pencil dancing across a sheet of paper in a series of messily conflated *m*s, Melanctha is without direction, which John Carlos Rowe (2003: 231) names "a genuine alternative to traditional rationality." Resisting conventional forms of consciousness, the story champions bodily feeling as the greatest "wisdom."

Stein struggles to translate what Melanctha describes as "felt" knowledge into linguistic form. Melanctha contrasts with her on-again, off-again lover Jeff Campbell, the town doctor. Despite Jeff's medical knowledge and predilection for rationality, Melanctha repeatedly calls him "stupid"—"Oh you Jeff, you always be so stupid," "Oh you so stupid Jeff boy" (Stein 1990: 398, 412). Melanctha understands stupidity as pertaining less to Jeff's cognitive capacities than to his evasion of bodily feeling. This circumvention occurs through Jeff's verbalization of their troubles: "You always wanting to have it all clear out in words, always, what every-body is always feeling," Melanctha complains (351). As Barbara Will (2000: 42) suggests, "Jeff expects a clarity from language which Melanctha refuses to mirror." While Jeff thinks, Melanctha feels. During one of many disagreements, Jeff attempts to explain himself once again:

> I don't stop thinking much Miss Melanctha and if I can't ever feel without stopping thinking, I certainly am very much afraid Miss Melanctha that I never will do much with that kind of feeling. . . . I certainly do think I feel as much for you Miss Melanctha, as you ever feel about me, sure I do. I don't think you know me right when you talk like that to me. Tell me just straight out how much you do care about me, Miss Melanctha. (Stein 1990: 411)

Jeff claims that Melanctha faults him for overthinking because it counteracts his ability to feel. He cannot grasp what he terms "Melanctha's meaning"; his "hard scientific reading" distracts him from her body-based knowledge, which positions sensory feeling *as* thinking (375). Slowly, Melanctha responds: "I certainly do care for you Jeff Campbell less than you are always thinking and much more than you are ever knowing" (411). To "learn" in "the darkness," which "covered everything all over," she adopts embodied modes of communication (failing, or perhaps succeeding, in the words of her friend Jane

Harden, to put her mind to "good use") (348). If the despairing (or mentally disabled) subject is deemed in the eyes of Janet and other leading psychologists as rhetorically deficient, Melanctha's sensory engagement replaces the standard, linguistic-based narrative that both science and literature position as crucial for humanizing representations.

When Jeff forestalls Melanctha's access to "real wisdom," she acquires knowledge through Jane, who, a decade older, "had had a good deal of education" and "had been two years at a colored college" before she was asked to leave for "bad conduct" (Stein 1990: 353). Together, the two women wander and then work "to really understand" (354):

> Melanctha sat at Jane's feet for many hours in these days and felt Jane's wisdom. She learned to love Jane and to have this feeling very deeply. She learned a little in these days to know joy and she was taught too how very keenly she could suffer. It was very difficult this suffering from that Melanctha sometimes had from her mother and from her unendurable black father. Then she was fighting and she could be strong and valiant in her suffering, but here with Jane Harden she was longing and she bent and pleaded with her suffering. (356)

In her chase for what Jeff terms "excitement," or external stimuli, Melanctha acquires "wisdom" through her body. Flesh becomes the conduit for acquiring knowledge—for "learn[ing] love," "know[ing] joy," and being "taught . . . suffer[ing]." Depressed not just emotionally but spatially, she is positioned in this scene as beneath Jane, where she is "kept down." "Real wisdom," Jane models, is "felt," positioned under one's feet and not in one's head. In their many communications, Melanctha calls for a refocusing on bodily sensation to recognize feelings that elide articulation through language.

Many critics have rightly read "Melanctha" as a racist imitation of Black life, in part for how it demonizes the Blackness of Melanctha's "unendurable . . . father" (348). Affirming a racial science in which Blackness and sensation are coupled (in *Notes on the State of Virginia*, Thomas Jefferson [1998: 146] claimed that enslaved people's "existence appears to participate more of sensation than reflection"), Melanctha as both a story and a character is made legible through the enactment of such stereotypes. Sonia Saldívar-Hull (1989: 188, 187) notes that the story exposes Stein's "class and race bias," revealing her belief in "in the 'unmorality of the black people.'" Stein's depression undoubtedly shaped her investment in narrating a woman's experience with chronic illness, and while as a Jewish American woman she was subject to anti-Semitism, her whiteness unveils the limits of her authorship in conveying the realities of Black life. At the same time, while Saldívar-Hull and other critics cast mindlessness as a state of abjection, Stein reclaims—in step with recent queer and critical race theories—the sensing body as a neglected source of knowledge production. "Dwell[ing] in the territory of the flesh," historian Amber Musser (2018: 3, 9) attends to Black and Brown peoples' "excess forms of embodiment," routinely objectified, as creating new "knowledge systems." She argues that excess is opaque, "what cannot begin to be conceived," just as the nineteenth-century Spiritualist or early twentieth-century psychiatric patient's extra, sixth sense refuses rational explanation (9). Influenced by Musser, my intent is not to defend "Melanctha's" racist representations but to suggest that the depiction in *Three Lives* of Melanctha's "wanderings after wisdom" model a mode of embodied and sensing expression that challenges authorship's privileging of the mind at the exclusion of the body (Stein 1990: 341, 248).[17] As Musser (2018: 11) explains, "Thought can be located outside of the linguistic, in and through the body and its movements."

Unlike Clifton, we might say that Stein remains reluctant to attribute her published work to forces beyond her making. In response to others' accounts of her writing as mindless, she responds by insisting: "I am a genius," pointing to a single individual wielding an exceptionally able mind (qtd. in Stendhal 1994: xi). But in *Lectures of America*, Stein ([1935] 1985: 170) upends our understanding of the genius as a solitary thinker, explaining, "One may really indeed say that that is the essence of genius, of being most intensely alive, that is being one who is at the same time talking and listening." If "talking has nothing to do with creation" (Stein 2004: 146), Stein, like Clifton, privileges voices exterior to the self, thus praising the collaborative mind—the one that "listen[s] with full feeling" (Stein 1990: 352)—as figured through the endlessly wandering body.

Extra Fingers

Stein's and Clifton's scenes of automatic writing reveal several differences—a clash between institutional and domestic spaces, the lavish Harvard laboratory versus the home in Buffalo—and a difference in subjects. Stein writes alone, her mind and body made the experimental object of her psychological study, while Clifton is surrounded by family, the Ouija board suturing three generations of Black women, some living and others dead. Spiritualism would undergo a revival in the 1960s, mainly by Black Americans like Clifton who embraced this era of "mediated" writing (Braude 1989: 29). In the 1970s, Clifton jotted received writings on scraps of paper, burned the edges, and then placed them in hidden spots like her shoe to find when she returned to a more conscious state. Shoes encase the part of the body farthest away from the head, which Western culture deems (as De Morgan's illustration suggests) the originator of knowledge. Melanctha's shuffling feet "wander" through town before conversing with Jane just as Clifton channels others' souls through the messages tucked atop the soles of her shoes. Eventually, Clifton would remove the folded scraps from their hiding places and stuff them into labeled envelopes. On one envelope, she explains that the message in her shoe was a response to a concern about the arrival of a check: "This was found in my (Lucille's) shoe" (Emory Special Collections). This description curiously bears parentheses around both "(Lucille)," which is meant to describe the shoe as hers, and a final addition, "(I think)" (written in small script), to show her uncertainty about the message's origin. Clifton reveals the thinking self (or poetic *I*) as insignificant— an afterthought to the enduring presence of the scrap itself.

Clifton's poems address the many visits from "the ones" who speak through her body:

we are the ones
who have not rolled
selves into bone and flesh
call us the ones
we will call you
one eye
field of feeling
singing ear
quick hand
we will make use of these (Clifton 2012: 614)

Describing the marriage of matter and spirit, the ambiguous "ones" shed "bone and flesh" ("flesh," they write, "is the coat we unfasten") to enter the bodies of the living (617). "The ones" carry no language. "Tongueless," they channel warnings through the medium's "morning cup":

neither dead
nor emigrant
we are just here
where you are" (624, 616).

As Erin L. Forbes suggests of nineteenth-century spirits, "Theirs is not the speech of abstract liberal subjects who 'speak, fact, and know' directly for themselves" (453). "The ones," as Clifton's ancestors, understand such voicelessness as redressing the insufficiency of human perception: "we have noticed / what you have ignored / we have not" (618). As medium, Clifton is awakened to these untapped sensations—a "field of feeling": how her hand hurries across the scrap or how her foot finds a message in its shoe (616).

Engaged in group travel, "the ones" transform the word *one* to mean many. Their consistent use of the pronoun *we* dismantles the singular scene of authorship as they bridge spirit with flesh and flesh with spirit. These bodily descriptors resemble the 1861 publication in the *Banner of Light*, which praises the "abnormal" body as conduit for the persuasive transmission of otherworldly messages. "The ones" discover the human subject to be wanting in its singularity: its "one eye," "singing ear," and "quick hand." Disembodied, such spirits "make use" of the poet whose body parts have lost their pairs. Here, impairment (materialized as bodily lack) enables the extrasensory excesses necessary to facilitate conversation between the living and the dead.

Clifton differs from the subject of "the ones" because of her extra (rather than missing) limbs, which she considers necessary for channeling the weight of her past.[18] Marina Magloire (2020) explains that the term *two-headed woman* (the title of Clifton's collection of channeled poems) is used in Black culture "to describe women gifted with access to the spirit world as well as to the material world." Nineteenth-century accounts of Spiritualism similarly feature "a 'second hand' [that] . . . would appear just above or behind the medium's own" (Rainey 1998: 134). These imaginative drawings of Spiritualists' anatomy were an embodied reality for Clifton, Thelma, and Sidney—three generations of women born with "two extra fingers" and two extra toes (Clifton 2012: 204). Clifton relays this "gift" in an untitled poem:

i was born with twelve fingers
like my mother and my daughter
each of us
born wearing strange black gloves
extra baby fingers hanging over the sides of our cribs and dipping
    into the milk

somebody was afraid we would learn to cast spells
and our wonders were cut off
but they didn't understand
the powerful memories of ghosts. now
we take what we want
with invisible fingers
and we connect
my dead mother my life daughter and me
through our terrible shadowy hands (196)

The trouble with six-fingered hands is that they assume too much space, their extraness overflowing the perimeters of the crib and falling into the milk cup. The hands are deemed extra not just for their additional digits but for their blackness, "strange black gloves" that thicken the women's embodied selves. Others' fear of the extra fingers prevents the children from keeping them. Like her mother, Clifton's additional fingers were removed at birth. As the poet grows, she settles a pen in the hand now missing its sixth digit. Even as they are cut away without her consent, the lost body part remains present as a threatening "shadow," the missing digits haunting the remaining ten: "They didn't understand / the powerful memories of ghosts." This disabled, embodied life returns in a new form. Years later, daughter and mother and grandmother will congregate and "connect" at the Ouija board: a living Clifton and her then living daughter touch the plastic planchette, welcoming their presence of their "dead mother" and grandmother "with invisible fingers."

Clifton's congenital disability manifests what Stein calls "xtra consciousness"; the poet explains, "I've always had a kind of sixth sense—especially when somebody talks about hands. Yes, a sixth sense . . . that deals with spirituality and with the sacred" (Rowell 1999: 68). With six fingers and six children, this preoccupation with the extraness of her own and others' bodies leads Clifton to insist that poetry is not the mind's doing: "It's not just intellectual. If it were, all people would be poets." She continues, "I don't even know how I write. . . . But I do know that it happens, and it comes to me" (Lamon 2007). Never formally trained in poem writing or literary analysis, Clifton tells her students:

Poetry . . . has to come from not just my head but from everything that I am. Now, in the academy . . . one tends to think of poetry as not only an intellectual exercise but . . . I'm interested in other questions. . . . Does it feel like a poem? . . . Because the whole truth is that we're not all just our head and what we think. Logic is very useful; so is feeling. (Rowell 1999: 61)

Clifton envisions the poet as akin to Stein's Melanctha, who also insists that "language is feeling more than thinking" (Rowell 1999: 61). By deprivileging intellect and insisting that bodies think as much as minds do, the twentieth-century poet communes with her father, who was not taught to write, and her mother, who could write but not spell (Holladay 2007). To envision language as sensation is to honor not just her parents but her enslaved ancestors who turned to the spirit world to convey the reality of violence done to their bodyminds. "No poetry," Clifton explains, "is all consciously done"; it flows from her "whole / alive twelvefingered" being (Hull 1997: 347; Clifton 2012: 594).

In her collection *Next* (1987), Clifton again defends feeling over thinking, dedicating "grandma, we are poets" to her grandson Anpeyo Brown, who is autistic and nonverbal. The poem presents the dictionary definition of autism interwoven with Clifton's (2012: 374) reexplanation of it: "the place before / language imprisoned itself / in words." While it is odd for a poet whose tools are words to cast them as prisons, Clifton's Spiritualist training recognizes what language misses in its capturing. Again shuttling between multiple voices, the entries from "Webster's New Universal Dictionary and the Random House Encyclopedia" intermix with Clifton's repetition of "say rather," which serves to correct cultural norms surrounding cognition. While the so-called authoritative account of language describes autism as a "failure to use language normally," Clifton proclaims that this "world of words" is not always the most intelligible; "I could not follow," the speaker says. Refusing to specify speaker from listener, the poem's opening is directed to Clifton herself: "grandma, we are poets." Clifton makes space for the mind's "circling and circling" apart from words to forge new possibilities for the present: to imagine an "external reality" where children occupy large rooms rather than small ones and Black men, refusing the "holes" from bullets, live rather than die. Falling under the genre of "xtraness" and the extrasensory, the poem returns us to the *Banner of Light*'s proclamation that the disabled bodymind "improve[s] upon the limitations of the normal."

Like Stein, Clifton dismissed cognitive ability as the locus of poem making, leading readers to deny the legitimacy of her writing (Rader 2020). In "in white America," Clifton (2012: 313) describes "com[ing] to read them poems"—*them* referring to white audience members who perceive the Black woman's reading as "a fancy trick" of "toss [ing] and catch[ing] as if by magic." In the white space of "white America," listeners focus not on what Clifton has written or what she speaks but on how her body behaves—the way she "juggles," her "eyes bright," and her "mouth smil[es]." While these white listeners "reduce" the poet to her body, Clifton emphasizes the inseparability of mind and body for Black women.[19] In *two-headed woman*, "for the mad" pays tribute to an extra head, which remains even as the white strangers have parted, and the speaker is left among friends:

> you will be alone at last
> in the sanity of your friends.
> brilliance will fade away from you
> and you will settle in dimmed light.
> you will not remember how to mourn
> your dying difference.
> you will not be better but
> they will say you are well. (313)

The poem returns to the powers of disability—in this instance, an unnamed and uncelebrated insanity. With madness cast as a "dying difference," "you" (the poem's speaker) feels alone among the sane after having entered the "dimmed light" of the living. Sanity robs "the mad" speaker of her "brilliance," its vibrancy stifled under the normalizing pressure of rationality. Like Stein, Clifton resists and revises definitions of "sense" grounded in Enlightenment-centered thinking, turning instead to what Hull (1997: 332) describes as "nonrational, nonwestern modes of apprehending reality." In Clifton's final interview before her death (when she is positioned at the tenuous threshold central to her understanding of Black life), Chard deNiord (2010) asks whether she sees her identity as a poet as tied to "craziness," and she replies, "Well, a little bit. Perhaps more than a little bit. Crazy could mean spirited, magical. It could be all these things." Clifton does not resort to pathology; just as she refuses to distinguish between the living and the dead, she does not parse "crazy" from "sane." As she ages, Clifton confesses to having difficulties with memory, but deNiord (2010: 13) assures her at the close of their conversation that she has "been sane the whole time [they have] been talking." Clifton, though, refuses what she is intended to take as a compliment: "To be sane in this world is crazy," she retorts (13).

Automaticity Then and Now

> The way that I can appreciate the words is to join them in whirling with them, quite in a big way of feeling the words style automatic.
>
> —Alex Kimmel, quoted in Amy Sequenzia and Elizabeth Grace, *Typed Words, Loud Voices* (2015)

Thus far, I have shown how rigid definitions of authorship, which rely on a singular voice to determine credibility, work to exclude disabled women's and, more specifically, disabled women of color's writing. By recasting authorship as a practice of the bodymind, we excavate collaborative and nonlinguistic forms of expression that too often elude critical attention. As a key component of disability history, automatic writing, in foregrounding sensation, challenges our understanding of authorship as exclusive to the thinking subject and listens to the many wanderings of the purportedly irrational messenger who crosses between this world and the next. By modeling forms of writing that exceed consciousness, Stein and Clifton make way for embracing the many forms of disabled authorship in our past and present.

Today, debates about the authenticity of disabled writers' voices persist, particularly among those who rely on facilitated communication (FC), a therapeutic technique introduced to the United States in the 1990s to assist nonverbal people in communicating via language.[20] Typically, the nondisabled person places their hand on the disabled person's arm to support their typing on a lettered keyboard. Scientists place FC in a longer genealogy of nineteenth-century Spiritualism to reveal the disabled person as influenced by external forces—either a visiting spirit or a communication facilitator. As William Paul Simmons, Janyce Boynton, and Todd Landman (2021: 149) explain, "The technique is now seen in the same light as Ouija boards, automatic writing and other writing techniques," which they describe as "well-intentioned but unable to stand up to scientific scrutiny." Scientists argue that facilitators produce the disabled person's writing, unconsciously moving their partner's limb to craft the message they wish to see rather than assist impaired individuals in conveying knowledge independent of nondisabled people's influence. Sociologist Mark Sherry (2016: 974) states, "The person who 'facilitates' the conversation directs the conversation; they are the authors, rather than the disabled person." Both sides of the FC debate rely on similar assumptions about authorship.[21] Although valiantly opposed, FC's believers and disbelievers embrace an ableist ideology that positions the mind as the locus of human agency—to be a message's originator, a person must express thinking through written language.

In more recent years, debates about automatic authorship in the form of FC have escalated to troubling allegations. In 2015, Rutgers University philosophy professor Anna Stubblefield confessed to having fallen in love with a mentally disabled man named DJ with cerebral palsy for whom she was serving as a communication partner. Their encounters raised concerns about sexual consent and whether it could be granted through the pseudoscientific phenomenon of FC. In court, Stubblefield defended the authenticity of their conversation— "I knew [DJ] was the author of his typing—why would I question that?"—and insisted that his impaired motor control prevented him from being able to engage in the physical act of writing, which would allow for self-expression (Enger 2015). Because FC does not qualify as evidence under New Jersey law, Judge Siobhan Teare convicted Stubblefield of first-degree aggravated sexual assault, "prov[ing] that DJ was incapable of consent" (Enger 2015).

This multimillion-dollar case is complicated for several reasons— because it raises questions not simply about authorship but also about the relationship between race and ability, more specifically, the relationship between a nondisabled, white facilitator with a PhD and a Black, disabled man to whom specialists assigned a low IQ (Enger 2015). A feminist-of-color disability studies critique would take issue with how DJ has been sidelined for his presumed inability. As reporter Daniel Enger (2015) explains, Judge Teare would "permit the prosecution to display DJ to the jury for a few minutes in his mute and spastic condition," as if others' perception of his body was proof that any claims of consent were untrue. Stubblefield herself—who, as Enger rightly notes, has dominated the press surrounding the case and eventual conviction—was not the only one on trial. Instead, the jury queried, Was DJ human enough to either agree to sex or to suffer the injustices of assault?[22]

Attention to the long histories of automatic writing asks us to devise new terms in the debate regarding the efficacy of FC and, more broadly, automatic writing—that is, to forgo the tracking of origins and authenticity and consider instead how meaning proliferates through and across the bodymind's sensations. By placing Stein and Clifton in conversation—having them communicate, like their nineteenth-century Spiritualist predecessors, across almost a century—we recognize the ableness ascribed to conventional forms of authorship, which neglect to honor embodied thinking. By contrast, automaticity foregrounds feeling, what nonverbal autistic writer Alex Kimmel describes via FC as "feeling the words style automatic" (Sequenzia and Grace 2015, n.p.). To center disabled people in the compositional scene is to imagine all the bodymind has yet to feel and all it has yet to write. In her meditation on Clifton's spirit writing, Magloire (2020) explains that the poet's poems "make . . . the pangs of [her] own embodiment as a Black woman easier to bear amid constant reminders of the perils of Black embodiment." She continues, "There is solace in the idea that this brown skin and these wide hips were made for listening to the voices that could not be erased by time, history, or death. Oh my body, make of me always a woman who listens." By listening, Clifton (and Stein via her understanding of the genius as listener rather than creator) demands a dually informed practice: disabled women recognizing what their bodies tell them while remaining aware of what is told by others through their bodies. "Xtra consciousness" for extra feeling, "extra limbs" for extra poem making. To listen to Stein and Clifton's many messages is to loosen our grip on the pen to see where our bodymind takes us.

Clare Mullaney is assistant professor of English at Clemson University, where she teaches courses on American literature, histories of editing, and disability theory. Her current book project, *A Word Made Flesh: Disability and Editorship in U.S. Literature and Culture*, reveals how both late nineteenth-century and present-day publishing networks recover writing about disability without erasing marks of authors' impairments or access needs from the page. Her work has appeared or is forthcoming in *Arizona Quarterly*, *J19*, *Journal of Literary and Cultural Disability Studies*, *Pedagogy*, *Atlantic*, and *Public Books*.

Notes

I am grateful to members of my steadfast writing group—Vivian DelChamps, Lindsey Grubbs, Jessica Horvath Williams, Jess Libow, and Sarah Nance—for their many careful suggestions. Thanks, too, to my colleague David Coombs for his helpful reading recommendations.

1   Hans A. Baer (1989) cites folklorist Gilbert E. Cooley, whose interview with psychic Rev. K.J. offers a helpful distinction between the terms *spiritual* and *spiritualist*. Rev. K.J. explains that spiritual people believe in divine influence to help the persecuted, whereas spiritualists believe that life extends into death. He explains of the spiritualists: "We believe . . . that those who are 'out of the body' are unable to communicate as spirits with those who are in the body" (116).

2   Erin E. Forbes (2016: 453) argues that Spiritualism is necessary for Black populations to counter "social and civil death." For an extensive account of the history of disability among enslaved populations in the United States, see Boster 2013.

3   Margaret Price (2015) introduces the term *bodymind* to challenge the Cartesian dualism that situates minds and bodies as separate and hierarchically distinct entities. A literalization of this concept, automatic writing imagines authorship as the work not only of the mind but also of the body and its sensations.

4   For a comprehensive history of women's sensitivity, see Wilson 2012.

5   My research reveals only one instance in which both writers are referenced simultaneously: an interview in which Hilary Holladay compares Clifton's work to Stein's, suggesting that they "view words as physical objects" (Holladay and Clifton 1988). Clifton is quick to disagree, expressing dislike for her modernist predecessor: "I'm not a particular fan," she confesses.

6   Offering a counter example to the West's reliance on this five-sense configuration, David Howes (2009: 3, 16) looks to the Cashinahua people, an Indigenous tribe in southern Peru, who believe that cognition resides in "the whole body [which] knows."

7   The abbreviation of the word *extra* as "xtra" conveys a tension between excess and lack; while the term means more, its abbreviation (the dropping of the *e*) signifies less.

8   As self-identified "big women," both writers also understand their large bodies as central actors in the compositional scene. In her poetry collection *The Book of Light* (1993), Clifton describes herself (if we assume, as many critics have, an autobiographical speaker in this poem) as a "big woman . . . rounder than the moon" (Clifton 2012: 426), and biographer Mary Jane Lupton (2006: 5) describes the poet as "a large-framed African-American woman." Stein famously relished food; as Wendy Steiner (1995) explains, "She loved to eat and her body showed it." Stein's contemporaries also equated the author's purportedly excessive corporeal form with her repetitive texts, with Wyndham Lewis describing her prose as "all fat, without nerve" (qtd. in Stimpson 1977: 68). For a more extensive account of fatness as activism rather than pathology, see Herndon 2002. For an account of the relationship between fatness and race, see also historian Sabrina Strings's *Fearing the Black Body*. Querying not only the relationship between women and weight but, more specifically, "how fatness became linked to . . . blackness," Strings (2019: 5, 70, 74) explains that mid-eighteenth- and early nineteenth-century "race-making projects" "underscored the purported racial distinctions in . . . body type . . . between black women and white women."

9   For another account of overlap between disability studies and sensory studies, see Corker 2001.

10   See Twain's *Jap Herron, A Novel Written from the Ouija Board* (channeled through Lola Hayes), Wilde's *Oscar Wilde from Purgatory: Psychic Messages* (channeled through Hester Travers Smith), and Yeats's *A Vision* (channeled through Georgie Hyde-Lees). Ludoph 2018 offers more insight into the latter example.

11   For an overview of this hierarchy of senses, see Fretwell 2018: 1.

12   In naming the social model of disability, which argues that disability inheres in bodies' and minds' interaction with material and social

environments, early disability studies scholars resisted the term *impairment*, which they believed confined disability to an individual. These models have since been subject to revision, allowing the realities of the impaired bodymind to come into new focus. See Kafer's (2013: 7) account of the political/relational model of disability where she undoes clear distinctions between impairment and disability.

13   While Stein expressed her reservations with surrealism, the movement similarly engaged with automatic writing to probe individuals' unconscious. For a comprehensive account of why critics should rethink the framing of surrealism as wholly misogynistic, see Conley 1996, which foregrounds disabled women's participation by showing how madwomen at the center of the movement queried the stark divisions between dream and reality.

14   Establishing a genealogy between the mid-nineteenth-century Spiritualist movement and the birth of twentieth-century psychology, Rachel Leah Thompson (2004) writes: "Psychoanalysis can be read as a form of secularized occultism."

15   For additional accounts of Stein and the senses, see Merrill 2009; and Chodat 2005.

16   Lucy Daniel (2009: 31) explains how Skinner uses Stein's proclaimed automaticity to both dismiss her intelligence and frame her as ill: "Because Stein's poetry resembled disassociated effects, it amounted to a proof of her own hysterical tendencies, her own 'degenerate' nature." For a helpful reading of Stein's response to Skinner's critique, see also Barbara Will's chapter "In Search of a Subject" (Will 2000: 21–47).

17   My notion of embodied thinking is similar to what studies in cognitive science call *embodied cognition*: the belief that "our cognition is influenced, perhaps determined by, our experiences in the physical world" (McNerney 2011).

18   Lupton (2006: 10) also explains that Lucille had "one bad eye"; since birth vision in her left eye was compromised. Lupton draws attention to Clifton's poem in *An Ordinary Woman* that begins with the line "lucy one-eye."

19   In her earlier poem "testament," Clifton (2012: 245) writes, "mother, I am mad. / we should have guessed a twelve-fingered flower might break," pointing to the many reaches of embodied life.

20   Such techniques are said to benefit not only autistic people but also those with cerebral palsy, traumatic brain injuries, and Down syndrome. See Simmons, Boynton, and Landman 2021: 146.

21   See also Mintz 2017: 1666, which similarly unveils "the many players of ableism at play in this case."

22   I am grateful to Jessica Horvath Williams for this insight.

References

Ambrosio, Chiara. 2018. "Gertrude Stein's Modernist Brain." *Progress in Brain Research* 243: 139–80.

Baer, Hans A. 2001. *The Black Spiritualist Movement: A Religious Response to Racism*. Knoxville: Univ. of Tennessee Press.

Banner of Light. 1866. "Third Quarterly Meeting of the Massachusetts State Convention." Vol. 20, no. 8: 2.

Biers, Katherine. 2013. *Virtual Modernism: Writing and Technology in the Progressive Era*. Minneapolis: Univ. of Minnesota Press.

Binet, Alfred. 1896. *Alterations of Personality*. New York: Appleton.

Boster, Dea H. 2013. *African American Slavery and Disability: Bodies, Property, and Power in the Antebellum South, 1800–1860*. New York: Routledge.

Braude, Ann. 1989. *Radical Spirits: Spiritualism and Women's Rights in Nineteenth-Century America*. Boston: Beacon Press.

Chodat, Robert. 2005. "Sense, Science, and the Interpretation of Gertrude Stein." *Modernism/Modernity* 12, no. 4: 581–605.

Clifton, Lucille. 2012. *The Collected Poems of Lucille Clifton, 1965–2010*. Edited by Kevin Yong and Michael Glasner. Rochester, NY: BOA Editions.

Conley, Katharine. 1996. *Automatic Woman: The Representation of Women in Surrealism*. Lincoln: Univ. of Nebraska.

Corker, Mairian. 2001. "Sensing Disability." *Hypatia: A Journal of Feminist Philosophy* 16, no. 4: 34–52.

Daniel, Lucy. 2009. *Gertrude Stein*. Chicago: Univ. of Chicago Press.

De Morgan, Sophia Elizabeth. 1863. *From Matter to Spirit: Ten Years' Experience in Spirit Manifestations*. London: Longman, Green, Longman, Roberts and Green.

deNiord, Chard. 2010. "Her Last Interview." *American Poetry Review*, May/June: 5–13.

Enger, Daniel. 2015. "The Strange Case of Anna Stubblefield." *New York Times*, October 25.

Forbes, Erin E. 2016. "Do Black Ghosts Matter? Harriet Jacobs's Spiritualism." *ESQ* 62, no. 3: 443–479.

Freidner, Michele, and Stefan Helmreich. 2012. "Sound Studies Meets Deaf Studies." *Senses and Society* 7, no. 1: 72–86.

Fretwell, Erica. 2018. "Introduction: Common Senses and Critical Sensibilities." *Resilience: A Journal of the Environmental Humanities* 5, no. 3: 1–9.

Garland-Thomson, Rosemarie. 1993. *Extraordinary Bodies: Figuring Disability in American Culture and Literature*. New York: Columbia Univ. Press.

Geurts, Kathryn Linn. 2015. "Senses." In *Keywords for Disability Studies*, edited by Rachel Adams, Benjamin Reiss, and David Serlin, 161–63. New York: New York Univ. Press.

Hare, Robert. 1855. *Experimental Investigation of the Spirit Manifestations, Demonstrating the Existence of Spirits and Their Communion with Morals*. New York: Patridge and Brittan.

Herndon, April. 2002. "Disparate but Disabled: Fat Embodiment and Disability Studies" *NWSA Journal* 14, no. 3: 120–37.

Holladay, Hilary, and Lucille Clifton. 1998. "She Could Tell You Stories." Poetry Foundation. https://www.poetryfoundation.org/articles/68875/she-could-tell-you-stories.

Howes, David. 2009. Introduction to *The Sixth Sense Reader*, edited by David Howes, 1–52. New York: Routledge.

Hull, Akasha. 1997. "Channeling the Ancestral Muse: Lucille Clifton and Dolores Kendrick." In *Female Subjects in Black and White: Race, Psychoanalysis, Feminism*, edited by Elizabeth Abel, Barbara Christian, and Helene Moglen, 330–48. Berkeley: Univ. of California Press.

Jefferson, Thomas. 1998. *Notes on the State of Virginia*. New York: Penguin Classics.

Judd, Bettina. 2019. "Glossolalia: Lucille Clifton's Creative Technologies of Becoming." In *Black Bodies and Transhuman Realities: Scientifically Modifying the Black Body in Posthuman Literature and Culture*, edited by Melvin G. Hill, 133–49. London: Lexington Books.

Kafer, Alison. 2013. *Feminist, Queer, Crip*. Bloomington: Indiana Univ. Press.

Katz, Leon. 1971. Introduction to *Fernhurst, Q.E.D. and Other Early Writings* by Gertrude Stein, i–xxxiv. New York: Liveright.

Kramnick, Jonathan. 2018. *Paper Minds: Literature and the Ecology of Consciousness*. Chicago: Univ. of Chicago Press.

Ludoph, Emily. 2018. "W. B. Yeats's Live-in 'Spirit Medium.'" *JSTOR Daily*, December 5. https://daily.jstor.org/wb-yeats-live-in-spirit-medium/.

Lupton, Mary Jane. 2006. *Lucille Clifton: Her Life and Letters*. Westport, CT: Praeger.

Magloire, Marina. 2020. "The Spirit Writing of Lucille Clifton." *Paris Review*, October 19. https://www.theparisreview.org/blog/2020/10/19/the-spirit-writing-of-lucille-clifton/#:~:text=Lucille%20Clifton's%20spirit%20writing%20makes,time%2C%20history%2C%20or%20death.

McNerney, Samuel. 2011. "A Brief Guide to Embodied Cognition: Why You Are Not Your Brain." *Scientific American*, November 4. https://blogs.scientificamerican.com/guest-blog/a-brief-guide-to-embodied-cognition-why-you-are-not-your-brain/?gclid=CjwKCAiA3pugBhAwEiwAWFzwdQVS5V3FD7muGWrRbpNpmzHvl3jrUSqS9ciJmNJ91JO-MbWFQ6ifUhoC6DEQAvD_BwE.

Merrill, Cole. 2009. "Remaking Sense: Gertrude Stein and the Names of the Father." *Women's Studies* 38: 84–99.

Mintz, Kevin. 2017. "Ableism, Ambiguity, and the Anna Stubblefield Case." *Disability and Society* 32, no. 10: 1666–70.

Morgan, Benjamin. 2017. *The Outward Mind: Materialist Aesthetics in Victorian Science and Literature*. Chicago: Univ. of Chicago Press.

Musser, Amber. 2018. *Sensual Excess: Queer Femininity and Brown Jouissance*. New York: New York Univ. Press.

Price, Margaret. 2015. "The Bodymind Problem and the Possibilities of Pain." *Hypatia* 30, no. 1: 268–84.

Rader, Dean. 2020. "'More than Me': On 'How to Carry Water: Selected Poems of Lucille Clifton." *Los Angeles Review of Books*, November 29. https://lareviewofbooks.org/article/more-than-me-on-how-to-carry-water-selected-poems-of-lucille-clifton/.

Rainey, Lawrence. 1998. "Taking Dictation: Collage Poetics, Pathology, and Politics." *Modernism/Modernity* 5, no. 2: 123–53.

Roudeau, Cécile. 2015. *"How the Earth Feels*: A Conversation with Dana Luciano." *Transatlantica* 1: 1–11.

Rowe, John Carlos. 2018. "Naming What Is Inside: Gertrude Stein's Use of Names in Three Lives." *Novel: A Forum on Fiction*. 36, no. 2: 219–243.

Rowell, Charles. 1999. "Interview with Lucille Clifton." *Callaloo* 22, no. 1: 56–72.

Saldívar-Hull, Sonia. 1989. "Wrestling Your Ally: Stein, Racism, and a Feminist Critical Practice." In *Women's Writing in Exile*, edited by Mary Lynn Broe and Angela Ingram, 182–98. Chapel Hill: Univ. of North Carolina Press.

Schalk, Sami, and Jina B. Kim. 2020. "Integrating Race, Transforming Feminist Disability Studies." *Signs: Journal of Women and Culture in Society* 46, no. 1: 31–55.

Sequenzia, Amy, and Elizabeth J. Grace. 2015. *Typed Words, Loud Voices: A Collection*. Autonomous Press.

Sherry, Mark. 2016. "Facilitated Communication, Anna Stubblefield, and Disability Studies." *Disability and Society* 31, no. 7: 974–82.

Simmons, William Paul, Janyce Boynton, and Todd Landman. 2021. "Communication, Neurodiversity, and Human Rights." *Human Rights Quarterly* 43, no. 1: 138–67.

Skinner, B. F. 1933. "Has Gertrude Stein a Secret?" *Atlantic Monthly* 153, no. 1: 50–57.

Solomons, Leon M., and Gertrude Stein. 1896. "Normal Motor Automatism." *Harvard Psychological Review* 3, no. 5: 492–512.

Stein, Gertrude. (1935) 1985. *Lectures in America*. Boston: Beacon Press.

Stein, Gertrude. 1990. *Selected Writings of Gertrude Stein*. New York: Vintage Books.

Stein, Gertrude. 2004. *Look at Me and Here I Am: Writings and Lectures, 1911–1945*. Edited by Patricia Meyerwitz. London: Peter Owen.

Steiner, Wendy. 1995. "Mother." *London Review of Books* 17, no. 20: https://www.lrb.co.uk/the-paper/v17/n20/wendy-steiner/mother.

Stendhal, Renate. 1994. *Gertrude Stein: In Words and Pictures*. Chapel Hill, NC: Algonquin Books.

Stimpson, Catherine. 1977. "The Mind, the Body, and Gertrude Stein." *Critical Inquiry* 3, no. 3: 489–506.

Strings, Sabrina. 2019. *Fearing the Black Body: The Racial Origins of Fat Phobia*. New York: New York Univ. Press.

Thompson, Rachel Leah. 2004. "The Automatic Hand: Spiritualism, Psychoanalysis, and Surrealism." *InVisible Culture: An Electronic Journal for Visual Culture* 7: 1–14.

Walker, Jayne L. 1984. *The Making of a Modernist Gertrude Stein*. Amherst: Univ. of Massachusetts Press.

Will, Barbara. 2000. *Gertrude Stein, Modernism, and the Problem of "Genius."* Edinburgh: Edinburgh Univ. Press.

Will, Barbara. 2001. "Gertrude Stein, Automatic Writing and the Mechanics of Genius." *Forum for Modern Language Studies* 37, no. 2: 169–75.

Wilson, Erin. 2012. "The End of Sensibility: The Nervous Body in the Early Nineteenth Century." *Literature and Medicine* 30, no, 2: 276–91.

Sunhay
You

The Sweetness of Race:
On Synesthesia, Addiction, and
Self-Possessed Personhood in Monique
Truong's *Bitter in the Mouth*

Abstract "The Sweetness of Race" examines the sensorial effects of lexical-gustatory synesthesia in Monique Truong's *Bitter in the Mouth* (2010). In this documentation of how words taste, whiteness becomes associated with the taste of sugar and its addictive properties. Throughout the novel, whiteness becomes legible as an object of addiction that defends against the failed ideals of self-possessed human personhood—a cornerstone to white supremacy. The novel then reveals opportunities to reorganize the senses and ideas of personhood as a means to disrupt particularly harmful appetites for racialized intimacies.
Keywords adoption, interracial love, multiculturalism, sexuality, nationalism

In her seminal work *Playing in the Dark*, Toni Morrison (1992) critiques how the history of slavery produces a visuality of race whereby blackness circulates as metaphors for danger and evil. She narrates the imperative of writing stories that challenge and transform such colored meanings, illuminating how the semantics of racism is intimately tied to habits of seeing (see Mirzoeff 2011). As if to anticipate Morrison's intervention, a politics of colorblindness rose to prominence in the aftermath of the Korean and Vietnam Wars with the dawn of transnational adoption (see Callahan 2011; Dorow 2006; Eng 2010; Kim 2010; Novy 2001; Pate 2014). David Eng (2010: 10) argues that despite its antiracist intentions, the colorblind politics of such adoption practices instead leads to the racialization of intimacy "by which race becomes occluded within the private domain of private family and kinship." Colorblind politics stresses how race can be unseen to reinforce the universalist ideals of abstract individualism, effectively evacuating race of any substantive meaning within the interracial family while containing the threats racial intimacies pose to

American Literature, Volume 95, Number 3, September 2023
DOI 10.1215/00029831-10679237   © 2023 by Duke University Press

white reproductive futurity. Under such logics of erasure, racialized intimacies can flourish in plain sight, evading notice or critique. Put differently, colorblindness simultaneously disavows and reinvests in a visuality of race, giving the lie to its purported liberatory aims.

The incapacity of colorblind politics to transform the meaning of race speaks to the impossibility of disorganizing racist logics without unsettling visuality as a hegemonic mode of knowing. Returning to Morrison's provocation, the question remains of how literature can disrupt the visuality of racist ideologies, especially how they idealize interracial intimacies (see Storti 2020). This article picks up this query through an examination of Monique Truong's *Bitter in the Mouth* (2010). The novel draws on synesthesia as a literary device to beget an unfamiliar semantic field within which to understand and articulate the effects of race and racism. The synesthetic capacity to confuse one sense for another unveils how race structures and is structured by habits of sensing other than the visual. At the same time, as the sounds of words trigger experiences of taste or color, synesthesia also disrupts the more direct associations between words and images. This interruption of linguistic-visual perception throughout the novel allows the racialization of intimacy to be perceived in terms of an addictive appetite for sweetness that can cloak and turn palatable the violence of racism. After analyzing how synesthesia suspends the visuality of race, the following sections interrogate the relationship between sugar addiction and racist appetites before detailing how Truong's novel charts other possibilities for relating across racial differences. These other ways of feeling and perceiving reconstitute the very meaning of interracial intimacy by divesting from abstract individualism and self-possessed personhood.

Synesthesia and the Visuality of Race

Bitter initially seems to concern the legacy of the Hammerick family in Boiling Springs, North Carolina, a name passed down for more than three generations with roots in slave ownership. Truong's protagonist and first-person narrator, Linda, is in line to inherit the Hammerick estates, except she is a transnational Vietnamese adoptee and hence not a true Hammerick. However, this fact about Linda's racial difference does not emerge from the text until the middle of the novel, when Linda receives her Yale diploma as "Linh-Dao Nguyen" (Truong 2010: 158). Up to this point, the narrative makes no visual reference to Linda's race, letting the reader assume Linda is white by virtue of her kinship ties. Linda's ethnic name is unimaginable prior to its discovery.

This narrative rupture incites readers to revisit the earlier half of the novel with the benefit of hindsight, to learn to sense race differently. Truong forces readers to examine how Linda had been expressing her difference all along through other sensory registers, creating another version of the novel itself. The story is best read twice—first for its shock value and then for a reeducation of the senses. In this second reading, the absence of visual references highlights other aspects of Linda's subjectivity, which might have been overshadowed by the fact of Linda's race. In the novel's opening, titled "Confessions," Linda's narrative primarily revolves around her lexical-gustatory synesthesia, the first secret she learns to keep from her family. She tastes spoken words. Her need to both express and contain this secret mobilizes her narrative. Privileging her synesthesia over race as the central object of her story, Truong asks readers to consider matters of taste and language as the prerequisite for understanding Linda's racialized subjectivity.

Synesthesia is a neurobiological condition that is highly responsive to social contexts in the sense that Linda's taste-word associations depend on her initial encounters with food and language (see Ramachandran, Hubbard, and Butcher 2004; Thomas 2017). As Linda explains, the "experiential flavors had to come first . . . only then could [the] tastes attach themselves to the words, without cause or consideration for the meanings of the words" (Truong 2010: 74). For instance, the name of her childhood friend Kelly triggers the sweetness of canned peaches, represented as "Kelly*cannedpeaches*" on the page (18). This sweet association not only foreshadows their future romance but also memorializes Linda's first encounter with her adoptive mother DeAnne's southern cooking.

The taste of canned peaches indexes Linda's affections for Kelly as much as her first memories of DeAnne and the South, making legible how the past bears on the present, how two distinct temporal-sensorial experiences can coexist. Literary scholar and historian Denise Cruz (2014: 718–19) notes that Truong's attention to the foodways of the South "resist[s] the dominant structures of racial visibility . . . [and] thus urgently promotes a reevaluation of how we understand, recognize, and imagine difference and community." Sara Gabler Thomas (2016: 42) affirms and builds on Cruz's insights, contending that "Linda's synesthesia replaces the racialized exterior (and textual representation) of her body as a route to epistemological certainty about her identity." This attention to how the multiplicity of perception disorganizes hegemonic modes of knowing difference and identity attunes readers to grasp the multiplicity of Linda's perspective as a Vietnamese adoptee—as simultaneously an unraced and raced subject of racialized intimacy. More than just a unique trait, Linda's synesthesia additionally mirrors how she circulates as a synesthetic object, as both an optimistic symbol of a colorblind era and a pessimistic reminder of the Vietnam War. Linda triggers competing perceptions of the present and hence unseats visuality as a stable denomination of meaning.

Truong's formal and narrative use of synesthesia clarifies how concurrent perceptions of reality press up against the limits of articulate knowledge. When Linda first tries to disclose her synesthesia to DeAnne, Linda hears her mother retort, "Linda*mint*, please*lemonjuice* don't talk*cornchips* like a crazy*heavycream* person*garlicpowder*" (Truong 2010: 107). In her reading of the scene, Amanda Dykema (2014: 118–19) highlights that while "*you* tastes of canned green beans and *Linda* tastes of mint, *I* is not associated with any taste. As such, it implies an unmarked subject (untouched by synesthetic production) and also establishes the subject as a fluid conception that cannot be stabilized, even by the process of synesthetic sensation." Dykema observes how synesthesia produces an embodied archive of knowledge and sense perception that disrupts the stability of the identitarian subject as a unit of both difference and community. There is no taste-word association that can lead to any epistemological certainty about Linda's subjectivity. The fact that *you*, *Linda*, and even *person* can be tasted in contrast to *I* merely deepens the mystery of who Linda could be. Linda's synesthesia presents a way of confronting epistemological limits, the threshold to "crazy" or the limits of linguistic and visual modes of comprehension.[1]

Any knowledge claim made about Linda (as you, Linda, or person) highlights an unknowability. If *you* and *Linda* are how the narrator is interpellated into being, the void of her *I* denotes the ontological impossibility of Linda's having an original and stable sense of self. Linda reveals to her readers that, while she learned to respond to "Linda" over "Linh-Dao," neither name was familiar. "'Linda' was the void. 'Linh-Dao' was the missing" (Truong 2010: 165). She implies that *Linda* indexes a subject that DeAnne would have preferred to call her daughter—a biological child that never existed and marks a void. Meanwhile, *Linh-Dao* cites a missing relation and person, a girl's missing ties to and knowledge of her birth parents and place of origin. Linda evades capture, irreducible to her racial otherness or racial origin, at once eliciting and rupturing scripts for racist love. Leslie Bow (2022: 196–97) defines racist love as "taking pleasure in a racial type constructed through (positive) symbolism," a pleasure "rooted in the reductive structure of typing, something it shares with racial profiling."

The racialization of intimacy that occurs at the behest of colorblind politics, embedded in the normalized appearance of "Linda" over "Linh-Dao," transforms the excesses of Linda's sociohistorical becoming into a simplified and consumable type, specifically as the assimilable model minority. Linda's narrative about her synesthesia, then, restores the excesses of racial meaning (the void and the missing) that circuit between her two names, presenting the crucible to the visuality of race and its attendant iconographic terms of "loving" recognition.

An Addictive Sweetness

In another synesthetic expression, "Hammerick*DrPepper*," Linda couples the whiteness of the Hammerick family with the soft drink Dr Pepper, an object of her adoptive grandmother Iris's sugar addiction. Sugar, and especially the US history of processed sugar, cites intentional efforts and desires to construct whiteness around the virtues of purity and refinement (see Abbott 2009; Kriz 2008; Mintz 1985). Offering deeper insight into this habituated way of associating whiteness with goodness, Catherine Keyser (2019: 1) writes that "whiteness, like refined sugar, is a technology . . . that relies upon the repression of corporeal abjection." She suggests that the process for stripping sugar of its molasses color concerns cleansing the commercial good of its ties to slavery such that sweetness can be enjoyed without the unpleasant reminders of laboring bodies. Intervening in these sensorial logics and repressions, Linda's synesthetic pairing "Hammerick-*DrPepper*" establishes whiteness in relation to the dark syrupy sweetness of Dr Pepper. The soft drink takes shape as an object of addiction that satisfies the compulsive and racist need to take pleasure in "the same old, same old" conceits about a racial world order (Bow 2022: 7). This other sensorial pairing foregrounds the racial intimacies and corporeal abjections upon which whiteness stands.

In the postbellum era, sweetness was considered "the most delicate taste sensation and simultaneously linked to unrestrained craving" (Fretwell 2020: 187). The paradox that sugar could be so refined and addictive restages how the vulgarities of slavery threatened any sense of white virtue. Literary scholar and theorist of emotion Erica Fretwell adds that the cult of white feminine domesticity developed as a means to neutralize this threat, to resolve and occlude traces of the abject Black body that laced any enjoyment of sweet desserts (189). The bourgeois white woman of the South was "to sublimate and perpetuate racial dominance by embodying the irrational appetites and drives that prove her inferiority to white men" (190). Reinforcing these observations, Linda introduces her grandmother Iris as a quintessential upper-class white woman of the South, with her piercing blue eyes. A model housewife of the 1940s, Iris had revered her husband and carefully monitored her weight and beauty "in order to keep [her husband's] eyes on her figure" (Truong 2010: 9). However, as Linda narrates, when he passed away Iris surrendered to her voracious appetite for sugar, cutting loose her sublimated corporeal abjection. Iris "lusted for sugar," and Dr Pepper was her worst vice (9).

Iris's blooming Dr Pepper addiction reveals how both abstaining from and indulging in corporeal excess gives shape to whiteness. In her study of artificially colored soda drinks, Keyser (2019: 35) claims that "the assumption that 'white' is the universal basis for all other colors, correlates suggestively with the racial ideology of unmarked whiteness. But the soda manufacturers take this assessment one step further, namely to lambast the affective and aesthetic emptiness of mere whiteness. . . . Whiteness has an inverse relationship to pleasure." In extension, whiteness inspires an insatiable hunger for the very wanton pleasures indexed by the excessive corporeality of racialized others. Along this vein, Linda goes on to suggest that Dr Pepper is what ultimately kills her grandmother, who had diabetes. Doctors had warned Iris that the soft drink would "kill [her] even faster than those doughnuts" (Truong 2010: 10). Iris dies after her third heart attack.

Iris's inability to quit her Dr Pepper habit raises suspicions around its addictive qualities beyond just its sugary sweetness. The synesthetic pairing "Hammerick*DrPepper*" insinuates that the brown liquid anchors the very meaning and white identity of the Hammerick household. Iris's addiction grows in the absence of her husband as if she needs to feed on the drink's racial meaning now that she is without another guarantor for her whiteness. In *Racial Indigestion*, Kyla Wazana Tompkins (2012: 185–86) presents a "link between white pleasure and black pain" in US practices of eating that are "oriented toward consuming and destroying that which seems to threaten the internal order of the majoritarian class." Indeed, Iris's Dr Pepper addiction enables her to contain and divert the threat of Linda's racial difference to the integrity of the Hammerick family.

The synesthetic association between Dr Pepper and Hammerick has roots in Linda's first experience of Dr Pepper, when Iris invites Linda to share in the guilty pleasure. The details and consequences of this event trace how Iris's taste for Dr Pepper allows her to take pleasure in her whiteness while containing the threat of Linda's racial difference. Linda narrates:

> As with most addicts, my grandmother Iris liked to share the experience. She was the one who gave me my first full bottle of Dr Pepper, straight from the fridge, not even bothering with a glass. . . . Iris took out a bottle for herself, and with three swigs she emptied every drop of its molasses-colored liquid.
>
> Don't tell anyone, she said as she dabbed the corners of her mouth with a paper napkin.
>
> About the Dr Pepper? I asked.
>
> No, you little canary, she replied. About how I let you drink it straight from the bottle. (Truong 2010: 9–10)

When Iris confesses that she should not have let Linda drink "straight from the bottle"—the secret that is to overshadow Iris's sugar addition—she brings attention to her own freedom to break class decorum in ways Linda cannot. Breaking from class etiquette only reinforces the freedoms that come with Iris's whiteness while diminishing Linda's claims to that same freedom. Invented in Waco, Texas, and established in 1885, Dr Pepper has historically been marketed as an emblem of the white nuclear family ideal (see Bellis 2019). In 1970, at the height of the Vietnam War and not long before Linda's adoption into the Hammerick family, a Dr Pepper ad featured a wedding photo of a white woman and man from the late 1800s (fig. 1). The text underneath tells the origin story of Dr Pepper's namesake. Far from what the image would seem to suggest, however, this origin story is a story of heartbreak. A young man had fallen in love with the daughter of his employer, a pharmacist by the name of Dr. Pepper. Facing the pharmacist's fierce disapproval of their plans to marry, the man left his hometown for Waco, without his sweetheart. He found another job as a soda jerk, where he invented a new soda drink that grew popular among the residents of Waco. The young man's loyal customers repeated the lore of Dr. Pepper and began calling the drink by this name, without whom it would never had been made.

In her seminal work *On Photography*, Susan Sontag (2005: 18, 85) claims that "needing to have reality confirmed and experience enhanced by photographs is an aesthetic consumerism to which everyone is now addicted," a realism that "creates a confusion about the real." However, the Dr Pepper ad complicates Sontag's insights by positioning the unique sweet taste of Dr Pepper as the object that can confirm and enhance the reality effects of the photograph and its attendant

Figure 1 A vintage Dr Pepper ad from the 1970s. Source: ClickAmericana

narrative racial fictions. If Dr. Pepper the pharmacist expresses classist attitudes that stratify members of the white race, the young man's later invention of Dr Pepper the drink proves how capitalism can overcome those divisions to buttress a unifying sense of whiteness. The title of the ad emphasizes this breakdown of class boundaries when it poses the rhetorical question, "What's a doctor doing in the soft drink business, anyway?" The nineteenth-century origin story and wedding photograph map onto the taste of Dr Pepper to direct America's past as a strict classist society into a more harmonious and prosperous future of a unified white racial class. The embodied practice of consuming Dr Pepper was arguably a project of "national embodiment [that] linked national formation to the consolidation of whiteness as the dominant racial position in the United States" (Tompkins 2012: 72). The unique sweetness of Dr Pepper turns whiteness into an immediate sensorial experience beyond just a story and aesthetic image. Therefore, when Iris clarifies the secret that establishes her intimacy with Linda, she effectively also warns Linda that she cannot participate in this conceit of white collectivity "straight from the bottle"—without regard for class decorum. Iris introduces Dr Pepper to Linda not in the sense of sharing but in the sense of consuming both in one full swig only to later demand that Linda "don't tell anyone" of the violence that took place. Her enjoyment of Dr Pepper facilitates the pleasures of such racialized intimacies.[2]

In effect, Iris's clarification around what Linda should keep a secret lends a subtle but cutting lesson about the boundaries of class and race. If Linda wishes to enjoy the taste of Dr Pepper, she must aspire to the virtues of upper-class decorum, cultivate a taste for this specific expression of whiteness, and learn to enjoy it so as to override the displeasures of her racial abjection. Iris's invitation had carried an insidious pedagogical intent to inspire Linda's appetite for Dr Pepper even while reinforcing Linda's incapacity to be white and hence truly enjoy drinking Dr Pepper as Iris does. Iris establishes her power to discipline Linda, sublimating her own undisciplined corporeal abjection, restaging scenes of racist pleasures awash with the sweetness of pop.

Interlude: Racial Melancholia and Addiction

Iris calls Linda a "little canary" right after saying "No" to Linda's query if Iris's secret concerns her Dr Pepper habit. Linda's question registers as a sign of danger as does a canary in a coal mine, implying that an explicit acknowledgment of Iris's sugar addiction threatens her very enjoyment of their intimate exchange. By the same token, this *no* forces Linda to serve as an alibi to Iris's ignorance on the matter and, in extension, her "innocent" racism. Iris's enjoyment of Dr Pepper therefore depends on the additional joys of disavowing its addictive and racist pleasures. Iris's addiction to Dr Pepper might best be understood as an addiction to racialized intimacies and the ability to then deny the vulgarities of such an appetite.

The psychoanalytic concept of melancholia offers an apt parable for the psychosocial processes involved in enjoying states of denial, especially as a means for negotiating the limits of white joy (Cheng 2001: 68). Across critical works on psychoanalysis, melancholia denotes a pathological response to loss in which a subject cannot find a satisfying substitute (see Cheng 2001; Eng 2010; Freud 1995). In such cases, a melancholic subject can fail to identify the very source of this loss. According to Sigmund Freud (1955: 245), "Melancholia is in some way related to an object-loss which is withdrawn from consciousness, in contradistinction to mourning, in which there is nothing about the loss that is unconscious." This withdrawal protects the subject from confronting the consequences of irreparable losses, such as the moral failures of an idealized object of love. Melancholia, then, clarifies how denial becomes an addictive state in and of itself and how Linda becomes an object that sustains such an addiction for the Hammericks. As much as this process is evident in the way Iris turns to sugar as a (inadequate) substitute for her husband, this process is most salient in DeAnne's response to her husband's infidelity and his failures to uphold the heteronormative terms of white belonging.

At the conclusion of the novel, DeAnne unveils the full story behind Linda's adoption. Linh-Dao was mysteriously found outside a burning house wrapped in a blanket, holding a letter from Linda's adoptive father, Thomas, addressed to Linda's birth mother, Mai-Dao. Upon identifying the abandoned child at the police station, Thomas had claimed Linh-Dao as his and brought her home to his wife, DeAnne. Glossing over the historical forces of the Vietnam War that might have motivated Mai-Dao to abandon her child, DeAnne simply narrates how she presented Thomas with two conditions for adopting Linh-Dao into the Hammerick household. First, Thomas had to reveal everything about his unrequited love affair with Mai-Dao. Second, he had to promise to "never speak about [Linh-Dao's] birth parents again" (Truong 2010: 278). Soon after, DeAnne renames Linh-Dao as Linda to further bury the details of Linda's birth parents (165). In her defense, DeAnne implores, "Otherwise how could I learn to love you?" (278).

The two conditions for Linda's adoption create secrets that ultimately intensify and occlude the deep attachments DeAnne has to the heteronormative ideals of whiteness. Across the two conditions, DeAnne first anticipates the obstacles that will prevent her from loving and raising another woman's child. She then forces a forgetting around the very existence of this other woman so that she can better embody the love a mother is supposed to have toward her child. The terms of belonging are set around actively ignoring Thomas' marital betrayal and how this betrayal breaks the prior terms of belonging set around racial logics of sexual reproduction. Denial becomes addictive for how it protects DeAnne from facing the breakdown of white belonging while enabling her to preserve its ideals as if they were never lost. As the missing and the void, Linda becomes a blank surface against which DeAnne can project and sustain her fantasies of white heteronormative love to cover up their impossible fulfillment. Hence, whiteness itself becomes a "type of haunted, ghostly identification" that is at once absent and present (Eng and Han 2003: 346).

This ghostly identification with whiteness maps onto how Freud describes melancholia as a mode of identifying with and subsuming objects of loss. The tainted ideal is swallowed whole by the melancholic subject so that she might sustain outward projections of the untainted ideal. DeAnne models this process when she turns the truth about Linda's birth parents into a secret, consuming and withholding the part of Linda most misaligned with ideals of white heteronormativity. DeAnne then becomes subconsciously addicted to Linda's "blankness" in order to sustain her attachment to whiteness. Linda's inability to be DeAnne's biological child becomes the constitutive but subconscious material of DeAnne's interiority, which she cannot consciously acknowledge if she wishes to sustain her projection and enjoyment of Linda's "blankness." Therefore, as Linda grows up to look more and more like Mai-Dao, DeAnne must persistently deny and unsee the spectral presence of this other woman. The melancholic subject becomes subsumed by the task of continuously evading the conscious realization of loss, which results in repetitive and cyclical behaviors akin to addiction.

Anne Cheng (2001: 8) notes that, while effective in protecting the psyche from realizing the source of loss, this ghostly identification usually triggers a self-destructive condition of "endless self-impoverishment" or self-hatred. The subject becomes personally responsible and identified with failed ideals. However, the first defensive measure of melancholia initiates a second that defends DeAnne against the pains of self-hate. DeAnne projects and excludes all the threats to her ideal objects of love upon the spectral figure of Mai-Dao and Linh-Dao. Cheng develops the concept of racial melancholia to account for this second defensive measure, how threats to American ideals of freedom and liberty not just are internalized and absorbed into the ego subconscious of white identity but then are subconsciously projected onto racialized others that can be permanently excluded as threats altogether (10–11). Hence, racialized others remain a part of the United States yet are often excluded from its national imaginary. Cheng goes on to claim that "dominant white identity in American operates melancholically—as an elaborate identificatory system based on psychical and social consumption-and-denial" (11). The ontology of whiteness as an ideal object of identification initiates states of melancholia within white-identifying subjects who must then continually colonize the interiority of racialized subjects as the repository of failed ideals that more accurately reflects the painful losses embedded in white interiority (see Cheng 2001: 176–78). In other words, DeAnne must repeatedly renew and deny her dependency on Linda to maintain the ideals of white collectivity.

The anticipatory defense mechanisms of racial melancholia reso-
nate with other psychological theories on addiction. For instance, psychological theories on the negative reinforcement model of drug
addiction posit that addicted subjects can be preconsciously or subconsciously primed to avoid the negative effects of drug withdrawal
(see Baker et al. 2004). This view allows us to consider how the defensive dispositions of melancholia function like addictions by continually anticipating and preemptively motivating subjects to avoid a conscious reckoning with loss. The workings of the subconscious are
such that the melancholic subject can get stuck in cycles of avoidance
and denial, unable to break those cycles by cognitive control or independent will alone. A more recent psychiatric study stresses the need
to understand substance use disorders as forms of chronic mental illnesses that demand structural interventions (see McCauley and
McLellan 2021). Such an understanding would privilege long-term
modes of community care that can transform the environmental fac-
tors contributing to substance and psychological dependencies (see
Wiss, Avena, and Rada 2018). These studies expose the shortcom-
ings of self-mastery and reason as guiding ideals for treating addictions, an insight reinforced in Linda's earlier narrative about Iris's
unreasonable appetite for sugar. However, melancholia also helps
DeAnne evade those very limits of self-possessed personhood, which
allows her to disavow her need for alternative modes of belonging and being in community. The defensive mechanism disables the
melancholic subject from transforming the very structures and environments that produce such unachievable ideals in the first place.
The dynamic between DeAnne and Linda then constitutes an endur-
ingly addictive form of racist consumption for disavowing the possibility of more satisfying and sustainable modes of being in relation
with others.

Linda's synesthesia offers a way to recognize racial intimacies as
psychic and defensive structures akin to addiction that exceed visual
metaphors. Such alternative strategies for representing and knowing
racism intervene in the ways visual metaphors fuel optimism around
the possibility of finding more and better objects to love as the means
to remedy the failures of the past, instead of expanding our psychic
capacities to live through states of loss. This reorientation further tar-
gets assumptions that transformation depends on visible changes
while stressing the need to develop more tools for facing the instabil-
ities of racialized subjectivities. In other words, the task of unraveling
structures of racism might involve strategies for sustaining a sense of
self in the absence of its security, when there is nothing to hold on to.

The Limits of Metaphor and Self-Possessed Personhood

The absence of visual cues throughout the first half of *Bitter in the Mouth* guides us to contemplate how the addictive cycles of melancholia take shape at the limits of metaphor. Even insights within Lacanian psychoanalysis stress how addiction refers to states of a-diction or an antagonism to processes of signification (Braunstein 1992: 257). In this sense, addictions mediate the ecstatic failures of linguistic-symbolic understanding. Cruz (2014: 722–23) additionally claims that the synesthetic expressions of word*taste* "represent disjunction and the failure of metaphor. . . . Indeed, the lack of correspondence between meaning and its representation underscores the difficulty of true empathy." Reinforcing this insight, Linda's first memory of a lexical-gustatory experience is of an unknown taste: "There was something bitter in the mouth, and there was the word that triggered it. . . . [But] I have not yet found a corresponding flavor in food or in metaphor. But such a 'match,' even if identified, would only allow me the illusion of communication and you the illusion of understanding" (Truong 2010: 15). Linda's synesthesia forces encounters with the failures of representation, especially in securing the meaning and experience of intimacy as empathy.

Critics of empathy highlight the political failures inherent to acts of perceiving the other as akin to the self, raising questions about whether such acts of feeling for another can adequately lead to justice or if it merely enacts violence by assuming that such transference of experience and feeling is possible, as if the self could stand in for the other (see Berlant 2004; Hartman 1997; Sontag 2003). The possessive logics of intimacy saliently frame these debates about empathy. To feel for another can entail an exchange or transfer of property or properties of feeling. In *The Intimacies of Four Continents*, Lisa Lowe (2015: 18) suggests that there is "a colonial division of intimacy, which charts the historically differentiated access to the domains of liberal personhood, from interiority and individual will, to the possession of property and domesticity." Indeed, Iris and DeAnne have access to the conceits of self-possessed personhood, interiority, and collectivity in ways that preclude empathy, the ability to have the very desire to know and address Linda as a complex person (see Gordon 2008). In contrast, Linda must wade through the mess of racist projections that populate and colonize her interiority, only to then confront the massive and unanswerable question of who she is distinct from her racial construction.

Throughout DeAnne's narrative about Linda's adoption story, she takes special care to defend Thomas, representing him as a sympathetic figure. DeAnne shares how much Thomas loved Linda, especially as she "began to look more and more like the young Vietnamese woman whom [he] had loved" (Truong 2010: 281). However, DeAnne's claim about Thomas and his love has the unintended effect of triggering Linda's memories of how the people of Boiling Springs never saw her for who she was (281).

> If they saw me . . . how many of the men would remember the young female bodies that they bought by the half hour while wearing their country's uniform in the Philippines, Thailand, South Korea, or South Vietnam? . . . Complicit, because they would rather not know the answer to that question, the mothers and sisters and wives of these men looked right through me as well. Instead of invisibility, Boiling Springs made an open secret of me. (171)

Through this remembering, Linda attends to how proclamations of love can hinge on racist forms of erasure and projection. DeAnne's defense of Thomas ends up reiterating how the specter of Mai-Dao masks the present-day existence of Linda in North Carolina, denying the violent contradictions of the Vietnam War. Linda's synesthetic objecthood, her capacity to trigger multiple histories and implicate those she encounters, occludes the very matter of her corporeal being. DeAnne demonstrates not love or sympathy but merely how Linda gets reduced and typified as a mere foil to white redemption.[3] However, the limits of metaphor and representation pose obstacles to "true empathy" only insofar as words and images remain the dominant modes for addressing difference and its perceived threats to white collectivity.

As much as lexical-gustatory synesthesia ruptures the limits of metaphor, it also offers the basis for a different kind of subject that does not seek to overcome or defend itself against the instability of representation and identification, or the incapacity of an object of love to sustain love. In other words, if the utility of words depends on reiterating their meanings and associations, stabilizing a collective memory around their uses, lexical-gustatory synesthesia foregrounds the body's materiality and its sheer capacity to feel in excess of those preestablished networks of meaning. Such a focus on the sensorial faculties of the body opens up an alternative site through which meaning transfers and empathy becomes possible in ways that deviate from colonial logics and mediate the pains of linguistic failure. This revision of the self presents an alternative mode of being, pertinent for grasping how the novel attends to the limits of Linda's own aspirations to articulate the truths of her experience.

Critical to this maneuver is first clarifying how writing, alongside the visual, functions as a privileged mode of communication and knowledge production that affirms the universality of the self-possessed subject. The material and embodied practice of writing facilitates this subject formation in ways that produce possessive constructions of identity, interiority, intimacy, and agency. An embrace of a subject's capacity to bear contradictory sensations and stimuli shifts psychic identifications away from ideal and visually stable constructions of identity to the resilient plasticity of embodiment, presenting different notions of safety that would allow the defensive mechanisms of racial melancholia to soften.

Linda's account of her earliest memories living in the American South begins with learning how to write English at the age of seven so that she can send letters to her neighbor Kelly. Linda notes that they "relied on carefully written letters to keep each other informed of [their] inner lives" (16). This practice is crucial to Linda's ability to communicate more clearly and more frequently without dealing with the onslaught of tastes. However, as much as these letters nurture Linda's intimate friendship with Kelly, they also cite the "the history of the Western act, scene, and product of writing" (See 2017: 7). The epistolary form involves various autobiographical acts that make legible a subject's interiority as a form of property that can be exchanged to establish relations of intimacy (also embedded in DeAnne's claim that "we always keep the secrets of those we love"). Sarita Echavez See argues that there is an "intimate union, a marriage, between writing and accumulation" (7). To pen letters is an act of "stylistic enclosure that coincides with land enclosure" (7). Beginning with the Renaissance period, letters and writing styles reflected the education and class of the writers in ways that justified their right to colonize other people and places. The ability to sign a piece of writing was equated to the right to claim ownership over oneself and others. These practices additionally grounded the self-possessed individual as a stable formation, an idealism most central to constructions of white identity as a site of salvation and safety.

An act of self-referential enclosure, epistles produce a sense of interiority that the author can possess in a material form, necessary for establishing a stable and secure sense of one's interior life and the very conditions for human intimacy. As mentioned earlier, Lowe (2015: 18) elaborates that modern and dominant notions of intimacy depend on this a priori status of the possessive individual. However, this process whereby the interiority of the possessive subject is produced as the basic currency for human connection is not so transparent or natural for Linda. She does not have the ready tools to express her inner life at the start of her life in the Hammerick household, considering that she emerges as a fully formed projection in the psychosocial drama of DeAnne's melancholia. The fact that crucial facts about her biography circulate as open secrets severely compromises the integrity of her interiority. In this sense, aspects of her interiority more accurately belong to other members of her adoptive family. As such, any of Linda's attempts at writing letters and, in extension, her narrative about her synesthesia necessarily rub up against notions of self-possessed personhood. Linda's sense of self comes to depend on her capacity to feel the permeable porosity of her body and senses.

Truong relies on another synesthetic form to represent how Linda negotiates her incapacity to achieve self-possessed personhood despite her demonstrated capacity for self-referential writing. Various historical vignettes from the 1966 history book *North Carolina Parade: Stories of History and People* interrupt Linda's narrative in ways that mimic how taste interrupts her speech. When Linda turns eight Thomas gives her the history book, hoping it will "foster a sense of security and belonging" (Truong 2010: 52). However, Linda gets caught off guard by seemingly inane details within the text that disrupt her ability to find a sense of belonging within the book's pages. These obstacles to Linda identifying with and as a part of North Carolina's history and people lead to their separate chapters where Linda restages histories within *North Carolina Parade* to better position herself within it. These historical revisions demonstrate how Linda intuits her partial access to the ideals of self-possessed personhood, especially as the currency for securing an intimate and safe sense of self and belonging. In particular, her revisions of the history of George Moses Horton, the first enslaved person to publish poetry, model how an embrace of instability and nonpossessive states of being enables associative connections to be made across sites of difference. The associative structure of her synesthesia extends to inform how she uses reading and writing to situate intimacy within a web of accidental and emergent relations such that the "essence" of her being can multiply across time and space. This webbing of self offers a mode through which she can never lose or be denied the existence and truths of her being.

In Linda's reading of *North Carolina Parade*, she first notes that the history of George Moses Horton chronicles the life of an enslaved man "who had earned extra money for his master by writing love poems for the young men of the University of North Carolina at Chapel Hill" (Truong 2010: 52). One of the first lessons Linda gleans from this book's version of Horton's history is how writing conventions can "reveal the truth and hide it at the same time" (141). Linda's story about this lesson begins with Horton selling fruits and vegetables at Chapel Hill: "George Moses was commanded to perform a trick . . . before [UNC students] would buy from him. . . . He opened his mouth, and a poem poured out. The young men thought it was a fine trick. . . . He told them in a low voice that the poem belonged to him. Of course, the moment those words were released into the open air the poem was no longer his" (142). In this retelling, Linda emphasizes the failure of poetry to demonstrate the author's mastery over the faculties of his mind and heart by virtue of his racialized status. Horton's poetry cannot lend any authority to his authorship and selfhood. As such, Horton gains notoriety as an enslaved person who can perform the faculties of a free person. However, the apprehension that these love poems reflect Horton's capacity to possess freedom then causes a young paying customer to panic. He suspects that Horton cannot possibly write these love poems if he did not already know the women they were for. Linda claims that this young man, "for a brief instance, felt jealousy. The slave knew his Julia" (188). The jealousy ultimately leaves the young man embarrassed over his irrationality as he remembers that "the slave was a slave. He couldn't possibly know his Julia" (188). The young man cannot imagine how Horton could have the faculties to love at all. This limit to the imagination, language, and empathy determines that Horton lacks interiority, the precondition for establishing relations of intimacy and love in the first place. Linda stages and confronts the lie that the English language can secure the author's ownership over oneself when the author is not traditionally a white property-owning man.

Linda goes on to narrate the seemingly minor detail that, to write his poems, Horton would first "feel the coolness of their coins in the palm of his hand. He would close his eyes to intensify the sensation" (Truong 2010: 187). He would tell himself that "freedom would feel like this" before writing his love poems (187). Linda constructs Horton's internal thought processes as a dynamic engagement with feelings and sensations that move across and through the surface of his body—his capacity to intensify the physical sensation of coins, to develop an internal sense of freedom, to imagine and feel the materiality of his thoughts. This depiction of Horton's interiority has two effects. First, Linda establishes that the young man misrecognizes Horton's poetry to be about love when it is about freedom. The very possibility of this misrecognition frees Horton from his audience's indictments against his capacity for and worthiness of love. Second, this misrecognition ruptures the possessive logic of intimacy and self-possessed personhood. Horton's interiority is based on his unbridled power to feel and the freedom he retains in his ability to transform a physical sensation into other sensations. Horton demonstrates how interiority is not a static object of knowledge or possession but something inherently changeable, moveable, and dynamic.

While one could argue that Linda evacuates Horton of any interiority given that she animates him with her own words and imagination, a potentially violent enactment of cross-racial identification, I argue that Linda sutures her interiority to his in a way that expands the very terrain of both their interior lives. The essence or vital part of their selfhoods becomes attached to the plasticity of embodiment itself, the capacity to amplify sensations and cultivate other senses that flow from pain to joy and even enables such contrasting sensations to be felt simultaneously. Interiority manifests as this conscious ability to feel differently about one's subjection such that the pains of racial violence cannot monopolize the meaning and life of a racialized subject. In animating Horton, Linda attends to how a subject's very consciousness—how one thinks and feels—cannot be possessed or evacuated considering its inherent capacity for movement and change, moving along and through the surface of bodies and texts, across time and space. In this manner, the possibility for life becomes attached to the plasticity of one's sensorial faculties instead of the stability of one's ideal object of love or identification. This account of Horton's and Linda's synesthetic mode of relating across difference clarifies how writing can lend new meaning to interiority and safety, in contrast to the kind of security assumed by self-possessed personhood and authorial authority.

Linda's relationship with Thomas makes the above contrast more apparent. Linda initially depends on Thomas to learn the English language when she first joins the Hammerick family. More specifically, she relies on him to spell out her first responses to Kelly, who begins writing Linda letters to welcome her to Boiling Springs. Later in her life, Linda learns that her father prized those memories of teaching Linda how to write. Thomas treasured that "something sealed, meant only for [Linda's] eyes, was shared with him, unsolicited and unprovoked" (Truong 2010: 18). Eliding the structural constraints that make Linda dependent on her adoptive father, Thomas remembers these mediations in terms of intimacy and exchanges of love. Thomas does not recognize how this relationship also enacts subtle forms of racial violence, how his efforts to teach Linda English can invalidate Linda's authority over her interiority. While reading one of Kelly's letters to Linda, Thomas shares that Kelly wants to know Linda's favorite color, to which Linda responds with "fire" (18). Thomas asks if Linda understands the question, suggesting the color red is a more appropriate answer. But for Linda, fire is the perfect answer, because it encapsulates the combination of colors she loves: red, yellow, orange, and blue. The interaction reveals how Linda's answer is unrecognizable to Thomas. He cannot intuit how Linda might experience the joys of color as the shifting movement between various colors. If Thomas expects Linda to name an object of love, she details a gesture of love. Furthermore, the irreducibility of fire into a color suggests that there are aspects of Linda's experiences that similarly cannot be reduced into a possessive form of knowledge that can be shared or exchanged. She exceeds the possessive logic of language acquisition and articulation.

The very mention of fire additionally makes an implicit reference to Linda's memory of her house burning down before her adoption, even as Linda claims early in her narrative that she erased all memories of her parents' death. She tells her audience:

> What took place inside that trailer home in the days and hours and minutes before the fire . . . was lost to me. Whoever carried me out, his or her face was blank to me. Whoever stayed inside, by force or by choice, became strangers to me. The years of my life with them, the life before *this* life, had been erased or, rather, my memories of them had been erased by my benevolent brain. The last word that this man or woman had said to me was the only thing that remained, as a taste of bitter in my mouth. A fire had made everything else about them disappear. (Truong 2010: 280)

However, her use of the word *fire* in her exchange with Thomas suggests otherwise. The scene creates an opening to consider how aspects of Linda's truths, her interior sense of self, shift and contradict one another to challenge the very limits of memory, English grammar, and the self-possessed subject. Linda's insistence that fire is her favorite color revives the contents of her forgotten memories in ways that foster new affective associations with an element of her most profound trauma, one that can grasp how the painful deaths of her parents can also signal the joys and beauty of fire. While the traumatic circumstances of her parents' death might have forced Linda's memory loss, she nonetheless cultivates a loving association between herself and her parents in the space of that need to forget.

The synesthetic form of Linda's and Horton's narratives demonstrates how intimacy takes shape even when a subject cannot possess and share her interiority in ways that make sense to others—the apparent preconditions for empathy. Between Linda and Horton, intimacy traces how subjects can feel past the constraints of memory, speech, and self-possessed personhood. This other paradigm stresses the power of the human psyche to know and feel one's environment differently than dominant projections of a white supremacist world. If anything, intimacy comes to denote the closeness between different senses of the world, how one's reality can easily open up to another such that the truths of Horton's and Linda's narratives never settle as fixed projections within the melancholic scenes of white identification. Hence, empathy becomes possible not based on our understanding of one another according to the linguistic stability of racial meaning and identity but based on our knowledge of the instability of any collective notion of truth and the opacity of being.

The Capacity to Feel Difference

In lieu of a conclusion, I would like to take us back to the opening of this article and its discussion of Kelly*cannedpeaches* and its erotic significance. A month after her grandmother's funeral, Linda is at Yale, "trying to focus on the discussion of the lesbian subtext in Carson McCullers's *The Member of the Wedding*, when the tears begin to fall" (Truong 2010: 13). Linda is suddenly reminded of her adopted grandmother's last words upon her deathbed: "What I know about you, little girl, would break you in two" (12). Linda then claims, "Another minute and a little skeleton key might have fallen out of her mouth" (13). As much as the skeleton key might refer to the secrets of Linda's origin, the context of this remembering suggests that the secret Linda fears most is the lesbian subtext to her own life. Therein lays another synesthetic crossing of the senses. If Iris poses race as the threat that will break Linda in two, Linda perceives the threat to be her desires for her best friend, Kelly. Matters of race cross into matters of lesbian eroticism. The secret that fuels Iris's threat doubles and produces a double vision. In one, race sits at the center as the force that sustains the sweet pleasures of whiteness itself. In the other, erotic desire takes center stage as evidence of how race can nurture other pleasures. This doubling allows us to return to another earlier scene of Linda lying in bed, whispering "Hammerick" to herself. As she relishes the phantom taste of Dr Pepper in memory of Iris and her passing, Linda also proves that she can enjoy the taste of Dr Pepper because there are other ways to enjoy it.

In her canonical speech on the uses of the erotic, Audre Lorde (1978) describes the erotic as a source of power that emerges from sharing a desire and purpose with another, the "electrical charge" of which does not distort "the enormously powerful and creative nature of that exchange." It names the joys of risking established ways of knowing and ordering a world to restore the plenitude of the human senses and their capacity to perceive other possibilities. In this manner, the erotic also attends to what Sontag (1966: 13–14) terms the "erotics of art," which pays attention to the "sensuous surface of art" that can contest how the "conditions of modern life . . . conjoin to dull our sensory faculties." If the melancholic scene of white identification involves anticipating and then reducing one's capacity to feel, Linda's sexuality results from her openness to feel joy in surprising places.

For instance, Linda remembers being eleven at a sleepover at Kelly's. In a bid to avoid the attention of boys, Kelly dares Linda not to brush her teeth for a week. Linda counters by daring Kelly to go to bed naked because to be naked was to be dirty of sin (Truong 2010: 71). Kelly accepts. In the following scene, they are in bed, looking at pictures of Dolly Parton while listening to her music. Linda shares that when they looked at her on the album cover of *Heartbreaker*, "we felt a vibration all around our bodies . . . the effect of experiencing pure joy" (71). Soon after, Kelly undresses herself and whispers that the sheets feel "slippery," to which Linda "gulps" and turns "breathless" (71). Linda joins Kelly under the covers and reaches for Kelly's hand. They "thought that holding hands would allow [them] to have the same dreams . . . the feeling of being closer" (72). As much as this closeness forebodes the dangers and pains of intimacy, expressed in the lyrics of the girls' favorite song, "Heartbreaker . . . sweet little love maker . . . couldn't you be just a little more kind to me," this scene also gestures to the power of art and play to induce surprising feelings. Significant to Linda and Kelly's erotic intimacy is that their racial differences magnify how neither of them fit into the white ideal. Linda notes that "Kelly was . . . awkward, fat, and shy" (17). She would grow up to be "an invisible fat girl" and a source of shame for her mother (67, 105).

Kelly's fatness makes her a nonnormative subject of whiteness in ways that position her in closer proximity to Linda. Their lesbian romance makes legible their capacity to feel their differences differently, to notice their overlapping experiences of racial-sexual abjection and mutual inabilities to transcend those experiences by turning to white privilege.

Initiating another process for making other affective associations across difference, Linda later learns that synesthesia is "hereditary and could be passed along via either the maternal or the paternal side of the family. The condition . . . was most often found in women" (222). Upon this discovery, the realization dawns on Linda that she most likely inherited her synesthesia from her birth mother. At the same time, the earliest tastes that accompany Linda's experiences of synesthesia come from DeAnne's southern cooking. Mai-Dao and DeAnne are coupled in Linda's most foundational experiences of her body, speech, and food. Though social conventions of white heteronormativity require that Linda privilege her white adoptive family as the basis of her identity, her synesthesia allows her to form an alternative attachment to the interracial lesbian coupling of her mothers. This new genealogy reformulates Linda's racial difference and multiple positionalities to affirm her relationship with Kelly.

Linda's synesthesia demonstrates how our capacity to develop new feelings and attachments can undo and remake the world. Lauren Berlant (2011: 263) adds that "the work of undoing a world while making one *requires* fantasy . . . to distort the present on behalf of what the present can become." Before DeAnne's last confession, Linda learns that she has ovarian cancer and undergoes surgery to remove her ovaries (Truong 2010: 208, 211). Linda goes on to claim, "We had children because they could be had. . . . We added to ourselves . . . because we desired, above all things, to outlive our bodies" (265). Children serve as vehicles for transcending death, making it beyond the scope of possibility. However, DeAnne and Thomas's legacy in the South will end with her. Linda observes how such failures of continuity inspire the sense that gravity is "no longer the law of the land" (180). Floating and drifting, as though a current were pulling her away from shore, Linda confronts feelings of loss as she becomes unmoored from the fantasy ideals of white identity and its melancholic effects. In this space of instability, the familiar turns strange. Different subjectivities and material realities can be sensed such that the present begins to contain more worlds than this one.

Sunhay You is an assistant professor of literary arts and studies at the Rhode Island School of Design, where she teaches courses on transnational Asian American literature and culture.

Notes

I would like to acknowledge Duke University's Gender, Sexuality, and Feminist Studies Postdoctoral Fellowship, which gave me the resources and time for completing this piece. In addition, conversations with members of the Minor Aesthetics Working Group at the Franklin Institute for Humanities nurtured the latter stages of writing. I extend my gratitude to Victor Mendoza, Sidonie Smith, Peggy Lee, and Jarod Lew for their incisive feedback and care.

1   It is critical that the very terms *addict* and *addiction* carry racial meaning and were deployed to further racist ideologies in the aftermath of the Opium Wars and Reagan's War on Drugs. While this article disrupts this racial imaginary by focusing on whiteness as a form of addiction, it is worthwhile to also consider how Asianness and the model minority emerge in relation to discourses on addiction (see Lee 2019).

2   The paradox that a national culture based on freedom depends on structures of racial exclusion dramatizes Lisa Lowe's (1996: 13) claims that "in a racially differentiated nation such as the United States, capital and state imperatives may be contradictory." The nation's need for racialized labor contradicts how the US has historically sought to achieve a unified national culture, bound to racialized and heteronormative logics of white belonging and kinship. This contradiction is then resolved by precluding racially differentiated people from proper citizenship. I suggest this resolution also manifests as an embodied experience of sweetness and sugar addiction in *Bitter*.

3   Yen Lê Espiritu (2014: 5) adds that "in the absence of a liberated Vietnam and people, the US government, academy, and mainstream media . . . produced a substitute: the freed and reformed Vietnamese refugees." Freed and reformed Vietnamese refugees redeemed the United States so that the nation could ostensibly get over the war. However, considering that Vietnamese refugees continue to be subjected to US racial-sexual violence after being "freed," they are also persistent reminders of the nation's failures to uphold its ideals. America's losses in the Vietnam War and its attempts at redemption produce the conditions for melancholia.

References

Abbott, Elizabeth. 2009. *Sugar: A Bittersweet History.* New York: Duckworth Overlook.

Baker, Timothy B., Megan E. Piper, Danielle E. McCarthy, Matthew R. Majeski, and Michale C. Fiore. 2004. "Addiction Motivation Reformulated: An Affective Processing Model of Negative Reinforcement." *Psychological Review* 111, no. 1: 33–51.

Bellis, Mary. 2019. "The Early History of Dr Pepper," *ThoughtCo*, July 7. https://www.thoughtco.com/history-of-dr-pepper-4070939.

Berlant, Lauren, ed. 2004. *Compassion: The Culture and Politics of an Emotion.* New York: Routledge.

Berlant, Lauren. 2011. *Cruel Optimism.* Durham, NC: Duke Univ. Press.

Bow, Leslie. 2022. *Racist Love: Asian Abstraction and the Pleasures of Fantasy.* Durham, NC: Duke Univ. Press.

Braunstein, Nestor. 1992. *La jouissance: Un concept lacanien.* Paris: Point Hors Ligne.

Callahan, Cynthia. 2011. *Kin of Another Kind: Transracial Adoption in American Literature.* Ann Arbor: Univ. of Michigan Press.

Cheng, Anne. 2001. *Melancholy of Race.* New York: Oxford Univ. Press.

Cruz, Denise. 2014. "Monique Truong's Literary South and Regional Forms of Asian America." *American Literary History* 26, no. 4: 716–41.

Dorow, Sara K. 2006. *Transnational Adoption.* New York: New York Univ. Press.

Dykema, Amanda. 2014. "Embodied Knowledges: Synesthesia and the Archive in Monique Truong's *Bitter in the Mouth.*" *MELUS* 39, no. 1: 106–29.

Eng, David. 2010. *The Feeling of Kinship.* Durham, NC: Duke Univ. Press.

Eng, David, and Shinhee Han. 2003. "A Dialogue on Racial Melancholia." In *Loss: The Politics of Mourning*, edited by David L. Eng and David Kazanjian, 343–71. Berkeley: Univ. of California Press.

Espiritu, Yen Lê. 2014. *Body Counts: The Vietnam War and Militarized Refuge (es).* Oakland: Univ. of California Press.

Fretwell, Erica. 2020. *Sensory Experiments: Psychophysics, Race, and the Aesthetics of Feeling.* Durham, NC: Duke Univ. Press.

Freud, Sigmund. 1955. "Mourning and Melancholia." In *The Standard Edition of the Complete Psychological Works of Sigmund Freud*, translated by James Strachey, 14:239–60. London: Hogarth Press.

Gordon, Avery. 2008. *Ghostly Matters: Haunting and the Sociological Imagination.* Minneapolis: Univ. of Minnesota Press.

Hartman, Saidiya V. 1997. *Scenes of Subjection: Terror, Slavery, and Self-Making in Nineteenth-Century America.* New York: Oxford Univ. Press.

Keyser, Catherine. 2019. *Artificial Color: Modern Food and Racial Fictions.* New York: Oxford Univ. Press.

Kim, Eleana J. 2010. *Adopted Territory.* Durham, NC: Duke Univ. Press.

Kriz, Kay Dian. 2008. *Slavery, Sugar, and the Culture of Refinement: Picturing the British West Indies, 1700–1840.* New Harvard, CT: Yale Univ. Press.

Lee, Peggy. 2019. "Turning Diaspora to Dirt: Addiction and Illness in Asian American Critique." *Women's Studies Quarterly* 47, no. 1: 151–68.

Lorde, Audre. 1978. "The Uses of the Erotic." Paper presented at the Fourth Berkshire Conference on the History of Women, Mount Holyoke College, South Hadley, MA, August 25.

Lowe, Lisa. 1996. *Immigrant Acts.* Durham, NC: Duke Univ. Press.

Lowe, Lisa. 2015. *The Intimacies of Four Continents.* Durham, NC: Duke Univ. Press.

McCauley, Jenna L., and A. Thomas McLellan. 2021. "Treating Addiction like a Chronic Illness." In *The American Psychiatric Association Publishing Textbook of Substance Use Disorder Treatment*, 6th ed., edited by Kathleen T. Brady, Frances R. Levin, Marc Galanter, and Herbert D. Klebar. 93–113. Washington, DC: American Psychiatric Association.

Mintz, Sidney W. 1985. *Sweetness and Power: The Place of Sugar in Modern History.* New York: Penguin Books.

Mirzoeff, Nicholas. 2011. *The Right to Look: A Counterhistory of Visuality.* Durham, NC: Duke Univ. Press.

Morrison, Toni. 1992. *Playing in the Dark.* Cambridge, MA: Harvard Univ. Press.

Novy, Marianne, ed. 2001. *Imagining Adoption: Essays on Literature and Culture.* Ann Arbor: Univ. of Michigan Press

Pate, Soojin. 2014. *From Orphan to Adoptee: US Empire and Genealogies of Korean Adoption.* Minneapolis: Univ. of Minnesota Press.

Ramachandran, Vilayanur S., Edward M. Hubbard, and Peter A. Butcher. 2004. "Synesthesia, Cross-activation, and the Foundations of Neuroepistemology." In *The Handbook of Multisensory Processes,* edited by Gemma Calvert, Charles Spence, and Barry E. Stein. 867–84. Cambridge, MA: MIT Press.

See, Sarita Echavez. 2017. *The Filipino Primitive: Accumulation and Resistance in the American Museum.* New York: New York Univ. Press.

Sontag, Susan. 1966. *Against Interpretation, and Other Essays.* New York: Dell.

Sontag, Susan. 2003. *Regarding the Pain of Others.* New York: Picador.

Sontag, Susan. 2005. *On Photography.* New York: Rosetta Books.

Storti, Anna. 2020. "Deidealizing Hybridity in Saya Woolfalk's World of the Empathics." *Frontiers* 41, no. 3: 147–77.

Thomas, D. M. E. 2017. *Texts and Textiles: Affect, Synesthesia, and Metaphor in Fiction.* Newcastle: Cambridge Scholars.

Thomas, Sara Gabler. 2016. "Queer Formalism: Synesthetic Storytelling in Monique Truong and William Faulkner." *Faulkner Journal* 30, no. 1: 39–61.

Tompkins, Kyla Wazana. 2012. *Racial Indigestion: Eating Bodies in the Nineteenth Century.* New York: New York Univ. Press.

Truong, Monique. 2010. *Bitter in the Mouth.* New York: Random House.

Wiss, David A., Nicole Avena, and Pedro Rada. 2018. "Sugar Addiction: From Evolution to Revolution." *Frontiers in Psychiatry* 9: 545.

**David
Pham**

Touching Ash in Vietnamese Diasporic
Aesthetics

Abstract Water has held a privileged place in theorizations of Vietnamese refugee being. Draw-ing from Ocean Vuong's chapbook *Burnings* (2010) and novel *On Earth We're Briefly Gorgeous* (2019) along with Tuan Andrew Nguyen's film *The Boat People* (2020), this article traces an alternative genealogy of Vietnamese diasporic aesthetics based on the element of fire. Theoriz-ing fire as another critical site of refugee passages, these works evince a pyric refugee onto-epistemology, one that conceives of fire and ash as explicit matter-metaphors of living and beauty that refuse the sensory diminution of racialized subjects as a result of US imperial and militaristic violence. Fire carries with it a destructive valence, and ash is taken as evidence of ruin and disaster. However, the explorations of fire and ash in both artists' work not only attest to the various onto-epistemological unravelings signified by fire and ash but also conceive of the possibilities and openings for a refugee poiesis that emerges in the aftermath of destruction. Both Vuong and Nguyen stage haptic encounters with ash that wrestle with questions of sensa-tion and subjectivity in the narration of personal and collective trauma. Paradoxically, these texts espouse the notion that any possibility of refugee futurity happens through contact with the subjunctive power of that which is insensible, ash.
Keywords Ocean Vuong, Tuan Andrew Nguyen, ash, beauty, refugee futures

> You must be ready to burn yourself in your own flame: how
> could you become new, if you had not first become ashes?
> —Friedrich Nietzsche, *Thus Spoke Zarathustra* (1961)

> The body is aflame. Tactile sensations are aflame . . .
> —Āditta-pariyāya Sutta (Aflame), SN 35:28

Two of the most sensational images of the Vietnam War era feature bodies burning alive. The first image, titled "The Ulti-mate Protest" and known also as the "Burning Monk," was taken on

American Literature, Volume 95, Number 3, September 2023
DOI 10.1215/00029831-10679251   © 2023 by Duke University Press

June 11, 1963, by Associated Press photographer Malcolm Browne and depicts the self-immolation of Buddhist monk Thich Quang Duc as a self-sacrificing gesture meant to bring attention to the religious persecution Buddhists experienced under the Catholic South Vietnamese government. The notoriety and attention that this image garnered globally were such that it became a topic of Thich Nhat Hanh's book *Vietnam: Lotus in a Sea of Fire* (1967), his historical account of Buddhism in the country leading up to the war. Taken almost a decade later, on June 8, 1972, the second image, captured by Associated Press photojournalist Nick Ut, is titled "The Terror of War" and pictures a group of young children running down Highway 1, frantically fleeing from Trang Bang village, which had just been hit by a napalm strike. The image's other title, the "Napalm Girl," references the central figure in its frame, nine-year-old Kim Phúc, whose clothes have burnt off and whose body has been scorched by the fire resulting from the napalm explosions. In a video for the New-York Historical Society's retrospective on the Vietnam War in 2017, Phúc reflects on this traumatic experience as follows: "That explosion happened just behind me. Then, suddenly, the fire [was] everywhere around me. And I didn't see anyone but the fire. My clothes burned off, and then my body [was] on fire" (New-York Historical Society 2020). Both of these images gripped the world, spurring international outcry over the war's grievous atrocities, and have since become two of the most iconic images of twentieth-century photography (see Miller 2004; Phu 2022).

The "Napalm Girl" photograph singularly conveys the ruthless brutality of US imperial aggression in Vietnam. Even more, it illustrates the nation-state's hold over the human sensorium as instrumental to the deployment of its regime of violence.[1] The orchestration of terror through the control of this sensorium, as made clear in this image, reveals the workings of subjection by way of the senses. Mimi Thi Nguyen (2012: 111) observes that this photograph of Phúc captures the "shattering figuration of her radical unmaking." The terror to which she is subject, reflected in her own words, captures a sensorial event whose violence and brutality language can only falter to describe, not least because it captures the ontological, epistemological, psychic, and sensorial foreclosures that she experiences at the moment of her unmaking. By analyzing Phúc's "radical unmaking" sensorially, we see that the photograph marks a threshold point at which her body senses too much and, because of the injuries she sustains from this bombing, will sense too little in the future.[2] Such violence brings her to the edge of subjectivity and, indeed, to the boundary limit of the human.[3]

The "Napalm Girl" holds an unfinished legacy within Vietnamese diasporic imaginaries to this day. What might it mean to return to this image of Phúc fifty years later, in search of a language that attempts to pry open the foreclosures to which she is subject? This is a language that, to be sure, does not seek to rescue her but aims to recognize her pyric violation as leaving a troubling legacy for Vietnamese diasporic aesthetics, one that ultimately recognizes the image as a progenitor to another elemental lineage of refugee passages based on fire. In this move, I wish to take heed of the pressing question that Saidiya Hartman (2008: 4) poses in "Venus in Two Acts" that arises from her own experience with the archive of transatlantic slavery: "How does one revisit the scene of subjection without replicating the grammar of violence?" The grammar of violence, as evident in the "Napalm Girl," is produced in and through the yoking of fire, sense, and subjectivity. And so, at the heart of such a fraught search for a language adequate enough to negotiate the image's grammar is the careful unyoking of these terms from the chokehold of empire in order to resignify them so that they mean more than ruin, disaster, and death for the imperial subject.[4] It is to see how metaphors of touch, as Mimi Thi Nguyen (2012) and Thy Phu (2012) have astutely pointed out, can themselves be given over to the service of empire.[5] Returning to this image demands, then, a kind of language that attends to the moments when metaphorical invocations of touch and sensation cross over into the material realm. In dealing with touch as it moves from immaterial feelings to material relations, this language attempts to link the senses to the imaginative capacities of the subjunctive, a "grammatical mood that expresses doubts, wishes, and possibilities," to counter the foreclosures issuing from this scene of violent unmaking (Hartman 2008: 11).

To resist the grammar of violence in the photograph means refusing to resuscitate both subjectivity *and* humanity so long as they are terms that remain under the purview of imperial governance. Rather than allowing for an investment in a narrative of subjective recovery and progress, the image's grammar of violence throws the subject into the interstitial space of unmaking, which becomes the only tenable place from which to wage a critique of empire. It is here where the human-as-subject returns, having been unformed or, perhaps more precisely, deformed by the imperial assault on the senses. The force that empire unleashes, however, is something that it fails to retain and that ultimately backfires, causing a slippage that opens up the possibility for theorizing the sensorial not merely as a conduit for colonial and imperial regulation but as a location for an embodied, materialist negotiation of its irreparable harms. Just such a project is carried out in the works of two contemporary Vietnamese diasporic artists, poet and novelist Ocean Vuong and multimedia artist Tuan Andrew Nguyen. Both artists deal with the refugee sensorium produced in and through the nexus of displacement, war, trauma, and memory in their respective productions. Notably, their works grapple with the ontological imprint left by fire on Vietnamese refugee being. Vuong and Nguyen directly confront the legacy of subjection by fire through their art and, in so doing, harness and appropriate fire's elemental force in cultivating a refugee poetics. Engaging with these artists, I propose, allows us to consider an alternative historical and aesthetic trajectory of refugee passages based on the element of fire.

The significance of tracing a genealogy of Vietnamese diasporic aesthetics from fire emerges from a context where dominant representational paradigms have drawn on the connection between refugees and water. Vietnamese diasporic aesthetics cohere around the motif of water, as reflected in memoirs, novels, poetry, and films such as Jade Ngoc Quang Huynh's *South Wind Changing* (1994), lê thi diem thúy's *The Gangster We Are All Looking For* (2003), Monique Truong's *The Book of Salt* (2003), Vu Tran's *Dragonfish* (2015), Quyên Nguyen-Le's *Nước (Water/Homeland)* (2016), Thi Bui's *The Best We Could Do* (2017), mai c. doan's *water/tongue* (2019), and Eric Nguyen's *Things We Lost to the Water* (2021). These works illustrate the cultural significance of water, or *nước*, to Vietnamese identity while also acknowledging the mass exodus of Vietnamese by boat post-1975 as a decisive historical circumstance that fundamentally shaped Vietnamese diasporic cultural production. For diasporic Vietnamese writers, according to Vinh Nguyen (2016: 67), "the sea and the boat become sites of return to re(-)member and (re)imagine personal and collective histories and identities that undulate on water." Through her performance art, Patricia Nguyễn (2017: 99) argues that water "is a critical site of analysis for *refugee passages*." Erin Suzuki (2021: 56) examines "refugee aesthetic production as an oceanic form." Evyn Lê Espiritu Gandhi (2022: 5) theorizes the primacy of *nước* to an archipelagic praxis that envisions decolonial solidarities among Indigenous peoples and refugee settlers that "challenge settler colonial states' monopoly over the land and sea." Scholars in the wider field of critical refugee studies have theorized the constitutive relationship between water and refugee subjectivity as well. For instance, as Suvendrini Perera (2013: 75) observes, "In all their complex affectivities and charged materialities, refugee bodies and oceans interpenetrate, in corpographies of enfolding, unmaking and remaking."

The attention given to water as a dominant motif in analyses of Vietnamese diasporic aesthetics, while critically important, risks overlooking the significance of fire as an equally compelling site to think through the onto-epistemological dimensions of the refugee. To suggest fire as an alternative basis for a refugee poetics is to admit to a kind of paradox, especially given the destructive valence attributed to fire. How can acts of making emerge in and through that which ostensibly burns, ruins, and destroys? Rather than shy away from the difficulties of such a paradox, both Vuong and Nguyen center it to illumine fire's productive and creative potentialities. Such a paradox is nowhere more evident than in the desire to touch fire and ash, a desire that undergirds the works of both artists. Touching fire risks burning and annihilation, while ash gives nothing back to one's touch. Though one may touch ash, it disperses as soon as it catches any breeze or wind. Both fire and ash can be seen, then, as confounding the haptic as its limit cases. Pressing toward these limits reveals the haptic as what Rizvana Bradley (2014: 133) calls "poetic minoritarian experience." As Bradley observes, "The haptic is not only experienced but performed *in* and *as* an otherwise dimension, always slightly out of reach and evading our complete understanding" (131). We may think of the haptic engagement with ash, then, as a gesture performed resolutely in the subjunctive mood.

At the limits of the sensorial and in conjunction with the paradoxes of fire emerges what I refer to as a *pyric refugee onto-epistemology*, or a particular kind of knowledge of living and being that comes from the refugee subject's encounter with fire and ash.[6] This is a knowledge of minoritarian life as one that is lived in and through paradox, contradiction, and limits. Not only is a pyric refugee onto-epistology attuned to life lived in the subjunctive, but it is also attentive to various crossings between life and death, trauma and healing, opacity and revelation, sense and insensibility. In the wake of imperial violence, its psychic trespasses, and its material harms, minoritarian life unfolds not through the reconciliation of these poles of experience but through a constant negotiation of their continual irresolvabilities. Of the various types of crossings that present themselves in the haptic encounter with fire and ash, the one that I wish to focus on is the crossing between matter and metaphor within the realm of aesthetics, a topic that has garnered significant attention in such fields as feminist science studies, new materialisms, and the environmental humanities. Recently, Christina A. León (2021: 358) writes that the work of matter-metaphors exhibits "how matter figures our poetic vision and how poetic vision may impact our material pursuits." In their introduction to the anthology titled *Elemental Ecocriticism*, Jeffrey Jerome Cohen and Lowell Duckert (2015) coin the term *matterphor* to describe the restless behavior of the elements in binding together language and materiality. According to the authors, "The elements whirl in unremitting itineracy, *etceteracy*, an invitation to lyrical drift and continuous conjoining" (11). In this article, I suggest that ash functions as a matter-metaphor of beauty to the extent that, in this crossing between the material and metaphorical, ash and beauty take on each other's qualities. Beauty in this guise is not about essence or artifice but is instead diffuse, resistant, and, above all, material. Ruminating on the beauty of ash, in turn, allows for an envisioning of refugee futures that, while never fully severed from the past, banish and incinerate overdetermined significations of race and coloniality that have spelled disaster, destruction, and death for so many of empire's Others.

This engagement with fire forefronts a kind of refugee poiesis that provocatively raises difficult questions about sensation and subjectivity in the narration of personal and collective trauma. Though attentive to these dilemmas, the artists' works are not solely preoccupied with the legacy of trauma and injury of the past but are deeply future oriented. Fire, for both Vuong and Nguyen, functions as a primary means to conceive of this future. Through fire, they begin to envisage refugee lifeworlds that honor the past without trying to transcend its traumas but, at the same time, not capitulating to them, either. In what follows, I trace the motif of fire as it appears in two of Vuong's texts, his first chapbook, *Burnings* (2010), and his first novel *On Earth We're Briefly Gorgeous* (2019). Then, I analyze Tuan Andrew Nguyen's short film *The Boat People* (2020) to illustrate how the feminist and queer refusals of empire performed in Vuong's writing are extended and amplified through Nguyen's film. A central through line across this set of works is their extensive rumination on ash as a sign of past catastrophe but also of insensible futurity. Before moving into close readings of these texts, the next section elaborates on philosophies of fire in connection to philosophies of beauty to draw out their resonances.

Elemental Beauty

In the context of empire, beauty becomes a property of personhood that can be gifted by the state as easily as it is taken away. The works of Vuong and Nguyen are less interested in this kind of beauty, as mere essence or artifice, and instead are invested in theorizing a beauty that is less manipulable. Their work, in fact, marshals a certain strain of discourse on beauty in the long history of Western aesthetic theory that emphasizes beauty's non-instrumentability (see Abrams

1991). Alexander Nehamas (2000: 402), for instance, sees the value of beauty in its indeterminacy: "Beauty is a call to adventure, a symbol of risk. It is the enemy of certainty." Anne Anlin Cheng (2000: 210) considers beauty "a gift that asks for nothing in return," observing that "this may be what is most terrifying about beauty: the possibility that it might ask for nothing and want nothing of us." Beauty's terror, as Cheng suggests, resides precisely in its autonomy from the realm of human social relations, to the sense that "we may not be able to own it, buy it, give it, or refuse it, even as we are profoundly moved by it" (210). But while the thought of beauty's uncontrollability may seem unsettling, critics like Cheng see it as providing an opening beyond the rigid confines of social hierarchy premised on discrete social identities of racial, gendered, class, and sexual difference.

Black feminist thought has long ruminated on the real, which is to say, material effects and consequences of beauty. Drawing from the poetry of Joy Harjo, Dionne Brand (2001: 193) observes, "The ruin of history visited on a people does not wipe out the steadfastness of beauty. Not a naive beauty but a hard one." Brand surmises that "for some, to find beauty is to search through ruins" (193). In *Wayward Lives, Beautiful Experiments*, Hartman (2019: 33) writes, "Beauty is not a luxury; rather it is a way of creating possibility in the space of enclosure, a radical art of subsistence, an embrace of our terribleness, a transfiguration of the given." Notably, the terror that attends to both Cheng's and Hartman's definition of beauty emphasizes its uncontrolled and unrestricted qualities. Beauty's waywardness as a dimension of its terrifying nature, and the ethos of ungovernability it fosters is something that Christina Sharpe (2019) conceives of as a method for living, one that is based on an "attentiveness whenever possible to a kind of aesthetic that escaped violence whenever possible." Beauty, in this recent turn advanced by Cheng, Brand, Hartman, and Sharpe, functions as a material force that intervenes in the real world and whose fugitivity offers an ethos for navigating the everyday violences of racial hierarchy and antiblackness.

The kind of beauty to which these critics offer witness, in other words, is one that neither derives from aesthetic judgments nor is a property of personhood. Rather, they theorize a kind of beauty in a pure, elemental state, one that I am suggesting is intimately linked to the pyric. The association of fire and burning with beauty and what it signifies—life and survival—may be unclear at first. However, as Gaston Bachelard (1964: 7) writes, "Fire is the ultra-living element" (see also Pyne 2019). Not only has it been vital to the continuation of societies, but fire has also been pivotal to the political contestation of their arrangements, particularly as processes of social reproduction depend on settler-colonial imaginaries of land (Nelson 2019).

Commentators have pointed out that fire, while evidently a life-sustaining resource, has also elicited uses that exceed strict necessity or self-preservation (Clark and Yusoff 2018: 16). Its characteristic exuberance and vitality also explains the abundance of metaphors associating fire with the excesses of human erotic desire. Nigel Clark and Kathryn Yusoff (2018: 9, 21) theorize the queerness of fire for how its "pyroerotic potentialities and untimely temporalities" alight "from its power to play upon the metamorphic possibilities that inhere in matter." Resonating with this premise, Anne Harris (2015: 46) attributes fire's play with metaphor and matter to its frenetic energy, observing that "it's as though the element becomes more restless, unable to stay in the realm of the real for too long, or perhaps it becomes impatient with our desire to separate metaphor and materiality, and fuses the two." Fire's transmutative potential, in other words, aligns with beauty's transfigurative possibilities. A materialist approach to beauty as one that searches for its presence within the physical conditions of living clarifies its elemental and specifically pyric basis.

Pyric Unravelings in *Burnings*

Fire has been a dominant elemental motif in Ocean Vuong's writing since the start of his literary career, beginning with the publication of his first chapbook of poetry, *Burnings* (2010). The opening poem of the collection is called "Ars Poetica." Set at sea, it thematizes fire and its limitless destructive drive as a backdrop to a scene of unlikely intimacy between two doomed individuals.

> When two ships emerge
> from a wall of fog,
> their sails lit with sheets of fire,
> there will be a traveler on each deck
> with the same face,
> watching flames reflect
> in the other's eyes. (Vuong 2010: 8)

The poem is narrated in the future imperfect tense, lending a sense of certainty to the speaker's vision of sublime catastrophe. The speaker foresees two ships whose sails are "lit with sheets of fire," and on each ship stands a traveler "watching flames reflect / in the other's eyes." These two travelers "with the same face" may be a split subject attempting to be whole again, two lovers straining for one final embrace, or a parent rescuing their child from harm. As made clear by the burning ships that "will moan and creek / beneath the fading weight" and whose "Windows will burst / into breaths of ember," they are running out of time, on the verge of catching fire. Determined not to "to see / the other burn," the travelers set up "a makeshift bridge" between each burning ship in one last, harrowing effort to reunite. They inch slowly toward each other on this flimsy plank of wood.

> Windows will burst
> into breaths of ember,
> while two hands reach out,
> the horizon shortening
> between their fingers.
> And if they should waver,
> if they should fall
> before they touch,
> may the sea receive them
> as it does two pearls
>   of soft rain. (Vuong 2010: 8)

Just as the poem reaches the height of its suspense, in which the travelers' "two hands reach out" with "the horizon shortening / between their fingers," the speaker precludes any sense of resolution by refusing to disclose whether their hands will actually reach each other. The speaker's withholding in the final lines of the poem is occasioned by a shift in grammatical mood from the future imperfect tense and its indicative mood to that of the subjunctive by concluding with a conditional assertion. The switch in mood halts the unfolding of catastrophe, at least for a time, wherein the travelers have not yet touched but still are not yet burned. The conditional *if* causes a wrinkle in teleology as the poem moves from reality to speculation. It is as though the speaker refuses to consign the travelers to annihilation with the speaker's own words. By deferring the inevitability of their dying, the speaker seeks to shift our attention to their two hands reaching out, a relation of touch and an assertion of life motivated by their mutual yearning for each other. In stopping at this exact moment, the speaker seeks to make this the last image by which they should be remembered. Touch offers the travelers some kind of solace in the face of existential threat.

The effect of the speaker's conditional assertions cannot be understated as it produces an opacity that maneuvers the poem into a state of atemporality. The world that the poem creates lurches to a stop right at the moment when the travelers might make contact. Their world becomes lodged between a touch that has yet to be realized and a touch that has yet to be denied. But knowing that the breach outside time cannot last, the speaker, in admiration of and compassion for these travelers, offers a blessing that the sea receive them softly, tenderly even, no matter what may come of their fate. The kind of instruction that the poem offers, given the title's reference to Horace, might pertain to how life and death travel together in constant, unresolved dialectical tension. The desire for life, figured through the travelers' outstretched hands and death, figured through fire's destructive burning, are indelibly linked. Consequently, the haptic and the pyric become linked as well. Though the poem begins with revelation, it ends with concealment. The speaker's opacity serves a second purpose, shielding the travelers from the indignity of a tragic death while critiquing the will to know. It is not for us to know what becomes of them.

If "Ars Poetica" depicts subjects ensnared in fire's destruction, the poem "Burnings" engages the speaker's transit through fire as one of potential freedom. In the poem, the speaker looks at a photograph of himself nestled between aunt and mother. Glancing at this picture conjures the speaker's memories of his experience in the liminal space of a refugee camp.

> Refugee camp in the Philippines.
> I sit, flanked by mother and aunt: my saviors.
> Here, they are young again,
> their bodies smooth and unscarred
> beneath the white garments illuminating
> from the shack's interior. (Vuong 2010: 10)

The speaker in the poem speaks affectionately about aunt and mother, calling them his "saviors," but as the poem progresses it is clear that this is not a conventional hagiography. Fond memories give way under the weight of melancholy and indignation. The change in the poem's mood begins with the seventh and eighth lines, where the speaker states, "No. This is not a metaphor / for angels." This plainly stated *no* functions as an articulated refusal to give testimony in support of facile narratives of refugee resilience, to which the photograph gives pretense by way of its depictions of cheerful subjects, where aunt and mother "are young again" and their bodies "smooth and unscarred." The speaker warns the viewer not to believe what they see: "the light in their eyes" or "the grins stretched / so wide." The real image, the speaker suggests, is one where there is "no room for joy" but only unmaking.

> Do not say our names. These faces
> cannot belong to the ruin they became.
> Do not say our names as this flame grows
> from the edge of the photo, the women's smiles
> peeling into grimaces, the boy spreading slowly
> into black smudge, filaments of fire
> dissolving into wind. No, do not say our names.
> Let us burn quietly into the lives
>   we never were. (Vuong 2010: 10)

"Do not say our names" is an interdiction repeated throughout the piece, which articulates the speaker's clear desire for opacity as an escape from scopic and linguistic capture, a refrain that renounces the trap of recognition and representation. The refusal of metaphor in the seventh line acts as both a refusal of narratives of resilience and a refusal of fire as mere metaphor. The language of the poem invokes the material, physical burning of the photograph in question to reveal the speaker's actual desires.

To consider further "the boy spreading slowly into black smudge" presses us into thinking about his transmutation into ash as an illustration of a refugee passage through fire. This transit evokes what Anne Harris (2015: 47) describes as the "intertwined ontologies" of fire and the human. As the poem's speaker intimates, however, not all intertwinings are consensual or easily embraced. Harris's overview of fire's entanglement with the human takes place within the context of Western history and thought, meaning that the connection being posited might more properly be understood as one between fire and western Man. This universalizing gesture leaves out an account of the specific, asymmetrical relations of imperial force through which figures like the refugee become intertwined with fire. Contrary to this, an understanding of imperial violation as pyric annihilation takes root as the basis of a pyric refugee onto-epistemology and translates into the speaker's recognition of the enmeshment of refugee being and ash as a fraught inheritance of imperial and militaristic violence. The pyric constitution of the refugee also upends any presumptions about the fully human status of the speaker, for it appears as though it is the ash, as much as the human subject, who speaks in the poem. The speaker moves through paradox to find some kind of freedom through the very element that has inflicted gratuitous psychic and physical harm. Working in this paradox, the kind of freedom that the speaker searches for finds no recourse in the human, accepting no way back to willful, sovereign, self-possessed subjectivity. Rather, it is a freedom premised on continuous unraveling and dispersal, where "the boy spreading slowly into black smudge" may finally find relief by "dissolving into wind." The speaker's interdictions culminate in a final request for solitude: "Let us burn quietly into the lives / we never were." Like the speaker in "Ars Poetica" who bestows opacity onto the travelers so as to protect them, the speaker here wishes for opacity for himself and his family. Burning into ash offers the only possible route to freedom.

To Sing of Fire: Inheritances of Ash in *On Earth We're Briefly Gorgeous*

While the second half of *Burnings* begins to explore fire and heat as metaphors of queer erotic desire, these metaphors attain full force in Vuong's first novel, *On Earth We're Briefly Gorgeous* (2019). The atmosphere of *On Earth* brims with fire, heat, ash, and smoke. Metaphors of fire and its corollaries not only describe the novel's setting in Hartford, Connecticut, but also are central to how the protagonist, Little Dog, defines his relationships to other characters. Of the many threads in *On Earth*, one of the most significant deals with Little Dog's growing consciousness of his own burgeoning queer sexuality. He uses the metaphoricity of fire and heat to describe his first intimate relationship with another teenager, Trevor, whom he meets one day while working a summer job in the tobacco fields in the outskirts of town. From the beginning of their relationship, he characterizes Trevor through fire. Little Dog, for instance, notices the "bits of brown and ember" in the irises of Trevor's eyes "so that, looking at them, you could almost see, right behind you, something burning under an overcast sky" (Vuong 2019: 97). He continues to notice and observe Trevor's pyric being throughout their complicated friendship.

The heat of their romance results in several pyrosexual encounters. Little Dog's memory of the first time he and Trevor have "real" sex back in the barn on the tobacco farm is one defining instance of their pyrosexuality (Vuong 2019: 199). That night, Trevor is responsible for tending to the coals to speed the curing process of the tobacco leaves in the barn's beams. He asks Little Dog to keep him company through the night. Their intimacy is tied to the immediate surroundings of the barn, saturated, as it were, by the heat from the burning coal piles. "All around us the heaps burned, glowing red and flickering each time a draft made its pass through the slats," Little Dog remembers (200). Deep into the night, Little Dog and Trevor yield to their desires. Little Dog gives himself over to Trevor: "I pressed myself into his sun-baked skin, still warm from the day in the field" (200). In his first act of penetrative sex, Little Dog experiences the dissolution of singular being. With Trevor, sex felt "as if we were two people mining one body, and in doing so, merged, until no corner was left saying *I*" (202). They experience intersubjectivity, where for Little Dog the pain of penetration transmutes "into an impossible, radiating pleasure" (202).

Little Dog's ecstatic reprieve from singular subjectivity is cut short when he realizes that he has accidentally released onto Trevor, filling him with shame. He readily braces himself for Trevor's wrath, yet this fury never materializes. Instead, he guides Little Dog to the river nearby to wash off. While in the water, both share a tender moment together: "Trevor put his hand on my neck and we stood, quiet for a moment, our heads bent over the river's black mirror" (205). In that moment of connection instantiated through Trevor's touch, he offers reassurance to Little Dog, telling him, "'Don't worry about that. You heard?'" (205). In a later recollection, Little Dog relays more of Trevor's affirmation to him that night: "'You good. You heard, Little Dog? You good, I swear. You good'" (215). Following Trevor's words is another sexually charged act, in which he uses his mouth to clean the stain left by Little Dog, "willed as a balm to my failure in the barn" (205). Through Trevor's pyrosexual eros, Little Dog is injected with its vital force: "I was devoured, it seemed, not by a person, a Trevor, so much as by desire itself. To be reclaimed by that want, to be baptized by its pure need. That's what I was" (206). Eros changes Little Dog multiple times over in the span of an evening. Channeled through Trevor, it takes Little Dog apart, puts him back together, only to undo him again. Through this dizzying cycle, Trevor maintains his care for Little Dog, all the while being the one who unravels him.

As a letter addressed to his mother, Rose, *On Earth* details both mother's and son's evolving relationships to fire. Its significance as a recurring motif that illustrates the pyric onto-epistemology of the refugee is signaled early in the novel through one of Little Dog's recollections as a young boy. Waking up in the middle of the night to the sound of Chopin filling the house, Little Dog gets out of bed to search for the source of the music. His investigation leads him to his mother's room, and initially, she is nowhere to be found. Upon closer inspection of the room, Little Dog discovers the music emanating from the closet. There, he finds his mother, breathing heavily. Sitting outside the closet, he recalls how "the door [was] etched in reddish light, like the entrance to a place on fire" (12). Little Dog sits outside the door for an indeterminate amount of time, waiting for Rose to return from her traumatic episode. Realizing his waiting would be in vain, he returns to bed shaken by this incident, entreating his mother to "'come back. Come back out'" after he tucks himself back into bed (Vuong 2019: 12). As one of Little Dog's core memories of his mother's struggles with posttraumatic stress disorder, the recollection dramatizes Rose's ontological suspension, shocked by her trauma into an arrested temporality of being. It exemplifies for him how "the war was still inside you" (4). Fire is not just a psychological destination but a physical place, one that lures Rose into total surrender and submission. In another recollection, Little Dog remembers when he is shopping for clothes with his mother at Goodwill. Rose gives him a white dress to look at and makes a request: "'Can you read this,' you said, 'and tell me if it's fireproof?'": (13) Even though he could not yet read, Little Dog confirms for her that it is indeed fireproof. To his lie, she responds in relief: "'That's so good to know, baby.' You stared off, stone-faced, over my shoulder, the dress held to your chest. 'That's so good'" (14). Fire haunts Rose and triggers her even in the most mundane of tasks. As witness to her pyrophobia, Little Dog sees how fire inundates both Rose's body and mind. Her conscious being is haunted by fire, such that the measure of Rose's living becomes defined by the degree to which she can protect herself from its caprices.

If Rose's subjection to fire defines the beginning of her character arc, then the end of it reveals a surprising turnaround, a miraculous personal achievement in which she manages to overcome her pyrophobia to deftly wield fire for her own purposes. *On Earth*'s penultimate chapter houses the novel's climax, presented as Little Dog's memory of a table in a room on fire. The room does not burn down in one quick instance. Rather, Little Dog remembers this burning in fragments, extended over the chapter and imbricated with other memories, such as when he visits his grandfather Paul the summer following his college graduation. Being juxtaposed with these other memories makes clear the surreal quality of Little Dog's memory of burning. It is less so a memory than it is a premonition, a vision of spectacular destruction in the subjunctive.[7] The chapter opens with this memory of the burning room:

> I remember the table. I remember the table made of words given to me from your mouth. I remember the room burning. The room was burning because Lan spoke of fire. I remember the fire as it was

told to me in the apartment in Hartford, all of us asleep on the hardwood floor, swaddled in blankets from the Salvation Army. I remember the man from the Salvation Army handing my father a stack of coupons for Kentucky Fried Chicken, which we called Old-Man Chicken (Colonel Sanders's face was plastered on every red bucket). I remember tearing into the crispy meat and oil like it was a gift from saints. I remember learning that saints were only people whose pain was notable, noted. I remember thinking you and Lan should be saints. (Vuong 2019: 219)

Throughout the letter, tables symbolize the diminution of life that the characters experience. For Rose, the kitchen table is a site where she is assaulted by her abusive husband (232). For Little Dog, the table has been a place of hiding. Paul, for instance, recalls finding him hiding underneath one after being bullied by his schoolmates when he was young (64). Tables function as a site of violence and as a repository of negative affect throughout *On Earth*.

Little Dog's reiterative declarations of "I remember" build propulsive force as part of a ritualistic incantation led by Lan, Little Dog's grandmother, that stacks his memories together into a pile of kindling. By gathering his memories of the early days of his family's resettlement, this accumulation gives form to a familial history characterized by need, charity, and ordinary pleasures. Burning these memories skirts the logic of personal and familial remembrance, as it is predicated on a desire to vanquish these memories rather than hold onto them. We learn from this passage that Lan is responsible for setting this conflagration, but she is not alone. Rose and Mai, her other daughter, also participate in this burning ritual:

I remember the room. How it burned because Lan sung of fire, surrounded by her daughters. Smoke rising and collecting in the corners. The table in the middle a bright blaze. The women with their eyes closed and the words relentless. The walls a moving screen of images flashing as each verse descended to the next: a sunlit intersection in a city no longer there. A city with no name. A white man standing beside a tank with his black-haired daughter in his arms. A family sleeping in a bomb crater. A family hiding underneath a table. Do you understand? All I was given was a table. A table in lieu of a house. A table in lieu of history. (Vuong 2019: 232)

The walls of the burning room recapitulate a family history with no origin, tracing back to a city "with no name" that is "no longer there." Theirs is a family history so vitiated by violence that ruin is all that's left for them to claim. They were not so much written out of history as bombed out of it. With nothing left but this table, a material symbol of negative affect, Lan, Rose, and Mai summon fire to set it ablaze regardless. Rose's relationship to fire is changed. Once an indication of peril and trauma, she now summons its transmutative force to create something else. As a material force, it burns the table down in a devastating display of its terrible beauty. Little Dog takes his turn in this ceremony once the fire razes the table to the ground:

> I remember the walls curling like a canvas as the fire blazed. The ceiling a rush of black smoke. I remember crawling to the table, how it was now a pile of soot, then dipping my fingers into it. My nails blackening with my country. My country dissolving on my tongue. I remember cupping the ash and writing the words *live live live* on the foreheads of the three women sitting in the room. How the ash eventually hardened into ink on a blank page. How there's ash on this very page. How there's enough for everyone. (233)

Little Dog crawls toward an object no longer recognizable in form. By dipping his fingers into the table's ashes, he touches a substance that unmoors him from his world. His interaction with ash is the quintessential encounter "with the infinite in/determinacy at the heart of matter" for ash is a paradigmatic example that represents "the abundance of nothingness" (Barad 2012: 216). Of ash and cinder, Jacques Derrida (2014: 55) writes that "the cinder is nothing that can be in the world, nothing that remains as an entity." Its negative ontology evinces ash's intrinsic opacity, for ash is never entirely graspable even as Little Dog may touch and manipulate it (Glissant 1997: 191–92). Little Dog's confrontation with that which withstands recognition and apprehension is acutely startling because it presents to him the terrifying reality of his own negated being. It mirrors back the untenability of selfhood within the parameters of his given world. In other words, ash unmoors him from the world precisely because it forces Little Dog to realize that his self has never fully cohered within it. Though undone by ash, Little Dog is not without desire.[8] Of ash, Michael Marder (2020: 156–57) writes:

> Ashes are meaningless within the everyday matrix of sense, unpresentable and unrepresentable on the grounds of *logos*. But they are, at the same time, the only things that survive, that outlive life itself, and that persist outside the bygone world consumed by fire. Ashes embody the anarchy of unclassifiable society . . . where everything

has been burnt beyond recognition and has slipped away from the reach of metaphysical hierarchies.

Little Dog's otherwise feeling for something else beyond his world guides his inscriptions of ash on his family members' foreheads. His pyric constitution gives him the license and the ability to alchemize through ash, transmuting the traumatic past into something different.

The beauty of Little Dog's inscriptions issues from his alchemical experiments with the materiality of language. The table is not just a symbol of negative affect but also a linguistic structure. Little Dog describes it as "a structure with words" (Vuong 2019: 222) and as "an inheritance assembled with bare mouths. And nouns. And ash" (232). As a linguistic apparatus, the table represents a particular worlding produced by a specific grammar that relegates the refugee figure to a space of deficit. When Lan, Rose, and Mai set it on fire, they transform the table into a linguistic heap of soot. Fire nullifies the grammar of deficit while breaking open the closed circuits of signification.[9] In this light, Little Dog's inscriptions can be viewed as an act of poiesis through his attempt to make language over. He touches his family with his words, anoints them with the injunction to live from the ashes of a language that could not previously account for their existence.

Little Dog's disclosure that "there's ash on this very page" reveals how his alchemy becomes embedded into the letter itself. It calls for closer scrutiny of this last passage as that which bears the material traces of Little Dog's linguistic invention. Another look at it draws attention to his striking use of anaphora, which occurs in triplets. The passage opens with the repetitions of *I remember* and closes with the repetitions of *how*. In the middle of the passage, *"live"* repeats three times and is significant even though it is not technically anaphoric. Connecting these parts of speech together forms a whole sentence, a latent message that nonetheless has been there all along: "I remember how [to] live." In this message written for his mother, Little Dog enjoins both of them to live on, to persist beyond a world that has failed them, in spite of what they have suffered. His alchemy signals his ability to use ash to "innovate around trauma" even as that trauma ostensibly defines his family's horizon of existence (Vuong qtd. in Nguyễn 2021).

This scene of sublime conflagration forms part of a wider constellation of otherwise smaller, quieter moments of subjunctive imagining in the novel. An insistent desire for an otherwise and an elsewhere is sharpest in moments such as when Lan is "thinking of another world," one "where there are no soldiers or Hueys and the woman is only going for a walk in the warm spring evening, where she speaks real soft to her daughter, telling her the story of a girl who ran away from her faceless youth only to name herself after a flower that opens like something torn apart" (Vuong 2019: 40–41). With his mother, Little Dog ponders: "Maybe in the next life we'll meet each other for the first time—believing in everything but the harm we're capable of" (192). And again, at the end of the letter, he thinks of her: "Maybe you'll be a girl and maybe your name will be Rose again, and you'll have a room full of books with parents who will read you bedtime stories in a country not touched by war. Maybe then, in that life and in this future, you'll find this book and you'll know what happened to us. And you'll remember me. Maybe" (240). While Little Dog's "maybes" offer no escape from the past that mother and son have forged together, the subjunctive yearning exhibited through his words exerts its own force that pries open the space of the novel, making Little Dog's existential question "Where have we been, Ma?" an expression of both lamentation and wish (137). His overtures to this future mark a radical act of selflessness whose solemnity is magnified by his own self-awareness that his place in this next world is not guaranteed. Still, he wishes for this world for his mother even if it would risk not being there with her.

"The Last Woman on Earth": Pyric Refugee World Making in *The Boat People*

If *On Earth* introduces the climactic scene of spectacular burning as an instance of apocalyptic revelation for the refugee, the work of artist Tuan Andrew Nguyen extends these ruminations by thematizing the paradoxical quality of apocalypse when its meanings are figured through ash. In this section, I analyze Nguyen's short film *The Boat People* (2020), which was the centerpiece of his exhibit *A Lotus in A Sea of Fire* at James Cohan Gallery in New York City. Set to the sound of experimental Balinese gamelan music, the film opens with five children emerging from the water, having made landfall in an unknown place after what appears to be a long, tiresome voyage on their yellow boat. With walking sticks in hand, these travelers enter the thicket of brush before them. Inside the brush, the travelers find objects left behind by those who once resided there, such as a Buddha statue built by Laotian refugees and replicas of parts of Angkor Wat. From there, the travelers find and search through what appears to be an abandoned settlement. Although the setting of the film is not apparent, one particular low-angle shot provides a clue as to what

Figure 1 The girl stands at the intersection of Uranium and Krypton Street. © Tuan Andrew Nguyen 2023. Courtesy of the artist and James Cohan, New York

may have occurred. Here, we see a young girl, the leader of the group and heroine of the film, standing at the corner of Uranium and Krypton Streets (see fig. 1). This shot alludes to nuclear catastrophe, whose occurrence appears to be confirmed by the voyagers' interaction with a locale that has so far been absent of human life. *The Boat People*, then, takes place at the end of the world. It centers the girl as a figure of the refugee in a state of utmost precarity and alienation, someone who must brave what is left of a world completely shattered and irredeemably destroyed by the ravages of imperial warfare.[10]

After finishing their explorations of the settlement, the voyagers rest, but while the boys are either dozing off or lounging around, the girl's expression remains focused and alert. Something beyond the camera's frame arrests her attention. As if pulled toward that object, she gets up out of her chair and walks out of the shot. In the next scene, the girl stands firmly, her gaze intently directed ahead of her. She begins to walk, and as the camera rotates around her, the object in question comes into view. As the camera focuses on this object, we see what she has been fixated by: the severed head of a Guan Yin statue nestled on the beach. As she walks across the expanse of glittering sand, drawing nearer to the object, the severed head of the Buddhist deity of compassion and mercy comes to life and transforms itself into the head of a woman.

Once the initial shock and surprise at each other's existence subside, the girl and the Guan Yin statue start a conversation with each other. The girl speaks in Tagalog while the statue head speaks in English. The girl tells the statue that she is a traveler. "I've been to many places," the girl says. "I look for things . . . And I've found many things." When the statue asks whether she is a thief, the girl responds by saying, "There is nobody left alive to steal from. The world is ours now. We seek the stories of our ancestors . . . Of who we once were." The statue, incredulous and baffled by the girl's responses to her questions, then asks about the rationale behind taking the objects she finds. To this, the girl replies and offers a correction: "We don't take things from anywhere. We only re-create them. We carve them out of wood. Then we burn them. And the ashes go into the ocean. We set them free." When asked who she learned this from, the girl tells the statue that her mother taught her this burning practice. Put another way, this act of burning is her maternal inheritance. This act, like Lan's song of fire, raises a conundrum, as burning contradicts modes of historical inquiry that consider the preservation of objects a sacrosanct principle.

Objects are central to the understanding of place, and their significance is nowhere more evident than in the very location where the travelers end up, which turns out to be the province of Bataan in the Philippines. "This whole region was engulfed in flames once. First as war, then as reenactments of wars," the statue relates to the girl. The objects the voyagers find, particularly in the museums they visit, attest to the nested histories of military conflict, settler-colonial occupation, and refugee reception and resettlement within the province (Espiritu and Ruanto-Ramirez 2020). For instance, the travelers find a large boat in the museum for the Philippine Refugee Processing Center, a monument to refugees' perilous escape by water. In the World War II museum, they find objects such as a machine gun, a gas mask, a pistol, and a machete. The travelers replicate these objects from both museums, making copies of them out of wood and then setting them on fire. With history in their hands, they would choose to burn these objects rather than keep them intact.

Fire leaves an onto-epistemological imprint on the girl, and much like Little Dog, its maternal inheritance bears significance. When pressed about her practice of burning the copies she makes, the girl recounts the story of her mother's death to the statue: "I remember when my mother stopped moving. When she became . . . dead. She was heavy. So heavy. I couldn't carry her anymore. My copies are light. . . . And they bring the past into the future. And burning brings nowhere to everywhere. I remember she told me to burn her so I

could keep going." Her mother's passing marks an occasion for burning that attunes the girl to multiple overlapping, conjoint dualities:
life and death, heaviness and lightness, past and future, nowhere and
everywhere, endings and continuations. These dialectical tensions
never resolve themselves but recursively enfold into each other. Her
disclosure resonates with what she relays to the statue earlier on in
their dialogue about her mother: "My mother told me that there are
many ways to burn. And that not all of them are bad." Placed in the
unfathomable position of having to burn her mother after she dies,
the girl experiences directly the finitude of life and the ephemerality
of being. Her mother's enigmatic words, however, do not exactly
dread the confrontation with one's own finitude. Rather, it seems as
though she accepts this end with peace. From this perspective, the
mother's wish to burn indexes a drive to go elsewhere, which in
effect instantiates a desire to abscond from the enclosures of subjectivity and humanity (see Nguyen 2012; Kim 2015; Jackson 2020). The
girl's burning of her mother's body exposes subjectivity's imperma-
nence, ambivalence, and mutability (Ngo 2011: 118). Teetering on
the edge of dissolution, the body consumed by fire is stripped of the
veneer of human and subject status, unveiling the inhuman matter into
which the body transmutes.[11] Perhaps the body is always already ash.
While certainly not easy, burning her body plays an important role in
the girl's grieving, and it also functions as the ultimate act of responsibil-
ity to her mother. She burns her body not to completely erase the bur-
densome memory of her mother but to make her memory light enough
that she herself can "keep going." Taken altogether, her disclosures to
the statue about her burning practice signify the basis of her pyric refugee onto-epistemology, one that intuits ash as a material conduit that
"brings nowhere to everywhere." An inheritance passed down by her
mother, the girl's pyric praxis reorients burning not as something
merely destructive and uncontrollable but as a force that can also enact
modes of care—cleansing, purifying, lightening in equal measure—at
the end of the world.

The allegorical resonances of fire and ash reach their apex in the
final moments of the film. The statue head, we learn, has been on a
lengthy journey toward the sea, where it hopes to find long-awaited
liberation after having been desecrated by looters and left stranded
for years. The girl helps the statue head complete this journey by taking it the final length to the shore, in her arms, a reversal of roles in
which the human girl is the one who intercedes on behalf of the deity.
Their embrace illustrates a compassionate intimacy grounded in the
girl's dutiful intent to release the statue head from its current form

Figure 2 The girl carries the Guan Yin statue head to the water. © Tuan Andrew Nguyen 2023. Courtesy of the artist and James Cohan, New York

(see fig. 2). Through the girl's touch, she makes a world with the statue, doubling herself into the statue as the statue doubles itself into her.[12] Once they reach the shoreline, their short-lived world together comes to an end, and she sets the statue head on fire with a torch. The final seconds of the film close with an extended shot of the statue resting on its side on the wet sand, where the peaceful ebb and flow of water laps up against the exuberant flash of flames that slowly consumes it (see fig. 3). As it burns away, the statue head reveals to us the prophetic quality of the girl's touch when she held it in her arms, for it is a touch that recognized and anticipated the necessary transmutation of being that the statue head had to undergo so that it might finally be free.[13] Her touch registers her conviction that fire will make the statue light, just as it did for her mother's heavy body. Even though the film does not show the complete transmutation of the statue head, we may speculate that when the girl sets it on fire, it still burns, disintegrates, and turns into ash, similar to the other objects that the girl and her crew have set on fire. Her desire to produce ash seems to evince nothing other than an indictment of empire and its global circuits of profit-driven accumulation, exploitation, and destruction, an expression of her desire to end the world, especially one that would desecrate the sacred. But her motivations are not geared solely toward pointless destruction. Nguyen notes that the girl is "the figure of the world maker indeed. She is not merely a survivor, but a creator—the bridge between the past and the future, the space between two worlds" (qtd. in Ingawanij 2020). Nguyen's appellation of *world maker* for the girl initially appears at odds

Figure 3 The statue head engulfed in flames. © Tuan Andrew Nguyen 2023. Courtesy of the artist and James Cohan, New York

with the burning rituals she conducts. If indeed a world maker, she is still at the same time a producer of ash, a proliferator of nothingness. Within this contradiction of creation and destruction, though, it becomes possible to recognize the girl's acts of burning as concerted efforts to extend the space of the interregnum. She routes questions of futurity in and through the very materiality of ash, thereby deferring and forestalling any clear vision of what may exist later on. Before the arrival of any future, she insists on an extended space of mourning for those that could not make it there in their earthly form.

The allegorization of futurity through ash cautions against any hasty move to divine the future. As Cathy Caruth (2013: 88) writes, "The figure of ash . . . refers us to events that may not have a simple referent, but are signs of the unimaginable past or the unimaginable future." This unimaginable futurity presents itself earlier in *The Boat People* when the girl walks on the glittering stretch of sand, upon her first time seeing the statue head—this sand might be thought of as a fitting analogue to ash. Though its abundance threatens to overwhelm, some grains of sand glimmer. As these shining grains suggest, though the indeterminacy and insensibility of ash signifies futurity as opaque, this recognition of opacity yields not to resignation but a renewed sense of possibility.[14] Ash invites an extended lingering in the interregnum between the time of ruin and repair. The ash that the girl makes will look not unlike these glittering grains of sand on the shore of the beach (see fig. 4). Like them, the ash will glimmer with an anticipatory illumination whose beauty lies beyond the grasp of

Figure 4   Glimmering grains of sand surround the statue head. © Tuan Andrew Nguyen 2023.
Courtesy of the artist and James Cohan, New York

human apprehension. From the ruins of one thing arrives the possibility of something else—what that is, we cannot be entirely sure.

A Speck of Ash

Vuong's and Nguyen's literary and filmic texts convey the continued hold the "Napalm Girl" has over Vietnamese diasporic aesthetics. As an image that visualizes the destruction of a lifeworld by fire, it precipitates another historical and aesthetic trajectory of refugee passages that contemplates the pyric nature of refugee being. In the photograph, empire inflicts its gratuitous terror not just on one person but on an entire family seen running for their lives. It is no surprise that the transits through fire depicted in *On Earth* and *The Boat People*, as aesthetic responses to this image, are narrated as familial ordeals. The mothers in each text carry an intimate, embodied knowledge of how it feels to burn, which they pass down to their children as a pyric refugee onto-epistemology. This knowledge of pyric being arises from their children's haptic encounter with ash. To touch ash is to touch that which has left this world. As a remnant of what was but no longer is, ash runs athwart of signification, meaning, and sense. Touching ash exemplifies "an analytics of touch that *cannot be*, let alone *appear*, within the onto-epistemological confines of the (moribund) world" (Bradley 2020). Ash draws its beauty from its terror as a substance that transfigures the given and jolts those who touch it out of "the everyday matrix of sense."

To revisit this photograph more than a half-century later is to stumble upon the unsettling abundance of ash produced in its wake, so much of it that "there's enough for everyone," in the words of Little Dog. Ash becomes the material for a refugee poetics, that which suffuses Little Dog's radical compositions. Like the world maker's burning rituals, his words are in the service of life but are, at the same time, always indebted to the dead. As Derrida (2014: 37) writes, "The sentence is adorned with all of its dead." Intimately aware of this fact, Little Dog's sentences are charred and scorched, yet they also evince his belief that "the end of the sentence is where we might begin" (Vuong 2019: 10). Following Little Dog's direction leads us to ash one more time, to the speck of it that feigns as a period on the page. If a world exists in a sentence, ash punctuates that world so that something else might yet follow.

David Pham is a PhD candidate in the Department of Ethnic Studies at UC Berkeley.

Notes

I thank Juana María Rodríguez, Darieck Scott, Salar Mameni, and Victoria Kahn for their support and feedback. Andrew Leong and especially Dorothy Hale provided incisive comments on the manuscript in its final stages.
1   Ronak K. Kapadia (2019: 9) writes: "The forever war is an assault on the human sensorium for citizens, subjects, survivors, and refugees of US empire alike." See also Rotter 2019.
2   Alex Harris's (2017) news reporting on Phúc's scar revision treatment: "'Before, sometimes things would touch me and I wouldn't know what it was,' Phan Thi said. 'Now, I can feel it.'"
3   As Trung Phan Quoc Nguyen (2020) argues, "Refugees are the instrumentalized *national detritus* of modern state sovereignty."
4   Critical refugee studies scholarship challenges the reductive framing of refugees. See Um 2015; Espiritu and Duong 2018; Nguyen 2019.
5   In her extensive discussion of the image of Phúc, Mimi Thi Nguyen (2012: 111) examines the affective relation between liberal empire and its subject through the sensorial register of touch. Like Nguyen, Phu (2012: 113) critiques how dominant discourses attached to circulating images of Phúc's scarred body reflect "the tactile dimensions of affect" by characterizing her scarring as a "touch point" for the Western viewer.
6   Kandice Chuh (2019: 78) brings attention to "the intimate and inseparable link between being and knowing, ontology and epistemology" in her theorization of "illiberal humanisms." See also Coole and Frost 2010.
7   The surreal quality of this sequence invites a reading of Little Dog as experiencing a reverie induced by fire. Bachelard (1964: 16) observes

that in this reverie "the fascinated individual hears *the call of the funeral pyre*. For him destruction is more than a change, it is a renewal."

8   For a discussion of eco-erotic intelligences, see Nelson 2017.

9   Maurice Blanchot (1995: 326) writes, "Take the trouble to listen to a single word: in that word, nothingness is struggling and toiling away, it digs tirelessly, doing its utmost to find a way out, nullifying what encloses it— it is infinite disquiet, formless and nameless vigilance." Derrida (2014: 37) writes: "An incineration celebrates perhaps the nothing of the all."

10 Black and Indigenous studies scholars have pointed out the failure of Anthropocene discourse to acknowledge how settler colonialism and transatlantic slavery have already been world-shattering processes for Black and Indigenous peoples. See Cornum 2020; and Yusoff 2018.

11 Yusoff (2015: 389) observes that "subjectivity contains both an anterior and interior non/inhuman excess."

12 For a discussion of touch as "a chiastic relation of reversibility," see Fretwell 2020: 225.

13 Within the tradition of Theravāda Buddhism, the Āditta-pariyāya Sutta, or Fire Sermon, is an account of the Buddha's warning to monks of sensory attachments to the world. See Bodhi 2000; and Āditta-pariyāya Sutta n.d.

14 Yusoff (2013: 213) writes: "And yet there is a force at the heart of relational thinking that is insensible to us; it is this very force that propels forth with a call for justice and solidarity, and risks itself to make such obligations possible. It is also a force that intuits other possible worlds."

References

Abrams, M. H. 1991. *Doing Things with Texts: Essays in Criticism and Critical Theory*. New York: Norton.

Āditta-pariyāya Sutta (Aflame). n.d. In *Saṃyutta Nikāya* (*The Connected Collection*), translated from the Pali by Thānissaro Bikkhu, 35:28. https://www.dhammatalks.org/suttas/SN/SN35_28.html (accessed May 10, 2022).

Bachelard, Gaston. 1964. *The Psychoanalysis of Fire*. Translated by Alan C. M. Ross. Boston: Beacon Press.

Barad, Karen. 2012. "On Touching—The Inhuman That Therefore I Am." *Differences: A Journal of Feminist Cultural Studies* 23, no. 3: 206–23.

Blanchot, Maurice. 1995. *The Work of Fire*. Translated by Charlotte Mandell. Stanford, CA: Stanford Univ. Press.

Bodhi, Bhikkhu, trans. 2000. *The Connected Discourses of the Buddha: A Translation of the Samyutta Nikaya*. Boston: Wisdom.

Bradley, Rizvana. 2014. "Introduction: Other Sensualities." *Women and Performance: A Journal of Feminist Theory* 24, no. 2–3: 129–33.

Bradley, Rizvana. 2020. "The Vicissitudes of Touch: Annotations on the Haptic." *b2o*, November 21. https://www.boundary2.org/2020/11/rizvana-bradley-the-vicissitudes-of-touch-annotations-on-the-haptic/.

Brand, Dionne. 2001. *A Map to the Door of No Return: Notes to Belonging*. Toronto: Vintage Canada.

Caruth, Cathy. 2013. *Literature in the Ashes of History.* Baltimore: Johns Hopkins Univ. Press.

Cheng, Anne Anlin. 2000. "Wounded Beauty: An Exploratory Essay on Race, Feminism, and the Aesthetic Question." *Tulsa Studies in Women's Literature* 19, no. 2: 191–217.

Chuh, Kandice. 2019. *The Difference Aesthetics Makes: On the Humanities "After Man."* Durham, NC: Duke Univ. Press.

Clark, Nigel, and Kathryn Yusoff. 2018. "Queer Fire: Ecology, Combustion and Pyrosexual Desire." *Feminist Review* 118, no. 1: 7–24.

Cohen, Jeffrey Jerome, and Lowell Duckert. 2015. "Introduction: Eleven Principles of the Elements." In *Elemental Ecocriticism: Thinking with Earth, Air, Water, and Fire,* edited by Lowell Duckert and Jeffrey Jerome Cohen, 1–26. Minneapolis: Univ. of Minnesota Press.

Coole, Diana, and Samantha Frost. 2010. "Introducing the New Materialisms." In *New Materialisms: Ontology, Agency, and Politics,* edited by Diana Coole and Samantha Frost, 1–43. Durham, NC: Duke Univ. Press.

Cornum, Lou. 2020. "Radioactive Intimacies: The Making of Worldwide Wastelands in Marie Clements's Burning Vision." *Critical Ethnic Studies Journal* 6, no. 1. https://manifold.umn.edu/read/radioactive-intimacies-the-making -of-worldwide-wastelands-in-marie-clements-s-burning-vision/section/efe07 ef7-fd8a-49ed-b769-029832999429.

Derrida, Jacques. 2014. *Cinders.* Minneapolis: Univ. of Minnesota Press.

Espiritu, Yến Lê, and Lan Duong. 2018. "Feminist Refugee Epistemology: Reading Displacement in Vietnamese and Syrian Refugee Art." *Signs: Journal of Women in Culture and Society* 43, no. 3: 587–615.

Espiritu, Yến Lê, and J. A. Ruanto-Ramirez. 2020. "The Philippine Refugee Processing Center: The Relational Displacements of Vietnamese Refugees and the Indigenous Aetas." *Verge: Studies in Global Asias* 6, no. 1: 118–41.

Fretwell, Erica. 2020. *Sensory Experiments: Psychophysics, Race, and the Aesthetics of Feeling.* Durham, NC: Duke Univ. Press.

Gandhi, Evyn Lê Espiritu. 2022. *Archipelago of Resettlement: Vietnamese Refugee Settlers and Decolonization across Guam and Israel-Palestine.* Oakland: Univ. of California Press.

Glissant, Édouard. 1997. *Poetics of Relation.* Translated by Betsy Wing. Ann Arbor: Univ. of Michigan Press.

Harris, Alex. 2017. "Vietnam War's 'Napalm Girl' Gets Pain Relief from Laser Treatment." *Seattle Times,* January 8. https://www.seattletimes.com/nation -world/vietnam-wars-napalm-girl-gets-pain-relief-from-laser-treatment/.

Harris, Anne. 2015. "Pyromena: Fire's Doing." In *Elemental Ecocriticism: Thinking with Earth, Air, Water, and Fire,* edited by Lowell Duckert and Jeffrey Jerome Cohen, 27–54. Minneapolis: Univ. of Minnesota Press.

Hartman, Saidiya. 2008. "Venus in Two Acts." *Small Axe* 12, no. 2: 1–14.

Hartman, Saidiya. 2019. *Wayward Lives, Beautiful Experiments: Intimate Histories of Social Upheaval.* New York: Norton.

Ingawanij, May Adadol. 2020. "Tuan Andrew Nguyen: '*The Boat People*'" (interview). https://www.vdrome.org/tuan-andrew-nguyen.

Jackson, Zakiyyah Iman. 2020. *Becoming Human: Matter and Meaning in an Antiblack World*. New York: New York Univ. Press.

Kapadia, Ronak K. 2019. *Insurgent Aesthetics: Security and the Queer Life of the Forever War*. Durham, NC: Duke Univ. Press.

Kim, Eunjung. 2015. "Unbecoming Human: An Ethics of Objects." *GLQ: A Journal of Lesbian and Gay Studies* 21, no. 2–3: 295–320.

León, Christina A. 2021. "Exorbitant Dust: Manuel Ramos Otero's Queer and Colonial Matters." *GLQ: A Journal of Lesbian and Gay Studies* 27, no. 3: 357–77.

Marder, Michael. 2020. *Pyropolitics in the World Ablaze*. London: Rowman and Littlefield.

Miller, Nancy K. 2004. "The Girl in the Photograph: The Vietnam War and the Making of National Memory." *JAC* 24, no. 2: 261–90.

Nehamas, Alexander. 2000. "The Return of the Beautiful: Morality, Pleasure, and the Value of Uncertainty." *Journal of Aesthetics and Art Criticism* 58, no. 4: 393–403.

Nelson, Melissa K. 2017. "Getting Dirty: The Eco-Eroticism of Women in Indigenous Oral Literatures." In *Critically Sovereign: Indigenous Gender, Sexuality, and Feminist Studies*, edited by Joanne Barker and Jessica Bissett Perea, 229–60. Durham, NC: Duke Univ. Press.

Nelson, Melissa K. 2019. "Wrestling with Fire: Indigenous Women's Resistance and Resurgence." *American Indian Culture and Research Journal* 43, no. 3: 69–84.

New-York Historical Society, dir. 2020. *The Vietnam War 1945–1975: "Napalm Girl."* YouTube. https://www.youtube.com/watch?v=OFUFRl1sMNU.

Ngo, Fiona I. B. 2011. "Sense and Subjectivity." *Camera Obscura* 26, no. 1: 95–129.

Nguyen, Mimi Thi. 2012. *The Gift of Freedom: War, Debt, and Other Refugee Passages*. Durham, NC: Duke Univ. Press.

Nguyễn, Patricia. 2017. "Salt | Water: Vietnamese Refugee Passages, Memory, and Statelessness at Sea." *WSQ: Women's Studies Quarterly* 45, no. 1–2: 94–111.

Nguyễn, Thị Minh Huyền. 2021. "Obliterating Form, Recasting Language, Elongating Time: A Conversation between Ocean Vuong and Dao Strom." *Diacritics*, October 13. https://dvan.org/2021/10/obliterating-form-recasting-language-elongating-time-a-conversation-between-ocean-vuong-and-dao-strom/.

Nguyen, Trung Phan Quoc. 2020. "The Labor of Absolution: National Detritus and the Op-Ed Form of the Vietnamese Refugee." *Critical Ethnic Studies Journal* 6, no. 1. https://manifold.umn.edu/read/the-labor-of-absolution-national-detritus-and-the-op-ed-form-of-the-vietnamese-refugee/section/19566799-6a7e-416a-9fae-3df25cf7875a.

Nguyen, Tuan Andrew, dir. 2020. *The Boat People*. Super 16mm transferred to digital.

Nguyen, Vinh. 2016. "Nước/Water: Oceanic Spatiality and the Vietnamese Diaspora." In *Migration by Boat: Discourses of Trauma, Exclusion, and Survival*, edited by Lynda Mannik, 65–79. New York: Berghahn Books.

Nguyen, Vinh. 2019. "Refugeetude: When Does a Refugee Stop Being a Refugee?" *Social Text* 37, no. 2: 109–31.

Perera, Suvendrini. 2013. "Oceanic Corpo-Graphies, Refugee Bodies and the Making and Unmaking of Waters." *Feminist Review* 103, no. 1: 58–79.

Phu, Thy. 2012. *Picturing Model Citizens: Civility in Asian American Visual Culture*. Philadelphia: Temple Univ. Press.

Phu, Thy. 2022. *Warring Visions: Photography and Vietnam*. Durham, NC: Duke Univ. Press.

Pyne, Stephen J. 2019. *Fire: A Brief History*. 2nd ed. Seattle: Univ. of Washington Press.

Rotter, Andrew J. 2019. *Empires of the Senses: Bodily Encounters in Imperial India and the Philippines*. New York: Oxford Univ. Press.

Sharpe, Christina. 2019. "Beauty Is a Method." *e-Flux*, no. 105. https://www.e-flux.com/journal/105/303916/beauty-is-a-method/.

Suzuki, Erin. 2021. *Ocean Passages: Navigating Pacific Islander and Asian American Literatures*. Philadelphia: Temple Univ. Press.

Um, Khatharya. 2015. *From the Land of Shadows: War, Revolution, and the Making of the Cambodian Diaspora*. New York: New York Univ. Press.

Vuong, Ocean. 2010. *Burnings*. Little Rock, AR: Sibling Rivalry Press.

Vuong, Ocean. 2019. *On Earth We're Briefly Gorgeous*. New York: Penguin Press.

Yusoff, Kathryn. 2013. "Insensible Worlds: Postrelational Ethics, Indeterminacy and the (k)Nots of Relating." *Environment and Planning D: Society and Space* 31, no. 2: 208–26.

Yusoff, Kathryn. 2015. "Geologic Subjects: Nonhuman Origins, Geomorphic Aesthetics and the Art of Becoming *In*human." *cultural geographies* 22, no. 3: 383–407.

Yusoff, Kathryn. 2018. *A Billion Black Anthropocenes or None*. Minneapolis: Univ. of Minnesota Press.

Shouhei Tanaka

Black Feminist Geohaptics and the Broken Earth

Abstract This article examines how literary imaginaries of the haptic in Black speculative fiction attend to the racial politics of the Anthropocene and the centrality of sensory praxis to ecological thought. Reading Alexis Pauline Gumbs's *M Archive* and N. K. Jemisin's Broken Earth trilogy, the article considers how ecological touch—or what Erin Robinsong calls *geohaptics*—emerges as a central literary trope that imagines new forms of sensory wayfinding and worldmaking that unearth and contest the epoch's racial ecologies of power. Expanding the concept's uses and forms, what the article terms Gumbs's and Jemisin's *Black feminist geohaptics* crafts new political forms of sensory dwelling and planetary futures of environmental liberation for Black life. Sense, these works show, makes legible and transforms the Anthropocene's geographies of power, unearthing how the categories of the human, inhuman, and more than human are generated and mobilized within the matrix of domination. Their works articulate the production of Black women's geographies within and against the racial, patriarchal, and colonial Anthropocene, orienting sense and touch as central political figurations for anticolonial and abolitionist ecological thought.

Keywords sensory studies, environmental humanities, African American literature, speculative fiction

> There's an air of the broken world—and revolutionary geology predicts this waft in time, this disruptive plume, insurgency's panache—that just keeps on tearing shit up and swirling it around. And it seems like there's always someone who can't help but ask how to survive intact in and as that solidity of waste and shame that comes at the expense of spirit.
> —Fred Moten, *Black and Blur*, 2017

> we broke the earth and now we fall through time. deep gashes in the ground. we scale the edges of our knowing. the smoother the worse, the more jagged the more better. what we stand on is not masonry. it is the torn place unhealed. the footholds come from how unclean the break.
> —Alexis Pauline Gumbs, *M Archive*, 2018

American Literature, Volume 95, Number 3, September 2023
DOI 10.1215/00029831-10679265   © 2023 by Duke University Press

In Alexis Pauline Gumbs's *M Archive: After the End of the World* (2018), a hybrid-genre speculative poem and archive that documents a postapocalyptic environmental future, geology is pictured as a wounded planetary body whose "deep gashes in the ground" shape the "jagged" and "torn" footholds of the broken earth (139). Footholds, as geology's sculpted bodies, become the site where planetary damage is made legible through touch, the mode through which, as the epigraph above states, "we scale the edges of our knowing" in the flashpoint of the Anthropocene. Touch, as the narrator-archivist tells us, reveals the knowledge that "the cracks where the earthquakes expressed themselves were exactly the same contours of the fissures in our minds and the breaks. all the breaks in our hearts" (9). This body-land dialectic cultivates connectivities between biological and geological life through touch: "do you know how long it takes to train hairs that would stand on end at any touch to become pores open with thanksgiving? . . . once upon a time the core of the earth made the magma solid, built crust around itself where dreams could safely plant and grow. we are of that lineage" (78). *M Archive* presents hapticity as a more-than-human heuristic that emplaces humans in intimate geological lifeworlds across vast time frames and geographies. As the narrator-archivist further notes, "If you could look close enough (or listen carefully enough, the critical geologists would have corrected), you could see the churning planet making herself brown" and feel the "energy close to the core of the earth where the planet felt more alive, soft, hot, and in production" (23). If you could look, listen, and feel more closely the animate planet in motion—this centering of embodied knowledge articulates a geophysics of sense in which haptic bodies conjure intimate forms of life with the earth and its sensuous materialities of embodiment, perception, and transformation. It conjures what Fred Moten (2017) writes as the insurgency of "revolutionary geology" that, materializing within the "air of the broken world," induces new domains of environmental judgment.

A different geophysics of sense appears in N. K. Jemisin's Broken Earth trilogy (*The Fifth Season* [2015], *The Obelisk Gate* [2016], and *The Stone Sky* [2017]), a speculative fiction series that chronicles a climate-ravaged Earth in the unknown future, characterized by seasons of massive climate catastrophes that continually transform a supercontinent named the Stillness. An Anthropocene allegory of everyday climate catastrophes, the trilogy introduces orogenes, a fantastical race of people who become crucial to human survival because they can seismically sense and shape the very geology of the continent through special sensory organs that grant them "awareness of the movements of the earth" (Jemisin 2015: 465). In one early scene, the trilogy's protagonist, Essun, and her companion Alabaster perform orogeny to quell an impending cataclysmic earthquake:

> She feels her own connection to the earth, her own orogenic awareness. . . . Alabaster has chained them together somehow, using her strength to amplify his own. . . .
>
> And then they are together, diving into the earth in tandem, spiraling through the massive, boiling well of death that is the hot spot. It's huge—miles wide, bigger than a mountain. . . .
>
> . . . But then it becomes easy, easy to smooth the ripples and seal the cracks and thicken the broken strata so that a new fault does not form here where the land has been stressed and weakened. She can sess lines of striation across the land's surface with a clarity that she has never known before. She smooths them, tightens the earth's skin around them with a surgical focus. . . . And as the hot spot settles into just another lurking menace and the danger passes, she comes back to herself. (127–28)

A contradictory grammar of animacy displaces the categorical divisions of human/nonhuman and life/nonlife, as Essun and Alabaster subdue the earth's rumbling strata in a meeting of equal force through orogenic terraforming. As Essun and Alabaster "dive" into the earth to smooth out erupting hot spots, minerals burst onto the narrative stage in an entwined dance of agency and affectivity. Showcasing geology as a sensory nexus of body-land relationalities, Jemisin's trilogy, like *M Archive*, imagines a sensuous geology whereby bodies intimately interface with inhuman lifeworlds through haptic wayfinding and place-making. *M Archive* and the Broken Earth trilogy show how emergent forms of life sitting at the conjuncture of geological and biological worlds materialize first and foremost through sense. Sense, as these works further show, makes legible and transforms the Anthropocene's geographies of power, unearthing how the categories of the human, inhuman, and more than human are generated across race, gender, and matter.

This article examines how literary imaginaries of the haptic in Black speculative fiction attend to the racial politics of the Anthropocene and the centrality of sensory praxis to ecological thought. In what follows, I consider how ecological touch—or what Erin Robinsong calls *geohaptics*—emerges as a central trope in Gumbs's and Jemisin's speculative climate fictions that imagine new forms of sensory wayfinding and worldmaking that unearth and contest the Anthropocene's racial ecologies of power. *Geohaptics* names the "extreme intimacy of ecological entanglement, via the air, water, and matter we take in and continually re-become," describing how sensory experiences "soften and move through borders of discrete or individual bodies or substances" (Robinsong 2018: 39).[1] Expanding the concept's uses and forms, what I term Gumbs's and Jemisin's *Black feminist geohaptics* crafts new political forms of sensory dwelling and planetary futures of environmental liberation for Black life. These works map the making of Black ecologies—the "foremost sites of ongoing injury, gratuitous harm, and premature death" and the "insurgent visions of an environmental future free of the relations and geographies engendered by the racial capitalocene" (Roane and Hosbey 2019)[2]— by pinpointing the epoch's forms of sensory necro/biopower, on the one hand, and mapping abolitionist, anticolonial ecologies fashioned through insurgent geohaptics, on the other. Demonstrating how the senses configure different forms of ecological relations that demarcate or undo the boundaries of the (in)human, these works read race as sensory assemblages of embodiment and perception that entwine with the disciplining of humans and nonhumans across race, gender, and matter. Black feminist geohaptics assembles new forms of attunement and animacy by ecologizing sense as more-than-human placemaking praxes that upend the ontological partitions between human/nonhuman, life/nonlife, and subject/object that underwrite Western colonial metaphysics. The attendance to Black women's geographies (McKittrick 2006) within and against the racial, patriarchal, and colonial Anthropocene articulates an ethics of ecological relationality and sensory freedom whose Black feminist and ecological frameworks are neither irreducible nor inextricable from one another—a coalitional theory of Black liberation, ecological alterity, and justice that Chelsea Frazier (2020) theorizes as Black feminist ecological thought (see also Ducre 2018). Their Black feminist sensory imaginations orient touch and perception as central political figurations for anticolonial and abolitionist ecological thought.

By illuminating sense's central role in mapping the Anthropocene's racial ecologies, these speculative fictions imagine new distributions of the sensible, the systemic apportionment of political power and life in which "aesthetic acts as configurations of experience . . . create new modes of sense perception and induce novel forms of political subjectivity" (Rancière 2004: 9).[3] What forms of animacy and attunement attend the broken earth of the Anthropocene, in which the entanglements of inanimate matter and racial formation generate categories of the human and inhuman? Touch, as Gumbs and Jemisin show, animates new attunements to more-than-human lifeworlds; in turn, non-human lifeworlds, equipped with their own repertoire of affectivity, agency, and autopoiesis, decenter the human sensorium as the proprietary seat of liberal humanist personhood. This haptic imagination orients sense and sensation as intersubjective forms and processes through which bodies encounter more-than-human forces, thereby displacing humanist perspective and power. Seen this way, the architecture of perception itself emerges as a reciprocal mode of more-than-human assembly that make personhood and placemaking possible as such. Black feminist relationality forges these novel ecologies by engaging, and undoing, the categories of the (in)human that propel the "matrix of domination" (Collins [1990] 2000: 18). Inventing alternative, speculative ecologies of more-than-human intimacies, *M Archive*'s and the Broken Earth trilogy's Black feminist geohaptics show how "geography, the material world, is infused with sensations and distinct ways of knowing," whose "alterability of space and place" (McKittrick 2006: ix) redefine the human as sensory praxis (McKittrick 2015). Sense becomes the modality through which abolitionist, more-than-human ecologies are felt, reimagined, and transformed.

Touching the Broken Earth

In the last decade, two dominant paradigms have animated environmental and Anthropocene studies, often in conflict and contestation: the school of new materialisms revitalizing the primacy of nonhuman ontologies and agencies, on one hand, and new and ongoing analyses of the epoch's ecologies of power via race, gender, disability, colonialism, and capitalism, on the other. In tandem with work critiquing the expunction of power and difference in dominant Anthropocene and new materialist theories, a growing body of work has productively interrogated the intersection of these two areas of critical inquiry.[4] Such approaches examine how nonhuman worlds, such as those of animals, minerals, energy, waste, and infrastructure, converge with and generate the political domains of race, capitalism, and colonialism. As Sylvia Wynter (2003: 260, 267) argues, forms of racial mattering and material formations of race are propelled by the "coloniality of being," whereby the formation of the white universal human subject is legitimized through racial hierarchies that coemerge with and coshape the "systemic stigmatization of the Earth in terms of its being made of a 'vile and base matter.'" In the case of antiblackness and its racial ontologies, Zakiyyah Iman Jackson (2020: 3) argues, "the fleshy being of blackness is experimented with as if it were infinitely malleable lexical and biological matter, such that blackness is produced as sub/super/human at once, a form where form shall not hold." Examining the production and disciplining of bodies, Mel Y. Chen's (2012: 55) theory of animacy engages the transmutation of racialized, gendered bodies into inanimate, abject matter under Western coloniality's animacy hierarchies, foregrounding how animacy is "a craft of the senses" that "endows our surroundings with life, death, and things in between." Put together, these adaptive configurations of race and matter manufacture the fantasies and fictions of the Anthropocene's racial ecologies.

Where and how, then, do these forms of life emerge? Dana Luciano (2015: 7) argues that the "most compelling contribution of the new materialisms is not conceptual or analytic, strictly speaking, but sensory," in which the attendance to nonhuman matter fundamentally posits "a reorganizing of the senses."[5] Seen this way, critical couplings of feminist, queer, decolonial, and critical race theories with new materialisms potentialize "rematerializations of race" in which racial formation is understood as "synthetic and syncretic" by tracing "its material-semiotic links to places where it no longer seems to be 'about' race at all" (Huang 2017; see also Tompkins 2016). Sensory thinking offers a vital entry point into these questions by examining the centrality of sense to the making of modernity and to how senses mediate the relations between self and environment, human and nonhuman, subject and object.[6] Such approaches not only understand senses as "assemblages of knowledge, narrative, and historicity that . . . reconceive of the ways in which human and nonhuman bodies alike affect each other simultaneously at and below the threshold of perception" but also work toward a "new critical sensorium . . . in which (white) Man is displaced as the prime locus of sensation" (Fretwell 2018: 7, 2).[7] Seen this way, race materializes as "assemblages of somatosensory experience and intersubjective affectivity" (Sekimoto and Brown 2020: 22) that shape, and are shaped by, various modes of ecological attunement and animacy.

Against this backdrop, ecological attunement and animacy translate into a politics of knowledge that raises the central question of ecology's scope as a field and object of study, in relation to its different epistemologies that bifurcate ecology as a domain of scientific versus embodied knowledge. In the former, for instance, the transdisciplinary field of Earth system science has produced new frameworks for understanding planetary ecological processes and systems through new technologies that amass climatological, geological, hydrological, and other environmental data. Similarly, across the earth sciences (geology, ecology, oceanography, hydrology), remote sensing has long provided environmental data by extracting, mapping, and visualizing information from environments through various satellite and sensor technologies. These domains of knowledge become powerful metaphors for engaging planetary thinking, providing "an (auto)biography of humans when humans have become a question for themselves" (Chakrabarty 2019: 30–31). In contradistinction to these approaches, many sensory theorists argue that such forms of scientific knowledge do not adequately apprehend or generate meaningful categories of environmental knowledge and judgment. They theorize instead forms of "intimate sensing" (Porteous 1990: 201) and "sensuous geographies" that center "the senses both as a relationship to a world and the senses as in themselves a kind of structuring of space and defining of place" (Rodaway 1994: 4; see also Serres 2008). This epistemological politics is central to Gumbs and Jemisin's Black feminist ecologies. In contrast to scientific knowledge, their geohaptic imaginations offer alternative embodied epistemologies that assemble more-than-human lifeworlds, an orientation made clear by the genre markers of *M Archive* as a "speculative documentary work" that is discovered by a future "post-scientist" (Gumbs 2018: xi), and the Broken Earth trilogy's fantasy mode as an epistemological critique of scientism. Their works read geology as the material and discursive domain through which the earth's deep-time histories are encountered and where the political ontologies of being and matter are coproduced and entangled with colonialism, race, and gender.

A speculative archive of poems comprising four main elemental archives—"Dirt," "Sky," "Fire," and "Ocean"—that documents the end of the world and emergent Black ecologies in the postapocalyptic future, Gumbs's *M Archive* illuminates the limits of environmental judgment borne out of scientific knowledge. One poem identifies the impetus of planetary ecological crisis as the insufficiency of recognizing the sociopolitical stakes of climate apocalypse:

> they never proved it, but we know. some of the hand-waving women had always known. some of the metaphysicians had been trying to say. no one took them literally. until the earth broke apart.
> and then. with the probe technology, with the accurate diagrams. with the skilled cave divers going deep into the fault lines. . . .
> . . . .
> … It became impossible to ignore. (Gumbs 2018: 9)

This passage pinpoints the failure of scientific knowledge—whether produced from probe technologies and diagrams or the study of fault lines—in preventing climate apocalypse and attending to the crucial environmental judgment that the "hand-waving women" and "some of the metaphysicians had been trying to say" all along. "Hindsight is everything," the narrator-archivist says, "if the biochemists had diverted their energies towards this type of theoretical antioxidant around the time of the explicit emergence of this idea . . . , everything could have been different. if the environmentalists sampling the ozone had factored this in, the possibilities would have expanded exponentially" (6). What, then, is this knowledge, the theoretical anti-oxidant to scientific knowledge? It is, as *M Archive* tells us, "black feminist metaphysics. which is to say, breathing" (6), a form of ecological relationality that holds "the reality of the radical black porousness of love (aka black feminist metaphysics aka us all of us, *us*)" (7). Prior to the proliferation of scientific data that verified the incontrovertible reality of environmental crisis, "it was the black feminist metaphysicians who first said it wouldn't be enough," that is, the fundamental Western-colonial fiction about "one body. the unitary body," since "one body was not a sustainable unit for the project at hand" and "not the actual scale of breathing" (6). By contrast, the relational metaphysics of *M Archive*—composed of the "black simultaneity of the universe also known as everything also known as the black feminist pragmatic intergenerational sphere" (7)—articulates a different form of felt intimacy with the earth:

> we took off our leaden clothes and we skipped out of our concrete shoes and we went barefoot enough to bear the rubble we had created just before. we let the sun touch us and felt what we had done to the ozone in our daze. we noticed that skin was just as thin as it should have been and all that we had been calling skin before were layers of accumulated scars.
>
> we touched each other's hands and found them warm and ridged with remembering. we traced the lines and found home again and again. home was like a pulse. home was where the hurt was. we lunged and pressed towards each other's chests. we let longing lead long past our labored lack. we held each other's hands. they did not break. (83)

In contrast to scientific knowledge, this geohaptic imagination—of people finding "home again and again" through haptic interfacing with the soft earth to feel its "lines" and "pulse"—opens new sensory geographies in which bodies come into contact with the earth's elemental ecologies of dirt, air, and water. It illustrates how touch, as a form of prosthesis, "invents by drawing the other into relation, thereby qualitatively altering the limits of the emerging touched-touching bodies" to index "a surplus or excess of the biological organism" (Manning 2007: xiv, 155–56). The reciprocity of remembrance and refuge forged through the fusing of bodies and the earth bears witness to ecological catastrophe and resilience through a praxis of situated knowledge and action ("to bear the rubble we had created just before," "we touched each other's hands . . . and found home again and again"). The description of their skin being "just as thin as it should have been" with "layers of accumulated layers" mirrors the broken earth's own bodily strata, linking violence against the earth and the body. This Black feminist spatial imagination shows how, as Katherine McKittrick (2006, ix) writes, the "earth is also skin."

M Archive's sensuous geographies open up the elemental genealogies and ecologies that make up the geographical and social afterlives of the Middle Passage. Written in close engagement with M. Jacqui Alexander's *Pedagogies of Crossing: Meditations on Feminism, Sexual Politics, Memory, and the Sacred* (2006), *M Archive* examines how the Middle Passage continues to inhabit the climate-ravaged future by showing that "the crossing was not only a geographic transfer of millions of people but also a movement of energies and elements into a relationship that persists, a material and conceptual relationship we navigate with the potential and compelled crossings we make in each movement" (x). This Middle Passage elemental afterlife is illustrated in a key poem wherein a group of "critical black marine biologists, scientists of the dark matter under fathoms," discovers the possible "causal relationship between the bioluminescence in the ocean and the bones of the millions of transatlantic dead": the magnesium and calcium of the transatlantic dead "has infiltrated the system of even the lowest filter feeders. so any light that you find in the ocean right now cannot be separated from the stolen light of those we long for every morning" in the ocean, "that place where the evolutionists and creationists all agree that life began" (Gumbs 2018: 11). Orienting the Middle Passage as a planetary afterlife, archive, and ecology, the poem cultivates new epistemologies of ecological dwelling that scientific knowledge cannot provide. Moreover, the knowledge of this elemental historical ecology is made legible through touch, as another poem illustrates wherein future Black oceanists dive into the depths of the ocean and immerse themselves within the deep fathoms that contain the elemental afterlives of the Middle Passage. This journey into the seafloor's elemental ecologies dramatizes Christina Sharpe's (2016: 41) analysis of the residence time of Africans in the Middle Passage: the "amount of time it takes for a substance to enter the ocean and then leave the ocean," in which Black people "exist in the residence time of the wake, a time in which 'everything is now.'" Notably, as they descend into the depths, the knowledge they discover develops as a form of sensory dwelling that forges new multispecies intimacies in the realms of the unknown and unknowable: training themselves "not to be afraid of going black. . . . they were not afraid to slow and evolve their breathing. they were not afraid of their kinship with bottom crawlers who could or could not glow. they were not afraid of being touched by what they could never see, never bring back to the light, never have a witness for" (Gumbs 2018: 10). Linking touch to ecological intimacy, knowledge, and wonder that allow bodies to "evolve their breathing" and expand their "kinship" to ordinary and extraordinary nonhuman forms and environments, the poem materializes history itself as an elemental archive written/created by sensuous matter and life forms. Geohaptics reads the Middle Passage as a future-anterior planetary archive and afterlife that continually remakes Black ecologies: it opens up, as Alexander (2006: 7–8) writes, the "urgent task of configuring new ways of being and knowing and to plot the different metaphysics that are needed to move away from living alterity premised in difference to living intersubjectivity premised in relationality and solidarity."

This Black feminist sensory praxis is exemplified in another poem in "Archive of Dirt":

> not big and blue. they were small brown women. the way their hair was silver heaven the way their skin was deep brown earth and how its texture mapped hills and valleys and tributaries of grace. it was there for anyone to see, really. or anyone to hear in the heightening or deepening tones of their voices, in the shaking vibration of their wisdom. if the people could not listen to the air all around them, if they could not place their hands on the cracked earth and know, they would only have had to pay attention to the small brown women who demonstrated it every day in language and action. (Gumbs 2018: 35)

Not "big and blue" but "small brown women"—this passage articulates an epistemological vantage point that begins not with the god's-eye view of the earth from outer space (the "blue marble" image) but with sensuous, situated geographies whose "more-than-human matrix of sensations and sensibilities" show how "bodies have formed themselves in delicate reciprocity with the manifold textures, sounds, and shapes of an animate earth" (Abram 1996: 22). This sensory becoming and worldmaking—"it was there for anyone to see," "anyone to hear"—unearths multiscalar Black women's geographies across place and planet in which ecological judgment emerges through felt experience, knowledge, and collectivity—what Audre Lorde ([1978] 1984) names as the primary register of the erotic. This body-planet dialectic is illustrated in another poem wherein the unnamed protagonist presses her body upon the earth, putting "her face directly in the dirt" that was "hard enough and soft enough to hold her" with "no back to brace her to loop up at the sky": "Part of the day she pounded the earth with her fists and screamed blame and despair. part of the day she let soil slip through her fingers and felt comforted. most of the day she just acclimated herself to solid breathing and seeing all there was. which was brown" (Gumbs 2018: 68). This passage stages a landscape of felt experience and knowledge—of blame, despair, and comfort—in which the wounds of the broken earth entwine with the woman's, as the materiality of the Middle Passage's elements and energies permeate the geographies of the future broken earth. Yet, by intimately lying on and with the earth, breathing and touching open up geographies that "cross into a metaphysics of interdependence" (Alexander 2006: 6). This is a conjuncture of grace and grief in which the "geographic meaning of racialized human geographies is not so much rooted in a paradoxical description as it is a projection of life, livability, and possibility" (McKittrick 2006: 143).

If *M Archive* "centers Black life, Black feminist metaphysics, and the theoretical imperative of attending to Black bodies in a way that doesn't seek to prove that Black people are human but instead calls preexisting definitions of the human into question" (Gumbs 2018: xi), Gumbs articulates this futurity by locating felt intimacies with the earth that resist the racial, colonial, and patriarchal terrains that shape Anthropocenic life. A similar geology of sense appears in Jemisin's Broken Earth trilogy in which the genealogies of slavery, antiblackness, climate apocalypse, and Black feminism entwine. Yet, as the next sections show, whereas *M Archive* envisions Black ecological futures borne from the postapocalyptic afterlife of the Middle Passage through the speculative documentary genre, the Broken Earth trilogy dramatizes the mythological animacies of nonhuman lifeworlds that inflect and generate emergent Black ecologies through its fantasy genre. In contrast to the radical forms of worldmaking cultivated through new reconceptions of sensory praxis and Black feminist metaphysics in *M*

Archive, the Broken Earth trilogy conjures fantastical sensory ecologies in which touch materializes as uncanny forms of terraforming that allow humans to encounter otherworldly geological lifeworlds.

Sensory Imperialism and Georacial Mattering

Chronicling the deep-time geohistories of a supercontinent subject to frequent cycles of climate cataclysms, Jemisin's speculative climate fiction exemplifies what Walter Benjamin (1968: 88) in "The Storyteller" claims as the central task of imagining "the transformation of epic forms occurring in rhythms comparable to those of the change that has come over the earth's surface in the course of thousands of centuries." In the world of the Stillness is the Sanzed Equatorial Affiliation, or Sanzed Empire, an elite race of humans who dominate and govern the continent and its diverse group of races and nations. The Sanzed Empire's success in mitigating and surviving massive climate catastrophes, known as Fifth Seasons, is made possible by their rule over orogenes, an enslaved race of people who have the special ability to "sess" (to sense) and terraform the continent's geologies. Due to special sensory organs located in their brainstem called "sessapinae," orogenes are equipped with fantastic forms of exteroception (sensitivity to the body in relation to external stimuli) that allow them to quell and control the Stillness's geologies, as well as attune to other environmental and affective phenomena such as "the presence of predators, to others' emotions, to distant extremes of heat or cold, and to the movement of celestial objects" (Jemisin 2015: 343). Providing the power to variously "see," "hear," "feel," and "touch" the earth in this way, orogeny's multisensory capacities transform touch into a kaleidoscope of overlapping sensory modalities and affectivities. Their enslavement under Sanzed rule is made possible by a special class of soldiers called Guardians, who have the special capacity to control and negate orogeny's sensory-terraforming powers. Against this backdrop, the storyline follows the protagonist Essun, a Black orogene woman who is in search of her lost daughter, Nassun. Together, the two eventually come to discover the nature of Fifth Seasons: the animate planet, known as Father Earth, perpetuates Fifth Seasons to punish humanity due to the loss of his companion, the moon. Through their power of orogeny, Nassun and Essun return the moon back into the earth's satellite orbit to thereby save the planet by abolishing the cycle of Fifth Seasons. By exploring the relationship of sense to geology through orogene racialization and ecological apocalypse, the trilogy orients race as an "assemblage of sensuous realities with texture, movement, rhythm, temperature, and weight" that "materializes as a bodily, affective, and sensorial *event*—something that *happens*, rather than something that *is*" (Sekimoto and Brown 2020: 3).

While speculative narratives abound featuring characters with earth-moving abilities (also known as elemental manipulation, semiokinesis, and geokinesis)—prominent examples include *Avatar: The Last Airbender* (2005–8) and the Terra, Sandman, and Avalanche series in Marvel Comics—the trope of geokinesis in the Broken Earth trilogy is distinctive for its environmental and racial significations. A key text that parallels Jemisin's sensory imagination in this register is Octavia E. Butler's Xenogenesis trilogy (*Dawn* [1987], *Adulthood Rites* [1988], and *Imago* [1989]), a speculative fiction series that features the Oankali, an alien race that possesses special tentacular sensory organs that allow them to extract genetic, emotional, and biochemical information from organisms through touch. The Oankali exemplifies posthuman futures in which novel life forms fashion new multispecies attunements and animacies through touch. Sensation acts as the dynamic site in which more-than-human relations are produced and evolve, and also where newly generated forms of racial and gender violence raise complex dilemmas of ecology and power.[8] Like Jemisin's trilogy, Butler's novels imagine speculative multispecies ecologies emerging in corporeal human-nonhuman contact zones. Whereas the Xenogenesis trilogy engages the themes of posthumanism, race, gender, and ecology through biological forms of sensory life, however, the Broken Earth trilogy explores geological forms of sensory life in which humans encounter the mineralogical worlds of inhuman matter. Along with orogenes and Guardians, the trilogy features fantastical mineralogical beings called obelisks and stone eaters, huge floating minerals that hover across the Stillness's skies and immortal stone figures that can travel through the earth's strata, respectively. This shift from biology to geology in Jemisin's trilogy crystallizes the racial politics of antiblackness, racialization, and minerality in the Anthropocene, or what Kathryn Yusoff (2018: 6, 9) calls the "geologies of race," in which race is understood as a geological formation whereby the "transactions between geology and inhumanism [materializes] as a mode of both production (or extraction) and subjection (or a violent mode of geologic life)." Critics have examined the trilogy's engagement with environmental injustice and Afrofuturism (see FitzPatrick 2020). Lisa Dowdall (2020: 151), for example, examines Jemisin's linkage of Afrofuturism and geology to argue that the trilogy "uses geology to question widespread cultural assumptions about the 'natural' divisions between race, species, and matter that underpin hierarchies of the human." This imaginary, I argue, centrally emerges through Jemisin's geohaptic imagination, in which sense mediates and transforms the animacy hierarchies of the Anthropocene's racial ecologies.

The narrative logic of orogene racialization and orogenes' terra-forming capacities drives the trilogy's georacial imagination. For millennia, orogenes are enslaved by the Sanzed Empire, who harness their orogeny to seismically control the supercontinent's geologies (quelling earthquakes, volcanic eruptions, and other seismic activities) and to create infrastructure such as roads, clearings, and architecture. Known as a race who are "born evil—some kind of agents of Father Earth, monsters that barely qualify as human" (Jemisin 2015: 124), orogenes are racialized as subhumans whose geokinetic powers emplace them in an adjacent animacy hierarchy with nonhuman matter. In the eyes of nonorogenes, otherwise known as stills, "they threaten, and manipulate, and use. They're evil . . . as Father Earth himself" (Jemisin 2016: 310). Through the twofold process of disciplining "inhuman life" (orogenes) to discipline inhuman matter (earth), the colonial logic of the Sanzed Empire illustrates how racialized extraction (harnessing orogeny) intersects with racial mattering (orogenes regarded as inhuman matter like the earth itself). Crucially, the historical origins of orogene racialization are traced back to the advent of Sanzed colonialism and cannibalism in the long past, when during a particularly hard season of food scarcity Sanzed communities—or "comms"—united to attack "comms of any lesser races" (Jemisin 2015: 417) to steal their resources, abduct people, and eat them. As the orogene Alabaster notes, "That's *when* they started calling us 'lesser races,' actually" (417), in which the dispossession, enslavement, and killing of orogenes led to the rise of the Sanzed Empire. Since orogenes are only legible and discovered as such when their sensory capacities are revealed to stills, orogene racialization is not biologically but sensorily marked. In this way, the narrative logic of orogene racialization and thingification registers "racializing assemblages," an understanding of race "not as a biological or cultural classification but as a set of sociopolitical processes that discipline humanity into full humans, not-quite-humans, and nonhumans" (Weheliye 2014: 4).

By focusing on a central cast of Black orogenes—Essun, Nassun, Alabaster, and others—the trilogy's racial allegory centers Black liberation and antiblackness even as the racial significations of orogenes also indexes other forms of racialization. Thus, while the trilogy does not posit an isomorphism between Blackness and orogeny, since orogenes of different racial identities exist, the allegorical register of orogene racialization nevertheless centrally engages (anti)Blackness, a figuration made apparent, for example, with the derogatory term for orogenes, *roggas*, connoting antiblack racial slurs.[9] Read this way, the Broken Earth trilogy is a speculative neoslave allegory that dramatizes the geological "afterlife of slavery" (Hartman 2007: 6) in a climate-ravaged future, in which orogenes struggle for liberation as they exist within perpetual states of enslavement, fugitivity, and climate catastrophes that continually generate new diasporas and crises. This allegorization is made clear by the nature of orogene enslavement: the Sanzed Empire kidnaps young orogene children across the Stillness to train them under the supervision of Guardians at the Fulcrum, a special academy where orogenes are disciplined to learn, control, and use their orogeny for the empire's ends. Moreover, many orogene mothers are forced to become "Breeders" for the Fulcrum to produce more children, while others are frequently sent off to various regions across the continent to perform various tasks for villages, towns, and cities. This enterprise of extracting and reproducing slave labor metonymically figures the Fulcrum as a plantation. The central storyline chronicling Essun's search for her daughter, Nassun, in particular resonates with the histories of US slavery, as the family narrative begins with a miscegenation and passing plot that leads to the fragmentation of Essun's family: upon discovering that her two children have inherited her orogeny, Essun attempts to train them to hide their orogeny from stills, as she has done herself. Eventually, however, her husband, a still, discovers their children's orogeny, beating their son to death and kidnapping Nassun. This plot line eventually turns into a fugitivity narrative, as Essun, along with Alabaster, flees to the small island of Meov off the coast of the Stillness, following their violation of Sanzed laws and escape from the Fulcrum. There they find refuge in an island community where orogenes can freely exist and live, and they eventually have several children. This sanctuary, however, is later destroyed when the Sanzed Empire discovers their whereabouts and invades the island. Rather than give her child Corondum away to a life of enslavement under the Fulcrum, Essun decides to kill him, a scene alluding to the history of the enslaved African American woman Margaret Garner, who similarly killed her daughter to save her from a life of enslavement. The trilogy in this way stages a speculative afterlife of slavery that keys in on the material conditions of sexuality, reproduction, and dispossession for enslaved Black women and the improvised forms of Black feminist mothering and fugitivity that resist and refuse the Sanzed Empire. In the storyworld of racial injustice, gender violence, and climate apocalypse wherein orogenes search for freedom and ecological sanctuary, the abolition of racial-colonial empire becomes inextricably entwined with the abolition of Fifth Seasons.

Powered by the entwined disciplining of racialized bodies and environments, the Sanzed Empire's control over the orogenic uses and limits of bodies culminates in a sensory imperialism that maintains mastery over life and land. As it turns out, orogenes are enslaved, disciplined, and killed through forms of sensory dominion implemented by Guardians, designated masters who train and surveil orogenes and ultimately reshape their orogeny for the empire's terraforming undertaking. Equipped with their own specialized sensory power through a surgical procedure and brain implant, Guardians possess sessapinae that are "repurposed, made sensitive to orogeny and not to the perturbations of the earth" (Jemisin 2016: 176). This procedure equips them with specialized abilities to incapacitate orogenes by negating their orogeny through proximity and touch, such that orogenes are no longer able to sess environments if they are inflicted by this haptic violence. Furthermore, in contrast to orogeny's ability to terraform external environments, Guardians can turn "orogeny inward" (Jemisin 2015: 290) through touch to implode the flesh of orogenes and kill them. This exteriority-interiority dialectic between orogenes' and Guardians' sensory powers stages contested forms of ecological worldmaking between centrifugal relationality (a liberatory haptics that indexes and generates more-than-human lifeworlds) and centripetal coloniality (an extractive haptics that seals and severs lifeworlds).

Sensory imperialism generates segregated domains of environmental habitability through racialized animacy hierarchies, shaping the making and maintenance of life and nonlife. Whereas the Fulcrum's training and breeding programs exemplify sensory biopolitics, the Sanzed Empire's sensory necropolitics culminates with the construction of node networks, hidden infrastructures installed all across the continent that seismically stabilize different regions of the Stillness. As Essun discovers to her horror during an expedition, node networks in fact consist of underground node maintainers: enslaved child orogenes who are lobotomized at a young age and imprisoned in underground facilities that harness their orogeny to stabilize local tectonics such as earthquakes and volcanic eruptions. Tied down to wire chairs equipped with food, medicinal, and waste tubes and put in a vegetative state through surgical operations that reduce them to their orogenic state, these imprisoned orogenes exist in a state of perpetual pain from their continual exertion of orogeny, until death. This somatosensory enslavement, in which orogenes housed within the strata of the earth are used to tame and discipline the earth itself, literalizes a form of necropolitical extraction in which racialized bodies are reified into the empire's infrastructures of ecological habitability. Sanzed dominion over lands and peoples is made possible through forms of georacial mattering that position both orogenes and the earth as abject, inanimate matter. Moreover, the empire operates through adaptive forms of social reproduction and killing: to ensure the prevention of future Fifth Seasons, the Fulcrum's breeding program secures an abundant population of orogenes to stabilize the Stillness; on the other hand, Seasonal Laws dictate that, if need be, orogenes must be killed during particularly harsh seasons in order to preserve, and become, resources for other humans. The trilogy's hybrid neoslave and Anthropocene allegory links slavery to geology through these vectors of sensory imperialism, such that slavery is understood as "a geologic axiom of the inhuman in which nonbeing was made, reproduced, and circulated" (Yusoff 2018: 5). In this way, the trilogy registers the transmutation of Black and other racialized bodies into inhuman matter as inextricably tied to the manufactured habitability of the imperial continent.

These segregated political domains of biological and geological life illuminate how Western colonial metaphysics sever ecological lifeworlds through extraction, accumulation, and dispossession. This racial-colonial matrix of domination—seen through the emplacement of orogenes in hierarchized taxonomies of life (Guardians, stills, orogenes, animals) and nonlife (orogenes, minerals, earth)—configures adaptive animacy hierarchies that arrange humans, nonhumans, and nonlife forms into different "orders of value and priority" (Chen 2012: 13). If Hortense J. Spillers (1987: 67) distinguishes "flesh" from the "body" to name the "zero degree of social conceptualization" that structures Black corporeality and subjectivity, the trilogy's augmented formulation affixes flesh to stone to explore forms of racialized mineralogical corporeality in the Anthropocene. This georacial interstice illuminates how Black women's bodies become "the principal point of passage between the human and the non-human world" (Spillers [1984] 2003: 155) that generates different racializing assemblages and animacy hierarchies (see also Hartman 2016). Chronicling the supercontinent's geological transformations across millennia, the trilogy imagines a

speculative geohistory of the planet that illustrates the mineraliza-
tion of race within the earth's strata. Like Gumbs's archival aesthetic in
M Archive that explores Blackness in relation to Earth's geohistories,
Jemisin's speculative geology shows how racial mattering and formation become part and parcel of colonialism's earth-shaping across
deep time frames, indexing antiblackness as a stratigraphic force
that shapes the habitability of the planet. By unearthing the contact
points between Blackness and the Anthropocene, the trilogy engages
the "problem for thinking of and for Black non/being" (Sharpe 2016: 5)
in the geological wake of slavery in climate-ravaged futures.

Sensory Insurgency and the Geological Network

Against the Sanzed Empire's regime of sensory imperialism, Jemisin's
trilogy envisions a form of sensory insurgency that assembles abolitionist, anticolonial ecologies. After their separate escapes from the
Fulcrum, Essun and Nassun eventually discover that their orogenic
terraforming power comprises only a small fraction of their larger abilities. Free from the Fulcrum's disciplining of orogeny, they learn and
cultivate another crucial form of sensory attunement that lies beyond
orogeny: the ability to sess and interact with magic, or what is also
called *silver*, "the stuff underneath orogeny, which is made by things
that lived or once lived" (Jemisin 2017: 242). Whereas Fulcrum-led
orogeny is predicated on human-dominated terraforming, magic is
powered by relational forms of worldmaking crafted together by nonhumans and humans. Perceiving the natural world anew with magic-
oriented sensoria, Nassun and Essun eventually learn to alter the
molecular composition of matter to heal and transform myriad life and
nonlife forms through multiscalar magic, among other things. As
Essun's mentor Alabaster teaches her, the Fulcrum's "methods are a
kind of conditioning meant to steer you toward energy redistribution
and away from magic," such that "you learn to think of orogeny as a
matter of effort, when it's really . . . perspective. And perception"
(Jemisin 2016: 203, 204). As a paradigm shift made possible through a
transformation in sensory perception and power, magic upends the
fictions of human exceptionalism and Western colonial metaphysics,
reimagining geological bodyminds (Schalk 2018) in which more-than-
human worldmaking emerges within the conjuncture of race, disability,
body, and geology.

   Significantly, Essun discovers the power of magic when she also
learns the origin story of Fifth Seasons and why they have existed for

millennia: long ago, an elite race of humans attempted to extract magic power from the earth's core to gain infinite energy, a project called Geoarcanity that attempted to "lock the raw magical flows of the planet into an endless cycle of service to humankind" (Jemisin 2017: 333). Like the Sanzed Empire's history, Geoarcanity was created through the enslavement of a special race of bioengineered life forms called tuners, who harness magic for energy extraction and distribution. The calamitous failure of the project, causing the moon's orbital displacement from the earth, led to the discovery of the earth as an animate planet, named Father Earth by humans. Angered by the loss of his child, the moon, Father Earth kick-started the cycle of Fifth Seasons. With this newfound knowledge of the planet's animacy and history, Essun senses that the "silver deep within Father Earth wends between the mountainous fragments of his substance in exactly the same way that they twine among the cells of a living, breathing thing. And that is because *a planet* is a living, breathing thing. . . . All the stories about Father Earth being alive are real" (242). Eventually, the trilogy's neoslave and climate allegories interlink as Essun's search for her long-lost daughter coincides with her new quest to unlock the Obelisk Gate, a network powered by the obelisks, to harness the planet's magic to bring the moon back into Earth's orbit and thereby permanently abolish Fifth Seasons.

Magic catalyzes insurgent sensoria whose perspectival and perceptual transformations fashion new forms of attunement to more-than-human worlds. As their magic power evolves, Essun and Nassun learn to connect to obelisks, which turn out to be network conduits and batteries whose "crystalline structure emulates the strange linkages of power between the cells of a living being" (Jemisin 2016: 136). Upon connecting to an obelisk, Essun discovers a geological network of magic spread across vast distances (narrated in second-person point of view):

> what you suddenly understand is this: Magic derives from life— that which is alive, or was alive, or even that which was alive so many ages ago that it has turned into something else. All at once this understanding causes something to shift in your perception, and
> and
> and
> You see it suddenly: *the network*. A web of silver threads interlacing the land, permeating rock and even the magma just underneath, strung like jewels between forests and fossilized corals and pools of

oil. Carried through the air on the webs of leaping spiderlings. Threads in the clouds, though thin, strung between microscopic living things in water droplets. Threads as high as your perception can reach, brushing against the very stars.

And where they touch the obelisks, the threads become another thing entirely. For of the obelisks that float against the map of your awareness—which has suddenly become vast, miles and miles, you are perceiving with far more than your sessapinae now—each hovers as the nexus of thousands, millions, *trillions* of threads. This is the power holding them up. (361–62)

This passage articulates a speculative multiscalar geohaptics—a new "map of your awareness"—in which the human sensorium extrudes beyond the corporeal boundaries of the body and expands into the elemental ecologies of air and sky, magma and cosmos. The new perceptual horizons of this geohapticity enable touch to map new temporalities and spatialities of the world that reconfigure the body's ontological terrestriality and unity. When Essun, in another moment, connects to a topaz obelisk, her body transforms into a more-than-human network that feels, inhabits, and ultimately becomes the elemental ecologies of the Stillness: "Then you're in the topaz and through it and stretching yourself across the world in a breath. No need to be in the ground when the topaz is in air, *is* the air; it exists in states of being that transcend solidity, and thus you are capable of transcending, too; *you* become air. You drift amid the ash clouds and see the Stillness track beneath you in humps of topography" (245). Haptic bodies not only inhabit space but also create and transform it through sense and sensation. By plugging into the geological network, Essun and Nassun experience touch as a posthuman praxis that unfurls the multiscalar interactivities and interconnectivities that comprise the planetary web of life.

In contrast to the Fulcrum's extractive node networks, magic's network form is powered by infrastructures of relationality and care. Magic, as Essun later learns, can also operate through forms of collective attunement called *parallel scaling*, networks that link orogenes together to "form a whole group working in parallel, in . . . a mesh" (Jemisin 2016: 356) to generate aggregate magic power. Magic's network logic, in this way, lays the groundwork for reconceiving the political ontology of life, land, and belonging. This new form of sensory attunement requires Essun to unlearn the Fulcrum's extractivist framework of orogeny: when she first experiences her attunement to an onyx obelisk, she wonders whether the connection is analogous to orogenes' servitude to Guardians—a bondage made of "chains" (89). As a friend corrects her, however, attunement to obelisks is fundamentally different since it is formed around a logic of attraction: the onyx is "drawn to your presence. . . . It lingers around you because it can't help itself" (89). This attraction is predicated on the recognition that minerals wield the agency to negotiate their own terms of attunement to humans, as illustrated when another character connects to an onyx obelisk:

> it snatches at my awareness the instant I come near, trying to pull me deeper into its rampant, convecting currents of silver. When I have connected to it before, the onyx has rejected me. . . . but now, when I offer myself and the onyx claims me, suddenly I know. *The onyx is alive*. . . . It *sesses* me. It learns me, touching me with a presence that is suddenly undeniable.
>
> . . . .
>
> So the onyx yields to me now because, it senses at last, I too have known pain. My eyes have been opened to my own exploitation and degradation. I am afraid, of course, and angry, and hurt, but the onyx does not scorn these feelings within me. It seeks something else, however, something more, and finally finds what it seeks nestled in a little burning knot behind my heart: determination. I have committed myself to making, of all this wrongness, something right.
>
> That's what the onyx wants. *Justice*. (Jemisin 2017: 332–33)

Staging the onyx's own haptic capacities to claim, learn, and touch human bodies, this moment articulates a nonhuman sensorium in which geology senses humans into being, upending the sensory episteme of liberal humanism in which embodiment and affect are understood to be the sovereign praxis and locus of the unitary human subject. It imagines a speculative stone sensorium that "undermines our fantasies of sovereign relation to environment" by showing how "stone sediments contradictions . . . [and] ignite[s] possibility, abiding invitation to metamorphosis" (Cohen 2015: 9, 6). As vibrant mineralogical life forms, obelisks autonomously grant or refuse attunement by determining the forms of reciprocity that will or will not cohere between connected parties, opening a traffic of affects and desires between humans and nonhumans (the communication, negotiation, and sharing of human "determination" and the onyx's "justice"). Transformed by Nassun and Essun's Black feminist spatial praxis, touch becomes a multiscalar technology that upends the anthropocentric bound-aries of perception and embodiment that deny sense and sensation as coconstitutive practices generated at the interface between bod-ies and more-than-human forces. Touch, in short, intuits and inhabits a sensate earth.

Unlocking magic and the earth's geological network in this way, Essun and Nassun's sensory insurgency become central to the trilogy's Black feminist spatial imagination. In the final climax, when Essun reunites with Nassun in a battle to determine whether to destroy the earth or to save humanity, the trilogy stages the fate of the planet's ecological future such that the abolition of climate apocalypse is inex-tricable from Black women's liberation from the racial-colonial-sexual matrix of power. When Essun connects to the Obelisk Gate and risks her life to save humanity, "what the onyx finds . . . is something differ-ent this time: Fear for kin. Fear of failure. The fear that accompanies all necessary change. And underneath it all, a driving need to make the world better" (Jemisin 2017: 381). As Essun and Nassun struggle over competing visions of the future by fighting over control of the Obelisk Gate through their magic power—activate the gate to bring the moon back into orbit or destroy the earth by turning everyone into stone to abolish further injustice, pain, and suffering—Essun finally sacrifices her life to save Nassun's own life, granting her power over the Obelisk Gate to decide the planet's fate. Turning into stone due to magic overflow, Essun shows "what mothers have had to do since the dawn of time: sacrifice the present, in hopes of a better future" (284). Upon realizing her mother's sacrifices to save both her daughter and the planet, Nassun decides to follow her mother's wishes to end Fifth Seasons and save humankind. Thus, the trilogy's ending imag-ines ecological futures in which the abolition of the Sanzed Empire, orogene liberation, and climate revitalization are forged and made possible through Black feminist praxis. This manifestation of Black feminist ecological judgment, borne from the conjuncture of Essun's mothering, care, and love for her daughter and her drive to abolish Fifth Seasons, shows how "the poetics of landscape, as a projection of black femininity . . . imagine[s] new forms of geography, seeing the world from an interhuman (rather than partial) perspective" (McKittrick 2006: 144). It centers the axiom that, "after all, a person is herself, and others. Relationships chisel the final shape of one's being" (Jemisin 2016: 1).

The geological network's figuration of ecological relationality is finally formalized through the trilogy's narrative architecture. Notably, the trilogy's multifocal narration switches between second- and third-person narration, along with an unidentified first-person master narrator (in *The Fifth Season*, for example, three separate plotlines narrating Essun's, Damaya's, and Syenite's stories are eventually revealed to be the same character in different stages of her life with different names). The trilogy's last installment finally unveils that the entire story is narrated by the stone eater Hoa, Essun's companion, after he has "reassembled the raw arcanic substance" (Jemisin 2017: 396) of Essun's being, following her sacrifice and death, to revive her anew as a stone eater. The trilogy is finally understood as a retrospective narration of the story to a new Essun who will eventually reanimate as a stone eater with lost memories in an unknown future—the climactic manifestation of a Black feminist ecology of extraordinary more-than-human bodyminds. In this way, the trilogy's narrative architecture itself materializes as a geological process—a stratigraphic text through which knowledge and history is transmitted through geology as medium and archive. This metafictionality poses a central paradox: how is Hoa able to gain access to Essun's and Nassun's interiorities and narrate their simultaneous whereabouts and actions? One possible answer points to the history of stone eaters themselves. As it turns out, stone eaters are the tuners who were a part of Geoarcanity millennia ago (the special race of bioengineered life forms who were built to harness magic) and who were then transformed into stone eaters following the catastrophe of the Geoarcanity project. As hybridized geological and biological beings who are able to "earthtalk" (101) through vibrations, tuners have the ability to "speak" through the earth via vibrations, temperature, and pressure—a form of geosemiosis powered by sensory communication through the earth. Seen this way, the trilogy itself manifests through the narrative logic of earthtalk, a geohaptic language—made communicative across vast distances through temperatures, pressures, and reverberations—that, like the geological network itself, is relational, felt, and boundless. As Hoa states in the trilogy's end, "I remind myself of why I continue to tell this story through your eyes rather than my own: because, outwardly, you're too good at hiding yourself. . . . But I know you. I *know you*. Here is what's inside you" (156). These metafictional addresses, found throughout the novels, dramatize a more-than-human affectivity in which bodies encounter one another through the earth as media infrastructure, even as such modes ultimately elide linguistic signification: "I wish that I were still a tuner, so that I could speak to you through temperatures and pressures and reverberations of the earth," Hoa declares; "to make this telling simpler, I will translate it all as words, except where I cannot" (166, 100). Speculative forms of sensory communication render language itself into sensuous form in Jemisin's trilogy to imagine a geohaptic textuality in which the reader encounters and intuits fantastical attunements with the sensuous earth.

Animacy, Attunement, Apocalypse

Gumbs's and Jemisin's geohaptic imaginaries illuminate the imperative of sensory thinking to the racial politics of the Anthropocene and the affordances of sensory aesthetics in Black feminist speculative fiction. Black feminist spatial praxis, these works show, becomes the transformative site of social life and environmental justice that invents new forms of animacy and attunement in the Anthropocene. These forms of sensory life and abolitionist planetary futures in *M Archive* and the Broken Earth trilogy are borne out of "cartographies of struggle" wherein "Black women's geographies and poetics challenge us to stay human by invoking how black spaces and places are integral to our planetary and local geographic stories" (McKittrick 2006: 146). Sensory praxis ushers in, as *M Archive* puts it, "a species at the edge of its integrity, on the verge or in the practice of transforming into something beyond the luxuries and limitations of what some call 'the human'" (Gumbs 2018: xi). This practice of transformation in these works is made possible by reading the planet as a sensate archive whose histories, materialities, and vitalities are made legible through touch. It is a practice of sensing for, with, and through the planet, in which "there are no sense-borders: sense is not a limit-concept. To sense is to world unlimitedly" (Manning 2007: 155). By sensing the racial ecologies of the Middle Passage, slavery, and fugitivity through time and space, these works understand geology as a site of healing and resistance in the afterlife of slavery and apocalypse of climate catastrophe. To feel the broken earth anew, these works show, is to reclaim Black ecologies from the wreckage of the Anthropocene, to refuse the severance of sense and life, and to retrieve new forms of liberatory life.

Mapping insurgent ecological futures within the Anthropocene's racial terrains of dispossession and ecological violence from below, *M Archive* and the Broken Earth trilogy enact what Fred Moten (2003: 229, 191) calls the dialectic of the "ensemble of the senses and the ensemble of the social" that names the conditions of possibility of "the drive for, and the knowledge of, freedom." Their Afrofuturist works illuminate abolitionist worldmaking as a form of reparative futurism on the broken earth, in which more-than-human relationalities are cultivated through an ethics of care, relation, and sensuality. Emplaced within the future conditional, these Black feminist ecological futures are predicated on the abolition of normative models of the human produced by racial-colonial power. Sense and sensation become infrastructures of care that forge novel ecologies of relationality emancipated from the matrix of domination. The manifestation of Black feminist ecological futurism in the postapocalyptic prolepsis of the present— as seen in *M Archive*'s future-anterior archival aesthetic ("we broke the earth and now we fall through time" [Gumbs 2018: 139]) and the Broken Earth trilogy's narrative cyclicality ("Let's end with the beginning of the world, shall we?" [Jemisin 2017: 1])—enacts a geophysics of Blackness whose "epiphenomenal time" (Wright 2015: 4) crystallizes the entangled past, present, and future within the thickened ontology of the present. Geohaptics unfurls multiscalar sensory worlds made legible within the movements between sense and ecology, touch and liberation. It assembles novel forms of ecological life within the broken earth that, as *M Archive*'s narrator-archivist insists, "multiply by every pore touched, every memory made skin again, every word of love and the lips that share them" (Gumbs 2018: 5).

Shouhei Tanaka is a PhD candidate in English at the University of California, Los Angeles. His work has appeared or is forthcoming in *PMLA*, *ASAP/Journal*, *Modernism/modernity*, *Modern Fiction Studies*, *ISLE: Interdisciplinary Studies in Literature and Environment*, and elsewhere.

Notes

1   For works on haptics, see, e.g., Merleau-Ponty 2002; Paterson 2007; and Jones 2018.
2   For an earlier work on Black ecology, see Hare 1970.
3   For Jacques Rancière (2004: 13), *aesthetics* names "the system of *a priori* forms determining what presents itself to sense experience. It is a delimitation of spaces and times, of the visible and the invisible, of speech and noise, that simultaneously determines the places and the stakes of politics as a form of experience."
4   For works on race and the Anthropocene, see, e.g., Vergès 2017; Pulido 2018; and Karera 2019. For works engaging geology and the Anthropocene, see Palsson and Swanson 2016; Povinelli 2016; Yusoff and Clark 2017; and Bobbette and Donovan 2019.
5   What Luciano (2015: 2) terms *affective geology* transforms the "necessarily speculative work of geology into a form of aesthetic and sensory experience."

6 For an overview of sensory studies, see Bull et al. 2006.
7 As Walter Mignolo and Rolando Vazquez (2013) argue, "The modern/ colonial project has implied not only control of the economy, the political, and knowledge, but also control over the senses and perception."
8 For a critical examination of Blackness in relation to posthumanism, new materialism, and animal studies, see Jackson 2020.
9 Jemisin describes the trilogy as a "Black female power fantasy" and clarifies that the trilogy "wasn't specifically depicting just the African-American experience" but "was drawing a lot of material from a number of different experiences of oppression" (qtd. in Hurley 2018: 470, 472).

References

Abram, David. 1996. *The Spell of the Sensuous: Perception and Language in a More-than-Human World*. New York: Vintage.

Alexander, M. Jacqui. 2006. *Pedagogies of Crossing: Meditations on Feminism, Sexual Politics, Memory, and the Sacred*. Durham, NC: Duke Univ. Press.

Benjamin, Walter. 1968. "The Storyteller." In *Illuminations*, translated by Harry Zohn, edited by Hannah Arendt, 83–109. New York: Schocken Books.

Bobbette, Adam, and Amy Donovan, eds. 2019. *Political Geology: Active Stratigraphies and the Making of Life*. Cham: Palgrave Macmillan.

Bull, Michael, Paul Gilroy, David Howes, and Douglas Kahn. 2006. "Introducing Sensory Studies." *Senses and Society* 1, no. 1: 5–7.

Chakrabarty, Dipesh. 2019. "The Planet: An Emergent Humanist Category." *Critical Inquiry* 46, no. 1: 1–31.

Chen, Mel Y. 2012. *Animacies: Biopolitics, Racial Mattering, and Queer Affect*. Durham, NC: Duke Univ. Press.

Cohen, Jeffrey Jerome. 2015. *Stone: An Ecology of the Inhuman*. Minneapolis: Univ. of Minnesota Press.

Collins, Patricia Hill. (1990) 2000. *Black Feminist Thought: Knowledge, Consciousness, and the Politics of Empowerment*. New York: Routledge.

Dowdall, Lisa. 2020. "Black Futures Matter: Afrofuturism and Geontology in N. K. Jemisin's Broken Earth Trilogy." In *Literary Afrofuturism in the Twenty-First Century*, edited by Isiah Lavender III and Lisa Yaszek, 149–67. Columbus: Ohio State Univ. Press.

Ducre, Kishi Animashaun. 2018. "The Black Feminist Spatial Imagination and an Intersectional Environmental Justice." *Environmental Sociology* 4, no. 1: 22–35.

FitzPatrick Jessica. 2020. "Twenty-First Century Afrofuturist Aliens: Shifting to the Space of Third Contact." *Extrapolation* 61, nos. 1–2: 69–90.

Frazier, Chelsea. 2020. "Black Feminist Ecological Thought: A Manifesto." *Atmos*, October 1. atmos.earth/black-feminist-ecological-thought-essay/.

Fretwell, Erica. 2018. "Introduction: Common Senses and Critical Sensibilities." *Resilience: A Journal of the Environmental Humanities* 5, no. 3: 1–9.

Gumbs, Alexis Pauline. 2018. *M Archive: After the End of the World*. Durham, NC: Duke Univ. Press.

Hare, Nathan. 1970. "Black Ecology." *Black Scholar* 1, no. 6: 2–8.

Hartman, Saidiya. 2007. *Lose Your Mother: A Journey along the Atlantic Slave Route.* New York: Farrar, Straus, and Giroux.

Hartman, Saidiya. 2016. "The Belly of the World: A Note on Black Women's Labors." *Souls: A Critical Journal of Black Politics, Culture, and Society* 18, no. 1: 166–73.

Huang, Michelle N. 2017. "Rematerializations of Race." *Lateral* 6, no. 1. csalateral.org/issue/6-1/forum-alt-humanities-new-materalist-philosophy -rematerializations-race-huang.

Hurley, Jessica. 2018. "An Apocalypse Is a Relative Thing: An Interview with N. K. Jemisin." *ASAP/Journal* 3, no. 3: 467–77.

Jackson, Zakiyyah Iman. 2020. *Becoming Human: Matter and Meaning in an Antiblack World.* New York: New York Univ. Press.

Jemisin, N. K. 2015. *The Fifth Season.* New York: Orbit.

Jemisin, N. K. 2016. *The Obelisk Gate.* New York: Orbit.

Jemisin, N. K. 2017. *The Stone Sky.* New York: Orbit.

Jones, Lynette A. 2018. *Haptics.* Cambridge, MA: MIT Press.

Karera, Axelle. 2019. "Blackness and the Pitfalls of Anthropocene Ethics." *Critical Philosophy of Race* 7, no. 1: 32–56.

Lorde, Audre. (1978) 1984. "Uses of the Erotic: The Erotic as Power." In *Sister Outsider: Essays and Speeches*, 53–59. Berkeley, CA: Crossing Press.

Luciano, Dana. 2015. "How the Earth Feels: A Conversation with Dana Luciano." Interview by Cécile Roudeau. Transatlantica 1: 1–11. https:// doi.org/10.4000/transatlantica.7362.

Manning, Erin. 2007. *Politics of Touch: Sense, Movement, Sovereignty.* Minneapolis: Univ. of Minnesota Press.

McKittrick, Katherine. 2006. *Demonic Grounds: Black Women and the Cartographies of Struggle.* Minneapolis: Univ. of Minnesota Press.

McKittrick, Katherine, ed. 2015. *Sylvia Wynter: On Being Human as Praxis.* Durham, NC: Duke Univ. Press.

Merleau-Ponty, Maurice. 2002. *Phenomenology of Perception.* Translated by Colin Smith. London: Routledge.

Mignolo, Walter, and Rolando Vazquez. 2013. "Decolonial AestheSis: Colonial Wounds/Decolonial Healings." *Social Text Online*, July 15. socialtextjournal .org/periscope_article/decolonial-aesthesis-colonial-woundsdecolonial -healings.

Moten, Fred. 2003. *In the Break: The Aesthetics of the Black Radical Tradition.* Minneapolis: Univ. of Minnesota Press.

Moten, Fred. 2017. *Black and Blur: consent not to be a single being.* Durham, NC: Duke Univ. Press.

Palsson, Gisli, and Heather Anne Swanson. 2016. "Down to Earth: Geosocialities and Geopolitics." *Environmental Humanities* 8, no. 2: 149–71.

Paterson, Mark. 2007. *The Senses of Touch: Haptics, Affects, and Technologies.* Oxford: Berg.

Porteous, J. Douglas. 1990. *Landscapes of the Mind: Worlds of Sense and Metaphor.* Toronto: Univ. of Toronto Press.

Povinelli, Elizabeth A. 2016. *Geontologies: A Requiem to Late Liberalism*. Durham, NC: Duke Univ. Press.

Pulido, Laura. 2018. "Racism and the Anthropocene." In *Future Remains: A Cabinet of Curiosities for the Anthropocene*, edited by Gregg Mitman, Marco Armiero, and Robert S. Emmett, 116–28. Chicago: Univ. of Chicago Press.

Rancière, Jacques. 2004. *The Politics of Aesthetics: The Distribution of the Sensible*. Translated by Gabriel Rockhill. New York: Continuum.

Roane, J. T., and Justin Hosbey. 2019. "Mapping Black Ecologies." *Current Research in Digital History* 2. https://doi.org/10.31835/crdh.2019.05.

Robinsong, Erin. 2018. "Geohaptics." In *Counter-desecration: A Glossary for Writing within the Anthropocene*, edited by Linda Russo and Marthe Reed, 39. Middletown, CT: Wesleyan Univ. Press.

Rodaway, Paul. 1994. *Sensuous Geographies: Body, Sense, and Place*. London: Routledge.

Schalk, Sami. 2018. *Bodyminds Reimagined: (Dis)Ability, Race, and Gender in Black Women's Speculative Fiction*. Durham, NC: Duke Univ. Press.

Sekimoto, Sachi, and Christopher Brown. 2020. *Race and the Senses: The Felt Politics of Racial Embodiment*. London: Bloomsbury.

Serres, Michel. 2008. *The Five Senses: A Philosophy of Mingled Bodies*. Translated by Margaret Sankey and Peter Cowley. London: Continuum.

Sharpe, Christina. 2016. *In the Wake: On Blackness and Being*. Durham, NC: Duke Univ. Press.

Spillers, Hortense J. (1984) 2003. "Interstices: A Small Drama of Words." In *Black, White, and in Color: Essays on American Literature and Culture*, 152–175. Chicago: Univ. of Chicago Press.

Spillers, Hortense J. 1987. "Mama's Baby, Papa's Maybe: An American Grammar Book." *Diacritics* 17, no. 2: 64–81.

Tompkins, Kyla Wazana. 2016. "On the Limits and Promise of New Materialist Philosophy." *Lateral* 5, no. 1. csalateral.org/issue/5-1/forum-alt-humanities-new-materialist-philosophy-tompkins.

Vergès, Françoise. 2017. "Racial Capitalocene." In *Futures of Black Radicalism*, edited by Gaye Theresa Johnson and Alex Lubin, 72–82. London: Verso.

Weheliye, Alexander G. 2014. *Habeas Viscus: Racializing Assemblages, Biopolitics, and Black Feminist Theories of the Human*. Durham, NC: Duke Univ. Press.

Wright, Michelle M. 2015. *Physics of Blackness: Beyond the Middle Passage Epistemology*. Minneapolis: Univ. of Minnesota Press.

Wynter, Sylvia. 2003. "Unsettling the Coloniality of Being/Power/Truth/Freedom: Towards the Human, after Man, Its Overrepresentation—An Argument." *CR: The New Centennial Review* 3, no. 3: 257–337.

Yusoff, Kathryn. 2018. *A Billion Black Anthropocenes or None*. Minneapolis: Univ. of Minnesota Press.

Yusoff, Kathryn, and Nigel Clark. 2017. "Geosocial Formations and the Anthropocene." *Theory, Culture, and Society* 34, no. 2–3: 3–23.

Book Reviews

In and Out of Sight: Modernist Writing and the Photographic Unseen. By Alix Beeston. Oxford: Oxford Univ. Press. 2018. xvi, 256 pp. Cloth, $78.00.

What Was Literary Impressionism? By Michael Fried. Cambridge, MA: Belknap Press of Harvard Univ. Press. 2018. viii, 400 pp. Cloth, $46.50.

In his introduction to *What Was Literary Impressionism?* Michael Fried reveals that he has been in pursuit of an answer to his book's titular question for more than thirty years. It is in part for this reason that so much of the book draws on Fried's previous scholarship dating back to the late 1980s. From relatively early explorations into the role played by disfigured and upturned faces in the literature Stephen Crane and Joseph Conrad to more recent examinations of monstrosity in H. G. Wells, portions of Fried's previous scholarship find their way into the present book and significantly inform the contribution it seeks to make, underscoring Fried's point, made early on in *What Was Literary Impressionism?*, that the path to publishing a "comprehensive (though by no means exhaustive) overview of English-language literary impressionism" had "lain open" to him for over a quarter century (23).

The result of Fried's decades-long effort is a book of considerable scope and ambition, presenting an impressively expansive account of literary impressionism that scans numerous works by the movement's major figures. Living up to its name, the book seeks to—and does—explain what Fried contends literary impressionism *was.* Admitting a sense of gratitude to the writings of Jacques Derrida, Fried lays out a theory of impressionism wherein a profound preoccupation with the scene and materiality of writing, and with writerly intensions, gives way to a "sheer literary intensity amounting at times to unbridled violence" (27). The generative subject of impressionist writing, Fried contends, is the act of writing itself, and the conscious awareness of and vigorous desire to suppress that core or generative subject on the part of writers is fundamental to impressionism's artistic undertaking.

American Literature, Volume 95, Number 3, September 2023

The book scans examples of symbolic images strung throughout the impressionist corpus that emblematize authorial suppression of the generative subject. For instance, maps, like those referred to in Conrad's *Heart of Darkness*, represent the "originary blankness at which or into which we ... [imagine] the author gazing" (56). Similarly, in Wells's *War of the Worlds*, maps denote the "palpable tension between the narrative as such and the scene of writing" (192). However, the motif that most attracts Fried's attention is that of the "disfigured upturned face" found most notably in works by Crane ("The Upturned Face," *The Red Badge of Courage*, *The Monster*) and Conrad (*Almayer's Folly*, *Heart of Darkness*). These faces, often of corpses, sometimes beaten beyond recognition, possessing at times a blankness and at others evidence of extreme trauma, represent the scene of writing, the surface on which writing occurs and, as such, dramatize the relationship—often deeply conflictual—between the writer and the page. In the coda that concludes his book, Fried argues that concerns regarding the "upward-facing page of inscription" (325) fall off dramatically after 1914, with modernists such as Gertrude Stein maintaining an emphasis on "seeing, flatness, and looking down" (326) but decoupling it from the conflictual and reader-centric practices of literary impressionism.

It is in part this interest in seeing, flatness, and, if not looking down, then certainly looking through and between on the part of modernists like Stein that Alix Beeston seeks to explore in her book, *In and Out of Sight: Modernist Writing and the Photographic Unseen*. Unlike Fried's nearly career-spanning monograph, Beeston's book began as her doctoral dissertation and, as such, catalogs a single burst of recent intellectual activity aimed at destabilizing "a host of gendered and racialized assumptions that have shaped the scholarship" of a handful of notable modernist writers (21). Theorizing an iteration of modernist writing dialectically (and, to a degree, causally) linked to the late nineteenth-century composite portraiture of Francis Galton, Beeston argues that the "segmented, serialized mode of narration and characterization" (4) found in the works of Stein, Jean Toomer, John Dos Passos, and F. Scott Fitzgerald constitute composite writing shaped by the "reiterated, sutured body of the serialized woman" (5). Beeston argues that the "multiple, compound, agglomerated" women found in Stein, Toomer, Dos Passos, and Fitzgerald derive from composite photography's "densely laminous and sequenced bodies" and are "coextensive with the reiterated, sutured bodies of the texts [they] ... populate" (5). By knitting together the "connective and disconnective tissue of modernist narrative" and the "woman-in-series"—that is, the figuration of the "conspicuous appearances and disappearances of female bodies"—Beeston interprets "composite modernist writing in relation to the aesthetic principles and ontological disclosures of serial or sequenced photography" (5).

Whereas the conventions of impressionism identified by Fried involve depicting downward gazes at stable albeit unsettling objects in order to match the writer's relation to the page, Beeston's intervention into modernism aims to show how the "textual principle of sequenced assemblage and juxtaposition" produces the "equivocality, ambiguity, and incongruity" found in Stein's *Three Lives*, Toomer's *Cane*, Dos Passos's *Manhattan Transfer*, and Fitzgerald's *The Last Tycoon* and "Cosmopolitan" (11). By examining what Beeston calls these authors' composite texts—texts consisting of unstable, sometimes murky images reminiscent of Galton's composite portraits (and not unlike the disturbing, uncanny faces central to Fried's analysis of impressionism)—Beeston advances a theory of literary modernism informed not only by what she sees in these images but also, crucially, by what exists in the fissures and gaps that exist between them. For instance, Beeston contends that the "interstitial construction" of Stein's *Three Lives* creates "blank spaces that separate and bridge [the] . . . serialized lives and deaths" of the book's female characters, Anna, Melanctha, and Lena (34). Similarly, she holds that the "composite logic" of Dos Passos's *Manhattan Transfer* "shows its debt to photographic technologies in its essentially iterative mode of narration and characterization" (109). Throughout this ambitious and deeply original book, Beeston makes a compelling case for the "photographic effect" in literary modernism "entering into the intimate, communal space of the in-between" to generate "moments of suspension in the social and political order of modernity" (195).

Whereas Fried's work in *What Was Literary Impressionism?* arguably aims to sew up critical discourse on the period, proffering the establishment of a foundational critical lens through which to view the impressionism of Crane, Conrad, Wells, and others, Beeston positions her critical adjoining of photography and composite writing as an unraveling of fixed assumptions about Stein, Crane, Dos Passos, and Fitzgerald. Taken together, these books bring into relief the profound self-awareness animating literary impressionism and dramatize how that self-awareness, intensely focused on the scene of writing and made manifest in the suppression of the generative subject, gave way, at least in part, to modernism's composite, serialized form of writing containing gaps and absences bespeaking the trauma of the figurative typologies of race, ethnicity, and gender. What is more, the contrasting objectives of these books, to offer a career-defining theoretical account of literary impressionism, on the one hand, and a novel disruption of the gendered and racial assumptions informing modernist scholarship, on the other, put on display to impressive effect the powers marshaled by accomplished scholars at different phases in their careers.

David Tomkins is professor of writing at the University of Southern California. His current book project, "Practicing Assemblage," draws on Deleuzian philosophy and post-process composition scholarship to devise new approaches to teaching advanced writing. He has also written on power dynamics, empathy, and performativity in writing classrooms; science fiction; and early twentieth-century American literature. In 2020 he co-organized the CCCC Regional Conference "Building Diverse Communities through Writing" held at the University of Southern California.

DOI 10.1215/00029831-10679279

The Origin of Others. By Toni Morrison. Foreword by Ta-Nehisi Coates. Cambridge, MA: Harvard Univ. Press. 2017. xvii, 114 pp. Cloth, $22.95.

Goodness and the Literary Imagination: Toni Morrison. Ed. Davíd Carrasco, Stephanie Paulsell, and Mara Willard. Charlottesville: Univ. of Virginia Press. 2019. viii, 262 pp. Cloth, $27.95.

For such a slight volume, *The Origin of Others* is a multigeneric surprise: a theory of others and motivations for othering; reflections on histories and episodes of race, racing, and racism; meditations by Nobel Prize–winning author Toni Morrison on her own works in light of such things; associated bits of memoir; quick readings of various authors, including Harriet Beecher Stowe, Camara Laye, and Flannery O'Connor; and perhaps most biting of all, commentary on colorism within US Black communities. Ta-Nehisi Coates in a brief foreword likens the book to *Racecraft*, the race-debunking volume by Karen Fields and Barbara Fields, but Morrison is interested in racial othering less as fictive ruse than as a product of self-alienation and insecurity. Her theme is the projection onto others of what the self cannot abide.

For scholars who study such matters, this will not exactly be news, but nor is Morrison's endeavor here to construct a grand new theory. *The Origin of Others* originated in her 2016 Charles Eliot Norton Lectures at Harvard, and the prose breathes with the life of its occasion, positing some functions of race making and adducing some of the ways the author inherited, disrupted (most of all in her writing), and imagined her way beyond them. Her earlier volume of literary analysis *Playing in the Dark* (1992) is the closest comparison to this one, but *The Origin of Others* burrows beyond works of literature into corners of everyday life and world making; as Morrison says, she attempted in her work to "annihilate and discredit the routine, easy, available color fetish, which is reminiscent of slavery itself" (53).

Strangers to ourselves, we other others to avoid becoming others, Morrison argues, skin color being the chief technology thereof. So severe is Morrison's angle of vision that in her first eight pages she equates the othering practices of her great-grandmother, Millicent MacTeer (who considered the lighter-skinned Toni and her siblings "tampered with," lesser), Old-South eugenicist Samuel Cartwright (author of "Report on the Diseases and Physical Peculiarities of the Negro Race"), and Thomas Thistlewood, upper-class English scion of enslavers in Jamaica who recorded his routine and extensive acts of sexual violation. Morrison differentiates them in outcome only; she renders the psychic motivations of othering as more or less the same. "The danger of sympathizing with the stranger is the possibility of becoming a stranger" (30), adrift on the wrong side of difference, she suggests before turning her gaze upon herself with characteristic rigor. Morrison tells of a pleasant encounter with an older Black woman fishing in the river near her home with whom she imagines becoming friends, but the woman never reappears. Finding herself perplexed and even bitter at the loss, Morrison reflects on the power of a stranger, and attendant processes of othering, to disturb, despite operating this time in the key of embrace, fantasy, even ownership: "I was longing for and missing some aspect of myself, and [not understanding] that there are no strangers. There are only versions of ourselves, many of which we have not embraced, most of which we wish to protect ourselves from" (38).

Morrison's glinting remarks on her own work match those she offers on other writers. She notes her novel *Paradise*'s premise of intraracial color hierarchy in its fictionalized Oklahoma Black world; she writes of her nineteen years at Random House editing Toni Cade Bambara, Angela Davis, Gayl Jones, Huey Newton, and even Muhammad Ali, whose varying sales figures inspired Morrison to gather materials for a truly attention-getting book—the one that became *Beloved*, whose titular murdered child Morrison calls the "ultimate Other"; she considered it an "opportunity to be and to become" this figure with "sympathy, clarity, and the risk of self-examination" (91). Her closing remarks widen to global scope, invoking borders, the refugee, the immigrant, and other Others while also keeping her focus down home. Morrison recalls sitting in church as a child as the offering plates came around collecting coins for Africa, a place that seemed at once "intimately connected to us and profoundly foreign" (100). It was one more call not to "deny the foreigner in ourselves and make us resist to the death the commonness of humanity" (110).

Goodness and the Literary Imagination, a volume containing Morrison's 2012 Ingersoll Lecture at Harvard Divinity School, as well as a dozen probing essays on her work and a 2017 interview, shares deep resonances with *The Origin of Others*. While focused principally on Morrison's religious ideas, it redoubles the gravitas of *Origin*'s emphasis on self-examination, which for Morrison exemplifies the idea of goodness, an idea, she says, that "fascinated" her. Evil gets all the glamour and pyrotechnics, Morrison acknowledges in the lecture, all the more reason to distrust its lure: "Allowing goodness its own speech does not annihilate evil, but it does allow me to signify my own understanding of goodness: the acquisition of self-knowledge. A satisfactory or good ending for me is when the protagonist learns something vital and morally insightful that she or he did not know at the beginning" (19). The essays' authors spend a fair amount of time on such properly religious tropes in Morrison's work as the Pan-African griot (Jacob Olupona), landscapes of demon and spirit (Tiya Miles), pietà iconography (Mara Willard), possession and dispossession (Matthew Potts), ministry and sermonizing (Stephanie Paulsell), Pauline theology and spiritual authority (Jonathan Walton), and eulogy (Gerald "Jay" Williams), but these ideas are vitally intermixed throughout with adjacent concepts, such as haunting, ghosts, flesh, captivity, silence, sound, and song (concepts and histories addressed frontally by Walter Johnson, Charles Long, David Carrasco, Biko Mandela Gray, and Josslyn Luckett). Their net effect is to enlarge the dimensions of Morrison country, where inner lives know the history that hurts, past suffering suffuses present vibrancy, and subjectivity meets infrastructure. (There is some perhaps inevitable talk about Morrison's work as sacred text and holy writ, but not enough to get in the way.)

David Carrasco's closing interview with the author broaches her conversion as a twelve-year-old to Roman Catholicism, "not for any sane reason but because my best friend was a Catholic"; with serene clarity (and conceptual chiasmus), Morrison avers that the Catholic church delivered an aesthetic dimension—"I was taken by the liturgy and the beauty"—that came through as well in hymns and sermons, but that it was the beauty of her mother's singing ("the most beautiful voice I've ever heard in my life, better than everybody else") that brought home the religious aspects registered in her writing, not to mention the very sound of language (229–30). There is a fascinating little turn on the language of naming and the nicknames of her father's friends—Duke, Lover, Cool Breeze, Jim the Devil—which Morrison says contained a "kind of teaching about the history of black people," as did, in another way, her own "legitimate" name, Chloe Wofford, which for Morrison is apposite with that of former Senator Harris Wofford and South Carolina's Wofford College—and thus, she says, "imbued with slavery" (234). Morrison's home in language and in her true name finds its correlative at volume's end in her Hudson River Valley home: "I finally found home. . . . It's where the comfort is, and the knowledge of belonging" (242). A comforting final note of resolution for an author to whom there were no strangers.

Eric Lott teaches American studies at the Graduate Center of the City University of New York. He is the author of *Love and Theft: Blackface Minstrelsy and the American Working Class* (1993; 20th anniv. ed., 2013), *The Disappearing Liberal Intellectual* (2006), and *Black Mirror: The Cultural Contradictions of American Racism* (2017).

DOI 10.1215/00029831-10679293

Brief Mention

Washington Irving and the Fantasy of Masculinity: Escaping the Woman Within.
By Heinz Tschachler. Jefferson, NC: McFarland. 2022. x, 275 pp. Cloth, $45.00.

Drawing on Jungian concepts of anima and animus, or feminine and masculine personality types, this study argues that the male figures in Washington Irving's body of work are "masculine archetypal images" that the author developed to compensate for his "feminine personality components." Irving's "feminine masculinity" is apparent in his use of pseudonymous identities as a form of self-concealment. Tschachler tracks Irving's struggle with masculinity as a series of responses to shifting notions of manhood that correspond with political and economic changes in the United States during the first half of the nineteenth century.

Gems of Art on Paper: Illustrated American Fiction and Poetry, 1785–1885. By Georgia Brady Barnhill. Amherst: Univ. of Massachusetts Press. 2021. xx, 288 pp. Cloth, $32.95.

Focusing on the impact that illustrators and bookmakers had on the development of American literature from 1785 to 1885, this study tracks the increasingly visual nature of the nation's print culture. Barnhill shows that illustrations had the power to heighten the perceived value of printed content and in this way helped to consolidate a distinctly American literary tradition. Many American authors and artists benefited from the increased use of illustration in volumes of poetry, literary annuals, and gift books. Barnhill pays special attention to developments in printing and image-reproduction technologies, which granted nineteenth-century audiences unprecedented access to fine art by American artists.

American Literature, Volume 95, Number 3, September 2023
DOI 10.1215/00029831-10679307   © 2023 by Duke University Press

Certain Concealments: Poe, Hawthorne, and Early Nineteenth-Century Abortion.
By Dana Medoro. Amherst: Univ. of Massachusetts Press. 2022. xviii, 213 pp. Cloth,
$90.00; paper, $29.95; e-book available.

Arguing that works by Nathaniel Hawthorne and Edgar Allan Poe "confront the
limitations and half-truths of medicolegal language surrounding abortion,"
Medoro begins by reading Poe's C. Auguste Dupin stories in context of the grad-
ual criminalization of abortion in the 1820s. Then, the monograph turns to how
Hawthorne's *The Scarlet Letter* (1850), *The House of Seven Gables* (1851), and
The Blithedale Romance (1852) interrogate privacy, legibility, and even the
nation by playing with concealments of bodies and bodily relations. Both writers, according to Medoro, unravel "hierarchies of life" and notions of manifestation via the obfuscation—and subsequent illumination—of abortion.

Carlyle, Emerson and the Transatlantic Uses of Authority. By Tim Sommer. Edinburgh:
Edinburgh Univ. Press. 2021. x, 270 pp. Cloth, $110.00; e-book, $110.00.

This book marshals the relationship between Carlyle and Emerson to trace
the development of transatlantic discourses of authority across the first half
of the nineteenth century. Adopting a "thematic and methodological plural-
ism" that blends philology, book history, sociology, and critical close reading,
it elaborates a "transatlantic comparativism" attentive not only to textual connections and conceptual relays but also to specific publication institutions and
concrete sites of performance. Part 1 explores British and American debates
surrounding racial identity and national history. Part 2 details print circulation
and publication histories. Part 3 attends to the cache and transformations of
public speech. Lastly, an epilogue recasts the foregoing material in light of
the US Civil War.

Up from the Depths: Herman Melville, Lewis Mumford, and Rediscovery in Dark Times.
By Aaron Sachs. Princeton, NJ: Princeton Univ. Press. 2022. xx, 472 pp. Cloth, $32.00.

This dual biography examines the life of Lewis Mumford in relation to the life
of Herman Melville, who was the subject of a landmark biography by Mumford in 1929. A pioneer in the Melville Revival, Mumford gravitated to the
nineteenth-century author to help him grapple with the ruptures and traumas
of twentieth-century modernity, and Sachs suggests that both writers offer a
model for responding to present-day upheaval with resilience. Mumford and
Melville understood modernity as an ongoing or continuous series of disconti-
nuities, a view that informs the innovative structure of Sachs's biography,
which alternates between its two subjects in short "jump-cut" chapters.

Sensing Willa Cather: The Writer and the Body in Transition. By Guy J. Reynolds. Edinburgh: Edinburgh Univ. Press. 2021. vii, 252 pp. Cloth, $110.00; paper, $24.95; e-book, $110.00.

Analyzing Cather's extensive writing career, this study argues that the author "wanted to make the body the very ground of art." For Cather, corporeal experience and especially the differentiation of impressions afforded by the five bodily senses were necessarily linked to textual representation and narrative. By drawing widely on Cather's fiction, reviews, essays, and personal correspondences, Reynolds situates Cather within the tumult of epochal transformations that spanned the aesthetic innovations of "late Victorian, Modernist, and pre-Postmodernist ages." In addition to incorporating newly available biographical archives, this inquiry explores critical discourses of disability studies, body studies, and queer studies.

The Eye That Is Language: A Transatlantic View of Eudora Welty. By Danièle Pitavy-Souques. Edited by Pearl Amelia McHaney. Jackson: Univ. Press of Mississippi. 2022. xiii, 164 pp. Cloth, $99.00; paper, $30.00; e-book available.

Illuminating "a global perspective of Welty's achievements," this collection brings together nine of Pitavy-Souques's essays on Welty's work. Beginning with a rumination on Welty's ability to "inspire" readers around the world, Pitavy-Souques explores the author's "concern with narrative technique" in stories like "A Curtain of Green" (1941). Later, the collection turns to essays that consider the structure of *The Golden Apples* (1949), Welty's relationship to modernity, mythology in "Circe" (1955), and more. The volume concludes by analyzing how Welty "grasps the very essence of humanity" and even crafts a form of humanism in her later, long-form works.

Underdogs: Social Deviance and Queer Theory. By Heather Love. Chicago: Univ. of Chicago Press. 2021. xiii, 224 pp. Cloth, $95.00; paper, $26.00; e-book, $25.99.

Providing a "renewed look" at the genealogy, methods, and frameworks of queer studies, this text illuminates queer thought's "important precedents in midcentury sociology," specifically deviance studies. The author considers Erving Goffman's *Stigma* (1963) as a surprising precursor to contemporary scholarship. Love then reads the work of Elisabeth and Nikolaas Tinbergen and Laud Humphreys as progenerating the refusal of essentialism, biologism, and stigmatization. Later, the study establishes Samuel R. Delany as an "inheritor" of deviance studies before connecting a postwar "descriptive view of sexual practices and sexual communities" to a "truly collective movement" in the future of queer studies.

American War Stories: Veteran-Writers and the Politics of Memoir. By Myra Mendible. Amherst: Univ. of Massachusetts Press. 2021. xv, 221 pp. Cloth, $90.00; paper, $28.95; e-book available.

Uncovering the "complex relationship between memory and politics in the context of postmodern war," this monograph argues that veterans' memories—and memoirs—serve a *"political* function" by affecting "the legitimacy of American power." To that end, the author examines narratives of "veteran activism," the power of shame in works like Philip Caputo's *A Rumor of War* (1977), issues of credibility and veracity in veteran writing, and the relationship between immigrant veterans and concepts of "honor." Mendible's work culminates by analyzing politics and poetics in Brian Turner's *My Life as a Foreign Country* (2014) and emerging stories from LGBTQ veterans.